SKETCH COMEDY

SKETCH COMEDY

Identity, Reflexivity, and American Television

Nick Marx

INDIANA UNIVERSITY PRESS

This book is a publication of
Indiana University Press
Office of Scholarly Publishing
Herman B Wells Library 350
1320 East 10th Street
Bloomington, Indiana 47405 USA

iupress.indiana.edu

© 2019 by Nick Marx

A portion of chapter 2 was originally published as "'Skits Strung Together': Performance, Narrative, and the Sketch Comedy Aesthetic in *SNL* Films," in *Saturday Night Live and American TV*, ed. Nick Marx, Matt Sienkiewicz, and Ron Becker (Bloomington: Indiana University Press, 2013), 213–232.

A portion of chapter 4 was originally published as "Expanding the Brand: Race, Gender, and the Post-politics of Representation on Comedy Central," *Television and New Media*, 17, no. 3 (March 2016): 272–287.

Both are republished here with permission of the author.

All rights reserved
No part of this book may be reproduced or utilized in any form or by any means, electronic or mechanical, including photocopying and recording, or by any information storage and retrieval system, without permission in writing from the publisher. The paper used in this publication meets the minimum requirements of the American National Standard for Information Sciences—Permanence of Paper for Printed Library Materials, ANSI Z39.48-1992.

Manufactured in the United States of America

Cataloging information is available from the Library of Congress.

ISBN 978-0-253-04414-3 (cloth)
ISBN 978-0-253-04416-7 (paperback)
ISBN 978-0-253-04425-9 (ebook)

1 2 3 4 5   24 23 22 21 20 19

For Louis, Jane, and Jill

CONTENTS

Acknowledgments ix

Introduction: Sketch Comedy and Reflexive Flexibility 1

1 From Radio Voices to Variety Choices: *The Colgate Comedy Hour* and Sketch Comedy in Early Television 40

2 "... and You're Not": *Saturday Night Live* in the Network Era and Beyond 61

3 Brand X: MTV's *The State* and Generation X in the Multichannel Transition 94

4 Sketch Comedy's Identity (Post-)Politics: *Inside Amy Schumer, Key & Peele*, and Comedy Central in the Post-Network Era 125

Conclusion: Sketch Comedy and Cultural Cohesion 147

Bibliography 153

Index 167

ACKNOWLEDGMENTS

I AM FORTUNATE TO HAVE HAD SO MANY smart and kind people support my academic endeavors. The ones with the most direct impact on this book began with my time as a graduate student, first in the Radio-Television-Film program at the University of Texas at Austin, then in the Media and Cultural Studies program at the University of Wisconsin-Madison. Much of the material for this book began in seminars at those universities taught by Mary Beltrán, Charles Ramírez Berg, Michael Curtin, Julie D'Acci, Michele Hilmes, Michael Kackman, Mary Celeste Kearney, Thomas Schatz, Jeff Smith, and Janet Staiger.

Jonathan Gray generously advised this project as a dissertation, and every day since then I have tried to emulate him as a scholar, teacher, and mentor. Matt Sienkiewicz has been a constant source of levity and wisdom on this project and so many others. Thanks to all of my wonderful colleagues in the Department of Communication Studies at Colorado State University, especially Kit Hughes and Evan Elkins, who provided insights and encouragement at key points throughout the writing process. Others to whom I'm deeply grateful for providing interviews, feedback, archival resources, or editorial assistance include: Art Bell, Kiah Bennett, Hye Seung Chung, Scott Diffrient, Maxine Ducey, Janice Frisch, Heather Heckman, Juliet Letteney, Derek Lewis, Jeffrey Sconce, Stu Smiley, Steven Starr, and Ethan Thompson.

Thanks to my family and friends for their steadfast support and unwavering enthusiasm along my meandering path through academia: my parents-in-law, Ramona and Tim Jarvis, for their curiosity and generosity; my brothers, Jason and Steven, for their camaraderie and compassion; and my parents, Kathi and Jim, for their unconditional love and guidance. Finally, thanks to my wife, Jill, for supporting me, for bearing with me, for moving with me, for moving with me the third and fourth times, for starting over with me, for ending up with me, for laughing with me, for laughing at me, and for somehow making the badass balancing act of professional, spouse, and parent look easy.

SKETCH COMEDY

INTRODUCTION

Sketch Comedy and Reflexive Flexibility

"We're a big-tent show," *Saturday Night Live* (*SNL*; 1975–) creator Lorne Michaels often says of the sketch comedy program's tendency toward broadly appealing humor for "a coalition of tastes."[1] When *SNL* booked Donald Trump to host in November 2015, Michaels certainly had this in mind. The outlandish celebrity was must-see television for all viewers, boosting the show to its highest-rated episode of that season. Perhaps due to the fact that many viewed him then more as a comedic curiosity than as a serious presidential candidate, *SNL* treated Trump with kid gloves in soft send-ups of his political inexperience and temperamental tweeting. This approach was consistent with Michaels's big-tent philosophy in the run-up to the 2016 presidential election, an approach built on the general absurdities of American politics rather than on specific critiques of any given candidate, party affiliation, or cultural identity.

Then, the shocking election of Trump to the US presidency set off waves of protests and political discord that, appropriately enough, proved to be a boon for American television and comedy. Late-night talk-show hosts feasted on his erratic and egomaniacal behavior, while scores took to social media to critique Trump with satirical memes and sardonic slogans. Regular political parodies buoyed *SNL*'s popularity after the election too, but did so in a way that exacerbated, rather than downplayed, Trump's divisiveness. Michaels's big tent had not collapsed as much as those gathered (and increasingly gathering) beneath it all congregated in one corner. *SNL* firmly situated itself on the anti-Trump side of America's cultural divide with sketches savaging his impulsiveness and penchant for peculiar outbursts online. "Just tried watching Saturday Night Live—unwatchable! Totally biased, not funny and the Baldwin impersonation just can't get any worse. Sad," the forty-fifth president of the United States tweeted in response.

The sketch that best exemplified *SNL*'s flexible politics in the fall of 2016, strangely enough, made Trump himself into mere background noise,

Fig. 0.1. Sketch comedians Dave Chappelle (left) and Chris Rock (right) laugh at the idea that electing Donald Trump is "the most shameful thing America has ever done."

reflexively positioning sketch comedy stars Dave Chappelle (*Chappelle's Show*, 2003–2006) and former *SNL* cast member Chris Rock as its primary identification points for political dissent. In "Election Night," Chappelle watches election returns with and sarcastically comments on his white friends' confidence that Hillary Clinton will win. Rock joins Chappelle in joking about their white friends' increasing dismay as Trump's lead grows. "This is the most shameful thing America has ever done," a white character obliviously proclaims when Trump's victory becomes official. The sketch ends with the two black comedians laughing together, knowing that white liberals are only beginning to feel a fraction of the anger and resentment that African Americans have long lived with. Then, the episode quickly pivots—as it has done for nearly half a century—to a prerecorded parody sketch, a live musical performance, and "Weekend Update."

This book examines sketch comedy as a genre within the American commercial television industry and as a cultural forum for comedians to articulate myriad ideas and identities.[2] I argue throughout that sketch comedy is defined by *reflexive flexibility*. By *reflexive*, I mean sketch comedy shows' tendency to joke about their own creative processes, differences from previous comedic traditions, and roles as arbiters of broader cultural debates. Perhaps more so than any other genre's relationship with the medium, television sketch comedy is first and foremost about television and sketch comedy, as when *SNL* solicits former cast members and other sketch comedians like Rock and Chappelle to host. By *flexibility*, I am referring to sketch comedy's malleability and modularity both as cultural texts and economic goods. Live sketch shows like *SNL* regularly swap out guests, cast members, and subject matter in order to address current events, while others like *Chappelle's Show* experiment with formal conventions and comedy taboos that critique dominant representations of race and gender. Television networks have also used sketch comedy to meet their ever-shifting industrial needs, inserting sketch shows into the schedule to initiate an edgy rebrand or removing selected bits from them for distribution online.

Of course, many other screen media formats are reflexively self-aware or have sudden changes in subject matter or scheduling. Taken together, though, *reflexive flexibility* makes sketch comedy a uniquely intense site of cultural struggle that manifests in comedians and networks fighting over their respective identities. This struggle over identities is so fierce that sketch comedy invites viewers to be reflexively flexible about their own identities too. As I explore later in this introduction through the work of cultural theorists like Pierre Bourdieu and Stuart Hall, sketch comedy uniquely captures the ways we occupy identities that are in the process of formation instead of being fixed and discrete. Sketch comedy—more than any other television genre—lays bare the process of identity formation, pokes fun at its contradictions, and invites us to debate its terms.

SNL's election-season treatment of Trump, for example, displays reflexive flexibility in several ways. The show's ability to pivot in tone regarding Trump (or any current event, for that matter) is due in no small part to *SNL*'s live, weekly production schedule, a rarity among scripted entertainment television programs. *SNL*'s use of social media in satirizing Trump also highlights the efforts of NBC—America's oldest broadcast network—to brand itself as attuned to the digital discourses of desirable young audiences today as networks grapple with declining ratings and distracted viewers. The comedic tone of the "Election Night" sketch, moreover, nimbly moves between the presumptuousness of privileged white voters and the bemusement of Chappelle and Rock before eventually centering their African American identities as the preferred frame for viewers to decode the confusion and anger of Trump's election. And throughout the election season, of course, *SNL* sought both acknowledgment and amplification of the show's voice in the national political conversation, whether in hosts' monologues, winking "Weekend Update" bits, viral clips of Alec Baldwin's Trump

Fig. 0.2. Alec Baldwin's impersonation of President Trump bolstered *Saturday Night Live*'s reflexive flexibility.

impersonation, interviews with Baldwin *about* his Trump impersonation, and rumors about Hollywood ringers ready to impersonate Trump cronies.

Reflexive flexibility is sketch comedy's way of manifesting the tension at the core of nearly all American television programs as both cultural and commercial works. As I explore throughout this book, sketch comedies often center on performers critical of dominant cultural, economic, or representational norms, only to have their ideas muddled by the profit imperatives of risk-averse television executives and networks. Of course, what qualifies as critical for an artist or risky for a network is highly contingent on the discursive contexts in which those agents operate. Rather than framing the art versus commerce tension as constant across the evolution of the genre, this book closely examines several key sketch comedy programs from American television history, their specific conditions of production, and the range of cultural meanings they generate.

Richard Pryor and Amy Schumer, for instance, use the format's brief comedic bursts to posit transgressive ideas about race and gender, but their comedic critiques are constrained by drastically different industrial practices. By the same token, a broadcast network might develop a sketch comedy in order to seem more edgy than competitors, as CBS did with *The State* in 1995, only to quickly cancel it for fear that the network could not safely contain the show's provocative jokes. The potential for impactful, incendiary, and immediate humor that attracts many comedians to sketch is the same quality that gives the format a much shorter shelf life than many other television genres. It is no accident, then, that most sketch comedies (with few major exceptions) tend to be fleeting, fraught with behind-the-scenes turmoil and fights between headstrong comedians and executives more mindful of the bottom line. By using the lens of reflexive flexibility and seeing sketch comedy as fundamentally self-obsessed, malleable, and modular, we can better understand how it has been a site of tenser struggle between the forces of art and commerce than many other television formats.

Indeed, my goal in using this analytic framework is to examine not only sketch comedy shows themselves but also the ways a variety of other voices—advertisers, creative laborers, fans, television critics, executives, and others—use the format's reflexive flexibility. To that end, I rely on as many different sources of evidence as I can, including close textual analyses of sketch comedy television shows; archival resources documenting network efforts to develop sketch comedies and refashion them as they air; interviews with performers and producers about the myriad competing approaches to working in sketch; and television industry trade journals chronicling their own version of sketch comedy's economic utility. This book thus positions the analytic domains of media text, industry, and sociohistorical context as mutually constitutive and in doing so aligns with the work of many scholars working in the media and cultural studies traditions.[3] I hope that this integrated approach offers my study a broad scope without sacrificing the details of what makes particular programs or comedians funny.

With this in mind, I have two major caveats before proceeding further. First, I limit this book's major case studies to television programs and media texts produced and aired primarily in the United States. Of course, dozens of highly influential and hilarious sketch shows have aired around the world to great acclaim, many of which I reference in passing. However, because this book ties sketch comedy's cultural import to the specific practices of the American television industry, attempting to account for dozens of global media economies would be too unwieldy. Second, although my integrated methodology allows for close examinations of key sketch comedy moments, programs, and practices, it does not support a comprehensive overview of the genre. That is to say, this book does not list and discuss the contributions of every notable sketch comedy to air on American television—the collective intelligence of the internet has done a fine job of that already. However, the book does have a historical structure, with each chapter closely examining a particular sketch comedy program within the social, cultural, and industrial contexts of its production. In doing so, I take a conceptual approach that understands sketch comedy as a cultural category whose meaning is equally constructed by television texts and their discursive contexts, not as a monolithic artifact with stable, unchanging characteristics.[4] Before examining sketch comedy conceptually—and given my emphasis on the format's flexibility thus far—having some baseline definitions in place will be helpful in exploring their broader implications.

In its use as a television genre, we might begin by defining sketch comedy as any program primarily composed of comedy sketches. Unfortunately, this definition is quite broad—undoubtedly part of the reason the format has been put to so many different cultural and industrial uses. If we look to scholarly resources for a definition, there is little addressing sketch comedy in and of itself in the way that I am attempting in this book. Another place to turn might be a consideration of sketch comedy television's basic building block—the comedy sketch. Fortunately, media and comedy theorist Steve Neale provides a useful starting point: "As the term implies, sketches are short, usually single-scene structures. They generally comprise a setting, one or more characters, and an internal time-frame within which the comic possibilities of a premise of one kind or another—a situation, a relationship, a conversation and its topics, a mode of language, speech or behaviour, or some other organising principle—are either pursued to a point of climax and conclusion (sometimes called a 'pay-off'), or else simply abandoned."[5] Neale's definition points to a number of key elements of a comedy sketch—its brevity, typical component parts, and desired effect. Additionally, it hints at the fact that what happens from sketch to sketch *within* a single episode—and even from episode to episode within a season or series run—of a sketch comedy program can vary even more in format and tone. Sketch comedy's modularity often makes the genre radically episodic, with viewers needing little to no knowledge of previous episodes and sketches in order to enjoy subsequent ones.

One common method networks and comedians use to manage this textual malleability and modularity is to organize the show under the aegis of a known personality, media practice, or cultural referent. *Saturday Night Live* announces in its title, for instance, both its daypart and production method. Without even viewing any of their sketches, audiences will know that *Mind of Mencia* (2003–2008) centers the stand-up comedian Carlos

Mencia as its primary creative voice, just as *Mad TV* (1995–2009, 2016) announces the satirical *Mad* magazine as its organizing text. Although there can be much variability among the sketches of a given episode or series, most sketch comedies still conform to television industry standards of thirty- to sixty-minute program length and commercial breaks. Program titles and length, then, are just two of the many ways that television industry discourses manage the volatility of sketch comedy's reflexive flexibility.

So too do longstanding storytelling conventions provide organizing principles for comedy sketches themselves. In general, most comedy sketches on television follow the formula described by Neale—establish a premise, explore it, then bring it to a climax. Although this pattern is common across virtually all forms of popular culture, it is the many malleable ways sketch comedy manifests this formula—as well as the reflexivity with which it does so—that makes the genre unique. In the next section, I explore some of sketch comedy's most commonly recurring textual aspects, including, but not limited to:

- cast members performing as themselves and as characters
- interstitial bits
- misunderstanding
- recurring characters
- breaking
- parody
- physical virtuosity
- absurdism
- blackout

I do so first—in the most reflexive and meta-sketch comedic way possible—by letting a comedy sketch define itself for us.

Sketch Comedy Definitions and Core Textual Traits

"Sketch comedy: What is it? What is required?" Dave Foley flatly intones to the camera in "Sketch Comedy" from the first season of the Canadian sketch show *The Kids in the Hall* (1989–1994). Right away, Foley's introduction highlights one of the core aspects of sketch comedy's reflexive flexibility: *cast members performing as themselves and as characters*, sometimes both within the same sketch. In "Sketch Comedy," Foley is both himself—regular cast member of the *Kids* troupe introducing a *Kids* sketch—and "himself," a parody of a television host, one bored of his job offering a peek behind the scenes. This dynamic is not always carried out with the layers of reflexivity of the *Kids* sketch; it more commonly manifests with cast members or guest hosts providing explanatory jokes or commentary in *interstitial bits* between sketches. *SNL*'s guest host each week assures viewers both at home and in the audience that "We've got a great show for you" before mentioning the musical guest and throwing to a sketch, while comedians like Schumer or Chappelle recycle parts of stand-up routines that frame an episode's prerecorded sketches. In its final season, *Key & Peele* (2012–2015) used interstitial bits to drop in on the eponymous stars, Keegan-Michael Key and Jordan Peele, on a (staged) road trip, joking about something tangentially related to each subsequent sketch.

In any case, sketch comedy performers—whether as regular cast members or as one-off guests—reflexively provide the baseline of familiarity from which the sketches themselves depart, using even shorter connective scenes to tie often disparate sketches together thematically among radically distinct episodes. In the rest of this section, I use *Kids*' "Sketch Comedy" both to highlight the through line of premise-conflict-resolution among sketches and to point to other variations among them. Doing so will help us better understand discussions of sketch comedy's cultural and industrial contexts later in this introduction.

Premise

"The first thing that is needed for a comedy sketch is a premise," Foley proceeds in "Sketch Comedy." The first minute or so of any comedy sketch usually introduces viewers to a funny world or worldview, fictional or reality-based, one designed to create comedic misunderstandings and outlandish interactions among its characters. In the *Monty Python's Flying Circus* (1969–1974) sketch "Dead Parrot," for example, a shopkeeper played by Michael Palin refuses to accept the return of the titular dead bird by a disgruntled customer played by John Cleese. The humor arises early on from the idea that a shopkeeper would sell a product so obviously defective and then refuse to accept its return. Similarly, the premise of John Belushi's Samurai Futaba sketches on early seasons (1975–1979) of *Saturday Night Live* has the recurring character exaggeratedly perform mundane tasks—carrying hotel guests' bags, slicing deli meet, repairing a television—much to the bemusement of onlookers. Both examples create a particular universe and quickly populate it with elements predisposed to clashing comedically.

Fig. 0.3. John Belushi portrays the recurring character Samurai Futaba for the second time on *SNL* in "Samurai Delicatessen."

The sketches also provide prime examples of two of sketch comedy's favored premises. "Dead Parrot" relies on a comedic *misunderstanding* between its two principal characters, affording them several minutes to humorously talk past one another and increase the tension of their miscommunication. Samurai Futaba is a *recurring character*, one whose premises have been developed in previous sketches and cue audiences to laugh for recognizing them. I explore recurring characters in sketch comedy—as a precursor to more conventionally episodic sitcom characters, as a way to win screen time over fellow cast members, and as a target of parody—in more detail over the course of this book.

Conflict

"The premise has been established. The comedic possibilities are inherent. All that is needed for this scene to progress is a conflict," Foley continues in the *Kids* sketch. After setting viewer expectations with a funny premise, most sketches introduce a conflict between two or more competing forces. It is here, in the sketch's middle section, that writers and performers have the most opportunity to devise unexpected narrative twists, improvise unscripted lines, break out of character, and generally find ways to escalate the scene in humorous ways.

In *The Carol Burnett Show*'s (1967–1978) "Supermarket Checker," for example, Harvey Korman plays a man anxious for Carol Burnett's chatty, fastidious clerk to complete his transaction so that he can rush home with a hot date. Burnett's titular checker delays Korman's character in increasingly frustrating ways—calling for a price check on incense, gabbing with a coworker—while he reacts with exasperation and watches other men chat up his would-be lover. Although "Supermarket Checker" features a relatively conventional conflict, *Burnett* would become somewhat notorious for its actors *breaking* out of character with laughter and derailing the fictional veneer of the sketch. Breaking is common across all scripted television, though it is normally edited out from the final product. In the case of *Burnett* and certain actors on other live sketch shows (Jimmy Fallon on *SNL*, for instance), breaking can become part of the pleasure of a sketch, reflexively reminding viewers that a sketch is often more about delivering laughter than exploring a conflict.

In a different vein, many sketches forgo a central conflict altogether in pursuit of a laugh. *Parody* sketches often rely on repeated references to some existing cultural artifact rather than on an escalation of tension. *In Living Color*'s (1990–1994) many parodies of musicians, for instance, feature cast members impersonating artists like Paula Abdul, Tracy Chapman, and Michael Jackson by exaggerating their outlandish dancing or performative quirks. The sketches—like the countless parodies of films, celebrities, or news events that have appeared on sketch comedy programs over the years—draw humor from their embellished reiterations of cultural iconography that is likely familiar to viewers already.

Other sketches might focus solely on the *physical virtuosity* of their actors, replacing the climax of an escalating conflict with the spectacle of a performance or comedic concept. Sid Caesar and Nanette Fabray emote and gesticulate wordlessly in their "Argument to Beethoven's Fifth" from *Caesar's Hour* (1954–1957), for example, and Ernie Kovacs's famous "Nairobi Trio" sketches (1957) provide perfectly timed punchlines through rhythmic miming.

As I explore more in chapter 2, comedy sketches in early television often relied on their performers' backgrounds using physical and sight gags in vaudeville and variety shows. Decades later, *SNL*'s Chris Farley shot to stardom by violently throwing around his famously fat frame in sketches like "Chippendales" (1990). Of course, there exists a broad range of creative choices for comedians wishing to flexibly develop a sketch's premise.

Generally, though, the middle section of a comedy sketch explores a funny idea before giving way to its climax and resolution.

Resolution/Punchline

"All that is required now for this to be a fully formed and well-rounded comedy sketch is a resolution . . . this is generally followed by a blackout," Foley deadpans at the conclusion of "Sketch Comedy." Much like many other narrative structures in popular media, the third part of a comedy sketch resolves its conflict and brings the scene to a close, usually doing so with an action, punchline, or gag that prompts a big laugh from viewers. Unlike other conventional narratives, comedy sketches are freer to experiment and take their endings to unexpected places, knowing that the next (likely wholly unrelated) sketch premise is right after the commercial break.

A news parody sketch from *Chappelle's Show*, for example, follows the story of Clayton Bigsby, a reclusive, fictional leader in the white power movement who is both black and blind. The sketch climaxes with Bigsby appearing at a book signing in full Ku Klux Klan regalia complete with a hood and gloves concealing his true race. As the black and blind Bigsby spews racist vitriol to his white fans, they implore him to remove his hood and reveal his identity. When Bigsby takes off the hood and his white fans see he is actually black, they react with horror and disgust, with one admirer's head exploding and spewing blood and brains everywhere. The climactic twist demonstrates *absurdism*, an aesthetic trait that became more common in the multichannel and post-network eras as sketch shows sought both to separate themselves from predecessors and to challenge similarly sketch-savvy viewers.

One device relatively unique to comedy sketches is the way their resolutions can be punctuated by a *blackout*, a hard cutting of light to the scene much more abrupt than a conventional film or television scene's dissolving or fading to black. The practice comes from sketch comedy's roots in live burlesque and vaudeville theater performances, one designed to prompt laughter and applause from the audience, as well as provide an opportunity for transitions among performers, scenery, and costuming. Foley's mordant joke in the *Kids* sketch is meant to bemoan the overuse of blackouts—and, according to *Kids*, the cloying, witless jokes that often accompany them— by sketch comedies still clinging to vaudevillian aesthetics. It also showcases *Kids*' cultural capital, reflexively proving that Foley understands previously consecrated comedic traditions enough to make fun of them. The blackout became such a common trope in many early television and network era sketch comedies rooted in live theatrical traditions that later comedians parodied or sought to abandon the device altogether in favor of humor addressing television itself.

Mr. Show (1995–1998)—whose very title is a satirical shot at vaudevillian comedy—regularly lampooned many of television's industrial and aesthetic norms, a characteristic common to many sketch comedies of the multi-channel transition and post-network era (as I explore in chapters 3 and 4). In the sketch "Pre-taped Call-in Show" (1997), for instance, a haggard talk show host played by David Cross sits at a cheap-looking desk adorned with a telephone, coffee mug, and ashtray overflowing with cigarette butts. "Let's try it again," he says into the camera, "It's really not that hard, OK? Our topic once again is the elderly. We're taping it now, and it airs next week. So if you're watching me talk about the elderly, don't call to talk about it, it's too late. Instead, call about cooking, which is next week's topic." A succession of confused viewers calls in to ask the host about pets, racism, and anything other than the elderly, as he explains with increasing exasperation the jumbled timeline for when the show is taped, when it airs, and when to call in. The sketch climaxes with a zoom in to a television screen beside the host's desk playing the "Pre-taped Call-in Show" episode currently on air, which has the host screaming that the topic viewers are calling about was covered last week, followed by a zoom in to another television in that episode reiterating the gag again, and so on. Instead of a blackout, the *Mr. Show* episode reflexively maintains the shows-within-a-show construction by indicating that viewers of *Mr. Show* are watching the "The Convoluted Television Network" before transitioning to a parody sketch of a horror movie.

Despite the preponderance of sketches playing with television's formal features, much of *Mr. Show* was shot before a live studio audience, though not broadcast live like many famed sketch shows before it—ones such as *Saturday Night Live* or *Your Show of Shows* (1950–1954). Certainly, as these and myriad other examples indicate, television sketch comedy's move from live theatricality to televisuality is not absolute. Live, sketch-based shows in the 1950s from Ernie Kovacs, for example, regularly toyed with the visual and technological affordances of television's early years, while more recent efforts such as *Maya & Marty* (2016) have sought to revive sketch comedy's live, vaudevillian roots. All of the programs discussed thus far, though, share the sketch as their basic building block, and all of their sketches share some form of the premise-conflict-resolution structure.

Fig. 0.4. Instead of ending with a blackout, *Mr. Show* sketches like "Pre-taped Call-in Show" reflexively toy with television's formal features.

Yet we're not much closer to identifying a concrete definition of a sketch as distinct from other comedic forms here than we were at the beginning of this chapter. As one writer puts it in describing sketch comedy's malleability: "A sketch should be short, though some are quite long. It should be simple, though many are complex. It contains more structure than improv, though it may be little more than a retro-scripted scene. It erects a fourth wall absent in stand-up, though it may tear that wall down. It should, above all, be funny, and still the best are often deeply serious."[6] In other words, there is no set formula for defining a comedy sketch, just as there is no set formula for determining whether or not something is funny. As the examples above indicate, there are many iterations of a comedy sketch, sketch comedy, and the affective outcomes they produce. Depending on the comedian, sociohistorical context, and production pressures a show faces, a sketch—and its presumed funniness—can flexibly take any number of forms. In order to understand these many forms, then, we must look beyond sketches as component pieces to the broader programs, aesthetic choices, and cultural and industrial discourses of which they are a part.

One way to do this is to examine television sketch comedy as a cultural production, one structured just as much by comedians' creative choices as they are by their conditions of creation. These conditions, according to the French sociologist Pierre Bourdieu, are constructed through a complex interplay among artists' cultural predispositions, the manner in which they express those dispositions, and the limits placed on both by an artform's material and economic constraints. I explore these constraints as they relate to sketch comedy throughout television history in this introduction's final section. In the next section, I consider the subjective and objective frameworks through which sketch comedians do their cultural work.

Sketch Comedy, Cultural Production, and Cultural Identity

If, as I suggest above, sketch comedy cannot be fully understood by looking only at the programs themselves, then we need a more thorough understanding of the specific forces bearing on sketch shows' creation. Accordingly, Bourdieu argues that the meaning of a cultural artifact—like a television show—is located both in the text itself and in the contexts of its production and reception. In doing so, he criticizes theoretical models that locate cultural meaning within the supposed genius of individual artists, a tendency he bemoans as the "charismatic ideology of 'creation.'"[7] At the same time, Bourdieu aims to avoid reducing cultural products to mere reflections of the social structures and dominant ideologies of their creation. In staking out this theoretical middle ground, Bourdieu posits the concept of field, structured social spaces where people jockey for resources in ways that create hierarchical power relationships. The field most germane to my study of sketch comedy is that of cultural production, which Bourdieu describes as "the system of objective relations between [cultural] agents or institutions and as the site of the struggles for the monopoly of the power to consecrate."[8]

The agents and institutions in the field of cultural production compete with one another not for economic capital—financial gain—but for cultural and symbolic capital, the prestige, celebrity, and competencies that consecrate certain artists and artworks over others. This formulation of capital is at the core of Bourdieu's better-known work on cultural consumption, *Distinction: A Social Critique of the Judgment of Taste*, which posits one's aesthetic choices as a social construction in much the same way that production is. Across both his theories of cultural production and consumption, Bourdieu is chiefly concerned with how cultural activities, ones seemingly based in individuals' conscious creative choices, are socially structured in ways that create and reproduce class hierarchies.

Given comedy's openness to interpretation, *Distinction* has provided a favored theoretical framework for many reception studies of comedic taste and power.⁹ Although this book suggests some of sketch comedy's interpretive possibilities, it is *not* focused on audience activities, nor does it utilize the same Bourdieusian fieldwork (such as surveys and ethnography) that many audience studies do. Instead, I examine sketch comedy as a field of cultural *production*, one with its own creative processes, historical conditions, and economic contexts shaping and positioning its "agents and institutions." In doing so, this book takes advantage of the flexibility inherent in Bourdieu's understanding of fields "as the site of the struggles for the monopoly of the power to consecrate." Bourdieu's characterization of these struggles as objectively determined provides tremendous insight into how artists closest in a social space—comedians on a weekly television production, for example—compete for the right to consecrate certain styles. Ultimately, though, field is limited in its capacity to explain the complex identity work of sketch comedy, a shortcoming I address through the framework of reflexive flexibility.

First, as a way to better understand sketch comedy production as a field, let's use the example of NBC's 30 Rockefeller Plaza as a Bourdieusian institution, home to several famous NBC programs such as *The Tonight Show with Jimmy Fallon* (2014–present) and *Saturday Night Live*. At first glance, the producers, writers, and comedians for both shows might seem to be in close competition with one another. After all, both occupy the late-night comedy genre and share Lorne Michaels as executive producer. Given Fallon's four-year tenure as coanchor for "Weekend Update," the temptation exists to view *SNL* simply as a farm team for bigger things beyond sketch comedy television shows (a dynamic I explore in chap. 3). When viewed through Bourdieu's framework, though, we see that the struggle to consecrate certain comedians over others is less intense between the two shows than it is *within* them. In order for a sketch comedian to ascend to Fallon's position on *Tonight*, for instance, she must first compete intensely with her *SNL* colleagues in order to win appearances in cold opens, nail key political impersonations, or develop recurring characters. Then, she must marshal her prestige for the role of herself at the "Update" desk, as Fallon did. Only once she has been consecrated among her peers on *SNL* can she compete beyond sketch comedy in movies or prime-time television—as Tina Fey and Amy Poehler have, for example.

Of course, the performers, writers, and producers—the cultural agents I examine throughout this book—of *SNL* and *Tonight* are in closer competition than, say, those of *SNL* and Marvel movies, just as the agents of those texts are in closer competition than agents in media versus those in clothing production. What makes sketch comedies particularly apt for field analysis are the many competing and contradictory ideas each agent brings to sketch comedy production and how quickly those ideas can change. I have already discussed above how sketch comedy's malleable formal conventions accommodate quickly shifting creative approaches and competition among comedians. Bourdieu's model additionally allows us to see how struggles within a field of cultural production like sketch comedy are embedded within bigger fields of political and economic power. We might understand the close competition among *SNL* cast members, for example, to be informed, but not determined, by the television industry's shift from broadcasting to narrowcasting or by the mood of political opposition to a given candidate. As Bourdieu notes, a cultural field "functions somewhat like a prism which *refracts* every external determination: demographic, economic or political events are always retranslated according to the specific logic of the field."[10] Keeping this interconnectedness of fields in mind helps us make better sense of the many struggles for capital among sketch comedy performers and programs, as well as their broader cultural import.

One of the central tensions of Bourdieu's model, then, is the degree to which a field of cultural activity like sketch comedy production is autonomous from the broader field of political and economic power enclosing it. Indeed, one of the goals of this book is to examine not only the competition for consecration among sketch comedians and programs but also how political and economic contexts do or do not shape this competition. Danielle Jeanine Deveau's exploration of Canadian stand-up comedy investigates a similar tension, one defined by the seemingly transgressive ideas of comics' performances within the field and the more conservative labor routines that reinforce dominant norms in the industry. Throughout her study, Deveau considers "the ways in which certain performers or career trajectories are consecrated, as well as the ways that performers mock or resist the authority of this consecration. Indeed, at times in their careers, performers seem to strategically render up much of their creative autonomy in order to advance into the cultural industries, with the end goal of regaining this autonomy once they reach sufficient levels of celebrity and/or consecration."[11] Similarly, my study examines the tensions inherent in sketch comedians' pursuit of various forms of capital and consecration, as well as their relationship to broader industrial constraints. In the four major case studies of this book, agents in the sketch comedy field again and again exhibit a maniacal drive to compete with one another for recognition, a game of one-upmanship to prove who best knows—and can mock—their sketch comedy antecedents, taking the field in a new direction. As David Hesmondhalgh pithily summarizes, this dynamic is centered on "a battle between established producers, institutions, and heretical newcomers."[12] These dual tensions—intense competition among sketch comedians, and the sketch comedy field's varying levels of autonomy from broader social power—constitute major analytical axes of this book.

As useful as it is as a starting point, though, Bourdieu's model presents a couple of challenges, ones for which reflexive flexibility strives to account. First, his division of the field of cultural production into two smaller subfields—small-scale and large-scale production—fails to anticipate the fluidity of these domains in television recently. Bourdieu conceives of small-scale production as having a high degree of autonomy from financial pressures, a place of "production for producers" where artists mostly talk to one another and jockey for symbolic capital.[13] Large-scale production, by contrast, has much less autonomy from economic pressures and is more commonly characterized by the motivations of commercial mass media like television. As Hesmondhalgh notes through the example of post-network "quality television," Bourdieu's division of the cultural field does not account for the "ability of large-scale production to disseminate consecrated culture" or how "restricted production has become introduced into the field of mass production."[14] In other words, field theory does not quite accurately capture how the production of a prestige program like *Game of Thrones* (2011–2019) can be informed by intense competition for symbolic capital—awards and critical praise—yet distributed for millions of viewers to see on a for-profit network. Reflexive flexibility offers one way to reconceive of small- and large-scale television production as complementary, not conflicting, industrial modes, a relationship I consider more closely in the final section of this introduction.

Another shortcoming of Bourdieu's model is its conception of the role of human agency in cultural production, one that does not adequately capture the centrality of identity in sketch comedy. At first glance, his characterization of a given cultural field as a site of struggles does echo my description of reflexive flexibility as a tug-of-war between comedians and networks over their respective identities. These agents, for Bourdieu, struggle not only for symbolic capital but also for advantageous positions to access capital, ones continuously generated out of a "space of possibles" that "define the thinkable and the unthinkable, the do-able and impossible for agents in the field."[15] In other words, creative activity is always circumscribed by one's position in a particular field of cultural production. In a literal, televisual sense, for example, a gaffer might light a sketch but cannot rewrite any jokes. In a more theoretical sense, Bourdieu clearly aims to delimit the potentially revolutionary nature of cultural production, instead making its meaning "dependent on the possibilities present in the positions inscribed in the field."[16] However, by pegging human agency to objectively defined positions, he leaves little room for understanding the processual nature of cultural production or how agents might occupy different identities and positions in a field simultaneously. This shortcoming becomes particularly apparent when considering how many sketch comedy agents are often in liminal positions, flexibly using the format both to explore their own creative processes and to critique their conditions of production.

The flexibility of positions within the field of sketch comedy production is clear when viewing them through the lenses of race and gender. Another example might help us flesh out how reflexive flexibility can supplement Bourdieu's conception of positions and creative agency. On the heels of vigorous public debates about and increased visibility for black activist movements in 2013, *SNL* came under fire for its lack of black women as cast members. "It's not like it's not a priority for us," Lorne Michaels flippantly commented while producers conducted an intense, behind-the-scenes search that would end in the hiring of Sasheer Zamata, Leslie Jones, and LaKendra Tookes.[17] That November the show addressed criticisms about its lack of diversity in a sketch, "Oval Office," starring host Kerry Washington as Michelle Obama opposite Jay Pharoah's President Obama. As the couple converses, press secretary Jay Carney (played by Taran Killam) interrupts to inform them that Oprah Winfrey would like to say hello. "So don't you think you should go and get changed . . . so that Oprah can come in?" Carney knowingly says to the First Lady, to which she flatly replies "Oh, because of the whole . . ." Washington-as-Michelle-Obama dashes offstage as onscreen text reads: "The producers at 'Saturday Night Live' would like to apologize for the number of black women [Washington] will be asked to play tonight." Washington returns in a new wig and bigger dress to impersonate Winfrey, then hurries offstage again after Carney informs her of Beyoncé's arrival. The scene reflexively ends—as so many half-baked *SNL* ideas do—with a cast member or celebrity grasping for a point by directly

Fig. 0.5. *SNL* guest host Kerry Washington impersonates Oprah Winfrey after portraying Michelle Obama minutes earlier.

addressing the audience, as activist Al Sharpton saunters onstage and sardonically states, "What have we learned from this sketch? Nothing."

The sketch exemplifies many of the aspects described above of sketch comedy as a Bourdieusian field. Its agents occupy clearly defined positions, with Washington as guest host and Killam and Pharoah as cast members. In fact, the latter two had toiled in secondary positions as featured players for several seasons before regularly winning coveted roles in 2013 in highly visible cold open sketches like "Oval Office." They jockey for the resources for consecration (laughs and applause from the live studio audience, critical praise for their impersonations), a process that undoubtedly began in the hallways of 30 Rock long before "Oval Office" aired. The sketch also demonstrates the logic by which *SNL* refracts external political and economic factors in specific ways. Just about every *SNL* cold open of the twenty-first century has similarly centered on political humor, an increasingly lucrative and demographically desirable topic for satirical television in the post-network era.[18] Finally, "Oval Office" highlights sketch comedy as a unique field of cultural production, one that comments on contemporaneous events in a scripted, radically episodic (and for *SNL*, live) format that asks audiences to find humor in both the sketch itself and its conditions of production.

Although field theory provides a strong foundation for examining sketches like "Oval Office," we need additional nuance to capture its complex race and gender identity work, particularly in Washington's role. Her position as network-television-star-and-guest-host is evident, but the sketch also reflexively jokes about other positions she occupies. This reflexive commentary occurs explicitly in the sketch's central comedic premise—Washington must make up for *SNL*'s lack of diversity by somehow simultaneously playing Obama, Winfrey, and Beyoncé. Implicitly, her performance not only reinscribes the position of black woman cast member back into *SNL*'s "space of possibles" but also joins and amplifies cultural voices critical of that very space. Just as Washington-as-Obama/Winfrey/Beyoncé moves on- and offstage in the sketch, so too is her position as an agent simultaneously located both within and outside of the sketch comedy field. It is precisely this simultaneity of identity positions, and the processual nature of their formation, that field theory fails to fully capture. In other words, field helps explain sketch comedy's reflexivity—its tendency to centralize itself in cultural production—but does little to help us describe its flexibility. Analyzing sketch comedy through the lens of reflexive flexibility requires understanding both its objectively determined conditions of production (like those described by Bourdieu) and the subjectivities of its producers. In order to do the latter, we must supplement field with a more thorough accounting of the subjectively formed identities that have become so central to modern life.

Identity has long been an urgent concern to scholars of media and culture, serving as a path of inquiry in studies of everything from onscreen representations to media production practices. Stuart Hall's examination of identity is most useful to us here in amending Bourdieu's framework and building a fuller understanding of sketch comedy's reflexive flexibility.[19] Though acknowledging its many contested meanings, Hall arrives at a definition of identity by reconciling two competing forces in how we operationalize the concept. On the one hand, we are capable of producing and performing any given identity position. On the other hand, we do so within a limited range of possibilities, ones to which we are interpellated by dominant cultural power. For Hall, one's race or gender is always in process, a "temporary attachment to the subject positions which discursive practices construct for us."[20] Identity is thus not a fixed endpoint where one can declare with permanence that she is a woman or an Arab or a heterosexual. Instead, an identity is the process by which those categories are both imposed on and produced by us.

The processual nature of identities, for Hall, means that they mark "difference and exclusion," functioning as temporary attachment points to various lived experiences "only *because* of their capacity to exclude, to leave out, to render 'outside', abjected."[21] In other words, declaring any given identity implicitly names as distinct its "silenced and unspoken other, that which it 'lacks.'"[22] Take, for example, the routine declaration of gender we have all made on a survey or application of any kind. Making that selection is a declaration of gender identity, one structured within the broader, dominant understanding that there are two options for gender and only two possible boxes to check. Selecting "woman," for instance, is not necessarily a disavowal or rejection of the masculine identity but rather an exclusion of it from the feminine one, a tacit declaration that it is distinct. Any given identity position is thus constructed both by our temporary attachments to it and by its constitutive other(s)*.

Hall's work has important implications for understanding how comedy participates in the construction of identities in powerful ways. Broadly speaking, comedic media are defined by their ability to unite various viewers around a shared joke or comedic referent—something those viewers all understand. As Andy Medhurst notes in his study of comedy and English identities, comedy "constitutes a repository of symbols that can be drawn on to indicate how, where and why people place themselves; it is a prime testing ground for ideas about belonging and exclusion."[23] Laughter—nearly always comedy's desired affect—physically reinforces this dynamic. It tangibly manifests where one can place oneself, as either a subject or object of comedic critique, as either on the giving or receiving end of derision. From either position, Medhurst suggests, invoking Hall, comedy allows "those inside any given identity category to shore up their sense of self by enabling them to use laughter 'to leave out, to render "outside," abject' those perceived as occupying contrasting or challenging identities."[24] Comedy thus provides a powerful way through which we occupy social positions on the basis of our identities.

Because identities only exist in fluid relation to other identities, fixing them to objectively determined positions within a field—as Bourdieu suggests—becomes challenging. The processual and sometimes simultaneous nature of identities in the sketch comedy field becomes particularly pronounced when considering their relationship to the broader economic field of the television industry. Here sketch comedy reveals not consistently hierarchical, but flexible, power relationships among the field's various agents. Often, sketch comedy programs inevitably support those from dominant identity groups, a dynamic evident in the way that a show or

---

* Given this book's emphasis on identity, I have strived, where possible, to use gendered language (e.g., woman and man) instead of sexed language (e.g., female and male). I hope that doing so highlights the ways in which sketch comedy and television contribute to the social construction of gender.

network simply publicizes itself. Before premiering several sketch comedies in the early 2010s, for example, Comedy Central released self-collected data conveniently finding that "more than music, more than sports, more than 'personal style,' comedy has become essential to how young men view themselves and others."[25] The network undoubtedly meant to assure advertisers that it would not alienate its valued longtime audience of young men before debuting programs starring women comedians. By explicitly distinguishing the identity of its desired audience, Comedy Central reaffirmed the cultural power that young men have historically enjoyed over those in other identity categories.

In other cases, television's commercial imperatives make sketch comedy's reflexive flexibility a bit more ambiguous. Herman Gray's study of FOX's *In Living Color*, for instance, reveals a range of deeply ambivalent black identities on the show, ones that both oppose and reinforce the network's efforts to appeal to a heteronormative black middle class.[26] In sketches like "Men On . . . ," in which cast members Damon Wayans and David Allen Grier crudely adopt the personas of homosexuals, sketch conventions like catchphrases anchor representations of transgressive gay blackness in the relative normativity of black heterosexual masculinity prized by FOX at the time. In a similar vein, the "Homeboy Shopping Network" sketches (which feature Damon and brother Keenan Ivory Wayans as destitute vagrants pitching garbage for sale to home viewers) confront the economic plight of the black lower class only to affirm a middle-class blackness able to revel in the joys of lower-class antics. For Gray, *In Living Color* posited black, heteronormative, middle-class viewers as its desired audience even as the show depicted oppositionally oriented black identities.

Still for other programs, identity in "sketch comedy is always about transgression," as Bambi Haggins argues in her look at *Chappelle's Show* on Comedy Central.[27] In sketches like "Racial Draft," "The Niggar Family," and the above-mentioned *Frontline* parody with Clayton Bigsby, the malleable sketch format allows Chappelle to maneuver among many transgressive representations of black identity. In other words, Chappelle's position within the sketch comedy field was rarely fixed, creating "partially translated enunciations of blackness that speak to various audiences on variable registers."[28] However, the dynamic proved unsustainable for Chappelle, as the comedian grew increasingly uncomfortable with the extent to which audiences reinterpreted elements of the show unmoored from their original context. (Chappelle was alleged to have been upset about a white studio

Fig. 0.6. Despite their transgressive racial representations, the broader meaning of *In Living Color* sketches like "Homeboy Shopping Network" was ultimately ambivalent.

audience member laughing at a racial epithet during taping, and he abandoned the show shortly after signing a lucrative long-term contract with Comedy Central.) The significance of *Chappelle's Show*, for Haggins, was less about transgressing mainstream black identities than it was about redefining them altogether, "making the margin the mainstream" in the process.[29]

The key for understanding the flexibility of identity formation in sketch comedy, then, is its relationship with television's various commercial mandates. On the one hand, networks strategically create and circulate sketch comedies with identities that serve their respective financial goals. Across nearly all historical periods, social contexts, and advertising models, networks have programmed sketch shows starring comedians and targeting audiences that support the social status quo. In this regard, sketch comedy has been and will undoubtedly continue to function much like many other forms of American media and popular culture. On the other hand, sketch comedy television programs have again and again centered on identities that deconstruct, destabilize, or transgress dominant ideological norms. As many examples discussed thus far have shown, sketch comedy is uniquely suited for comedians to differentiate their ideas from those of other generations or identity categories, and for viewers to imagine their place in the world in powerful new ways. In addition to serving as a site through which individuals articulate flexible identities, sketch comedy also provides examples of the day-to-day production and promotional decisions in the television industry that structure those cultural discourses. In order to understand the mutually constitutive relationship of these cultural and economic domains, finally, we need to examine their industrial and historical contexts more.

Sketch Comedy and Television Industry Identities

Thus far I have used reflexive flexibility to flesh out the malleability of sketches and sketch shows themselves, as well as the identities a range of cultural agents express when producing sketch comedy. In this final section, I historically contextualize those creative practices in order to better track the broader relationship between television's various economic models and the cultural meanings they generate. Sketch comedy's specific role in this capacity, I suggest, has been to help television's executive, promotional, and advertising personnel quickly and cheaply negotiate the industry's fickle financial imperatives. Just as sketch is a Bourdieusian site of struggle for cultural consecration among comedians, so too has it been a contested space for television's myriad business-minded agents to flexibly meet (or not meet) the industry's many financial demands. As my subsequent analyses make clear, sketch comedy's industrial modularity is ideally suited to serve short-term economic goals such as rebranding and experimentation, rather than provide the comparatively reliable long-term financial returns of many other television genres.

In structuring this book chronologically, though, I do not wish to trace a straightforward evolution of sketch comedy from the dark ages of crude technologies and insular understandings of audiences to the enlightened contemporary moment of technological convergence and viewer empowerment. If anything, examining the industrial history of sketch comedy reveals that many of television's new best practices are recycling, not replacing, existing ones. For instance, sponsors have recently resurrected early television's live, event-driven scheduling and integrated advertising models in an effort to reach viewers who are skipping over or avoiding conventional commercial breaks more and more. Recent variety-sketch comedy programs such as *Rosie Live* (2008) have similarly strived to mimic the genre's early roots in an effort to re-create early television's live, collective viewing experiences. Particularly when viewed in the context of the often recursive practices of the television industry, sketch comedy's reflexive flexibility becomes even more salient.

In the remainder of this introduction, I situate sketch comedy within television's various economic models across four eras, each with a set of dominant production, distribution, and promotional practices.[30] Each section provides industrial and historical context for a corresponding case study later in the book. More importantly, though, this overview supplements the above analyses of sketch comedy's cultural functions with a more thorough understanding of their conditions of production.

Early Television: 1940s–1950s

In television's formative years as an entertainment medium, sketch comedy was not yet the recognizably distinct genre that it is today. Instead, comedy sketches often constituted parts of longer variety programs, which might also have included songs, dancing, monologues, or a number of other acts. Comedy sketches' role in this era was to act as a site of formal experimentation within these broader programs. Sometimes, this simply meant that comedians previously trained in theatrical performance would attempt to directly translate their stage acts for television viewers. For others, sketches laid the conceptual and character groundwork for what would later become situation comedies. In most cases, comedy sketches in early television helped comedians, producers, and networks flexibly explore television's formal features, even if it meant borrowing liberally from other media.

Indeed, as Michele Hilmes's work has shown, early television relied heavily on the creative and commercial infrastructures of radio before it.[31] Short, bit-driven comedy acts took a number of forms on radio that could be simulcast on television, reworked to accommodate visual gags, or stretched into recurring narrative scenarios to fill radio's, then television's, voracious appetite for content. The role of sketch-like comedy in broadcasting's formal experiments on radio and early television, though, is often lost in histories lauding the era's famed live, single-sponsored anthology dramas.[32] Programs such as *Kraft Television Theater* (1953–1955), *Four Star Playhouse*

(1952–1956), *Ford Theater* (1952–1956), and *Lux Video Theater* (1954–1957) featured both original teleplays and ones adapted from the New York theater community that, as famed NBC producer Fred Coe noted, served a "mission to bring Broadway to America via the television set."[33] Visually, much early prime-time television displayed the live and theatrical sensibilities for which anthology dramas came to be so fondly remembered. Culturally, as Coe indicates, the genre provided early television with a sheen of prestige distinct from that of film and bolstered the notion of television as a shared national experience.

Many early television comedies were similarly rooted in live, theatrical, New York–centric aesthetics, particularly comedy-variety shows featuring an array of comical, musical, and performance segments. Calling any of these shows sketch comedies, however, is not quite accurate. Still, comedy-variety forerunners to sketch programs of the network era and beyond displayed many of the same characteristics of reflexive flexibility as later programs more commonly categorized as sketch. A number of early television comedy-variety shows, for instance, flexibly moved from stage to radio to television, or they were simply performed on more than one medium simultaneously. Comedians such as Lucille Ball, George Burns, Gracie Allen, and Jack Benny (among many others) combined their experience in previous performance contexts with the new affordances of live, broadcast, visual humor. In doing so, they explored a range of comedic styles and production practices that were both utterly derivative of other media and uniquely shaped by television's nascent industrial norms. In order to understand the later arrival of sketch comedy in the network era, then, we must examine early television's flexible integration of comedic modes and material from other sources, a practice largely brought about by the need for new content for weekly live broadcasts.

Producers and performers working in comedy-variety during early television implemented a number of strategies for dealing with the demands of weekly live broadcasts. One of these was a practice long in use in the film industry, itself having gone through the transition from silent to sound films in the 1920s and 1930s. Although film comedians like Charlie Chaplin and Buster Keaton had great success in film's silent era, producers of sound film sought out performers who could supplement physical comedy with humorous repartee too. Hollywood studios turned to vaudeville performers like the Marx Brothers to meet these new demands, (sometimes awkwardly) integrating comedy sketches and reflexive bits of banter from their stage acts into the more conventionally plot-driven scenarios of classical Hollywood narratives. The resulting anarchistic comedies provided a forum for Hollywood films to experiment with various performance and production practices as they transitioned into the sound era. Additionally, as Henry Jenkins suggests, the convergence of vaudevillian stage techniques with Hollywood's existing industrial norms encourages us to think about comedy "atomistically, as a loosely linked succession of comic 'bits.'"[34] In doing so, we can better see how early television comedy-variety performers on television—many of them with backgrounds in vaudeville—applied a similar logic to their programs, recycling old bits from their stage shows in the new context of live, modularly segmented television broadcasts.

Television's roughly equivalent proto-genre of anarchistic comedy films came to be known as vaudeo (video vaudeville), a term that highlights the format's negotiation of vaudevillian stage humor with the specifically televisual demands of weekly live broadcasts.[35] While it borrowed bits from performers' stage acts and deployed them in a comedy-variety context, vaudeo also tinkered with recurring characters in sketches and other scenarios that provided programs with some semblance of consistency. In many ways, vaudeo was a sort of generic common ancestor to variety, late-night talk shows, sitcoms, and sketch comedy, with many performers using vaudeo to experiment with what would and would not translate from their other work to television. Indeed, for decades before television, comedians performed their stage shows in regional runs to theatrical audiences, so they could afford to repeat material from show to show. However, television's power to simultaneously broadcast the same joke or routine to a national audience of millions compromised comedians' ability to repeat performances each week. As a result, many vaudeo performers and executives devised ways to anchor their programs in recurring scenarios to which performers could return each episode, laying the groundwork for what would eventually become the situation comedy. Taking a close look at the transitional vaudeo genre, then, provides important context for how later sketch comedies would similarly negotiate television's industrial flux.

In chapter 1, I consider sketch comedy's roots in vaudeo in a case study of *The Colgate Comedy Hour* (1950–1955), which ran for six seasons in the early 1950s on NBC led by a rotating cast of star comedians such as Eddie Cantor, Dean Martin, Jerry Lewis, Bud Abbott, and Lou Costello. Combining the atomistically swappable bits and sketches of vaudevillian stage acts with the recurring scenarios of the sitcom, *Colgate* is an excellent example of how sketch comedy in vaudeo manifested many of the tensions surrounding early television's transition from live chaos to recorded stability. I trace these tensions by examining original production notes and correspondences among the producers, writers, and cast of *Colgate*, highlighting the competing creative visions each had for the show and the ways they reflexively manifested on stage. In the end, the case of *Colgate* provides a deeper understanding of television's flexible formal experimentation as both a live and recorded medium. Moreover, it exemplifies many of the aesthetic sensibilities against which later generations of sketch comedians would define their own comedic and cultural identities.

Network Era Television: 1950s–1970s

By television's network era, programs that might properly be defined as sketch comedies—at least more so than any other generic label—began to emerge. Many, such as *Rowan and Martin's Laugh-In* (1968–1973), *The Flip Wilson Show* (1970–1974), and *The Carol Burnett Show*, hewed closer to the comedy-variety conventions of early television, integrating studio-set sketches among a broad mix of entertainment segments. In doing so, these shows aligned with the network era's governing logic of broadly appealing, "undifferentiated programming options."[36] For *Saturday Night Live*, by contrast, comedy sketches were the program's focal point in its mix of music, monologues, and short films. Moreover, *SNL* distinguished itself by using sketches to explore aesthetic possibilities that other comedies would (or could) not. Within its first several seasons, it became clear that the only connection *SNL* sought to either its comedy-variety contemporaries or to early television vaudeo shows was its liveness.

But if liveness—with all of its production perils and creative possibilities in comedy-variety and vaudeo—defined television early on, the financial stability and viewing predictability of filmed and rerun programs became its industrial imperative in the network era. Given television's voracious appetite for programming, the industry quickly realized the advantages of moving shoots to the controlled environs of Hollywood studios, editing in post-production, broadcasting programs across the country via their affiliate stations months later, and charging sponsor-funded advertising agencies a premium for thirty seconds of access to a national audience of millions. Indeed, the broadcast networks ABC, NBC, and CBS, which came to be known as the big three, dominated American commercial television as the only game in town by taking a financial stake in every aspect of a program's lifecycle. At the same time, the big three exerted creative control over content in order to appeal not only to the most sizable swath of viewers possible but also to advertisers seeking to sell to it. This industrial structure narrowed the medium's creative possibilities and routinized its production practices. It also normalized television as an integral and intimate part of Americans' leisure time thanks to a "regime of repetition"—reruns—that regularly wove television stories and characters into the everyday lives of many Americans.[37]

It is during the network era that American television earned the reputation, perhaps unfairly, as an idiot box, boob tube, or, as then-FCC chairman Newton Minow infamously described it in 1961, a "vast wasteland." Among other programming forms, Minow bemoaned formulaic sitcoms "about totally unbelievable families," a gesture to the many network era sitcoms that created a perception of America as predominantly white and middle class.[38] David Marc argues that network comedies of the 1950s and 1960s purposely sought to repress any markers of cultural identity in order to create a homogeneous mass audience appealing to advertisers.[39] *The Dick Van Dyke Show* (1961–1966), for instance, produced by Carl Reiner, had initially written the lead as a Jewish show businessman. But, after a failed pilot, producers cast Dick Van Dyke as a white, middle-class family man who lived in the suburbs and worked in New York City. "Magicoms" such as *Mr. Ed* (1961–1966), *Gilligan's Island* (1964–1967), and *Bewitched* (1964–1972) suppressed the rising social tensions of the 1960s through escapist stories that simultaneously worked to reinforce conservative ideologies about race and sexuality. Similarly, comedy-variety programs like *The Ed Sullivan Show* (1948–1971) packaged crowd-pleasing musicians alongside family-friendly comedic acts. For the most part, network era comedy sought not to alienate any large part of the viewing audience with risqué humor or representations, particularly in prime time. Because of the three-network bottleneck, as well as advertisers' desire for a mass audience of undifferentiated viewers, strategically safe comedy provided a predictable and profitable industrial norm for years.

As the late 1960s and 1970s arrived, though, many comedies featured comparatively contentious material, a move that signaled a shift on the part of some programs to targeting young adult audiences. Sitcoms such as *All in the Family* (1971–1979), *The Mary Tyler Moore Show* (1970–1977), and *Maude* (1972–1978) directly addressed issues like abortion, race relations, and the

Vietnam War, often in a way that highlighted intergenerational clashes on the subjects. In the same vein, the comedy-variety show *The Smothers Brothers Comedy Hour* (1967–1969) featured recurring characters like Goldie O'Keefe, a hippie homemaker who dispensed advice on how to get rid of "unsightly roaches." The program's coded references to marijuana subversively addressed the burgeoning American counterculture in a way sanitary enough for prime-time television, though one that led to clashes with CBS and the show's cancellation after three seasons.[40] In many cases, networks began to recognize the power of programming specifically for young adult audiences, a strategy in which sketch comedies would play an integral role for decades to come.

Indeed, it was a sketch comedy that gave one of the most prominent voices to a new generation of young comedians and paved the way for thinking about the genre beyond the boundaries of prime-time television. *Saturday Night Live* debuted in 1975, fittingly enough, as a weekend replacement for reruns of Johnny Carson's *Tonight Show* (1962–1992) and immediately sought the kind of cultural consecration that would distinguish it from Carson. Although broadcast live like its vaudeo predecessors and sharing many of the socially relevant themes of its sitcom contemporaries, *SNL* still strove for something different through a new type of identity work. The program's aggressive, confrontational comedic style both spoke to and helped create in its baby boomer audience a sense of separation from the comedy of previous generations. *SNL* would go on to become such a dominant presence in sketch comedy across subsequent decades that, inevitably, its original boomer audience no longer found itself clearly defined as the desired young adult audience. In its stead was another group of young viewers—Generation X—equally eager to distinguish itself by embracing an ironic distance from (in contrast to boomers' aggressive confrontation of) earlier sketch comedy aesthetics.

As the longest running sketch comedy show in American television history, *Saturday Night Live* has been the subject of countless books, feature-length articles, and oral histories. As such, it is difficult to find a new entry point for analysis of the program, particularly from a scholarly perspective. Despite—or perhaps because of—this hagiographic body of work on the show, significant gaps remain, as I explore in chapter 2. One of these is the way *SNL* cast members sought symbolic capital by demonstrating both knowledge and rejection of the already consecrated comedic traditions of previous generations. This dynamic privileged humor constructed around the identities of comedians who were straight, white men such as Chevy Chase and John Belushi, performers who aggressively competed with cast mates for airtime. In the first part of the chapter, I examine both the on-screen work and offscreen commentary of performers such as Gilda Radner, Laraine Newman, Garrett Morris, and Richard Pryor (host of one of *SNL*'s most memorable early episodes) who were marginalized by early *SNL*'s struggles for consecration. In doing so, I disagree with accounts of early *SNL* as a progressive, new comedic voice by demonstrating how its cast members' struggles for consecration ended up reinforcing—not undermining—existing social power inequalities based in race and gender.

In the second part of chapter 2, I consider how this same struggle for consecration—individual cast members competing with one another for air time—flexibly positioned *SNL* as a stepping stone to media and cultural opportunities beyond the show. This dynamic not only complicated network-era notions of television's medium specificity but also set an example for *SNL* cast members in later decades seeking to work in other media. Famously, or perhaps somewhat infamously, Chevy Chase left the show after his first season to pursue a career in Hollywood movies that can generously be called a mixed success. Myriad *SNL* alumni would follow in Chase's footsteps over the years, a television-to-film trajectory of stardom not entirely unique to *Saturday Night Live*. What makes *SNL* stars' departure for film worthy of close attention is the way their post-*SNL* careers continue to be understood as an extension of the show. The malleability and modularity of *SNL* carries over to the work routines of its alumni as well, affording them the flexibility to create comedy that collapses the boundaries of medium specificity.

Critics' reviews for many former *SNL* stars' film work, for instance, might rigidly characterize the sketch comedy–like moments in a film narrative as distracting or disruptive to its main story. Rather than take this interpretation at face value, I contextualize these moments by exploring their origin in the field of production decisions behind early *SNL* sketches, interviews with cast members, and analyses of their later films. From its first season, I suggest, the program established a reach beyond television that both set it apart from other network-era comedies and positioned sketch comedy as amenable to the flexible, transmedia movement of content so key to television in later years. Connecting this industrial strategy to sketch comedy aesthetics onscreen has important implications for how performers, networks, and viewers would understand the genre for decades.

Television's Multichannel Transition: 1980s–1990s

After the network era, sketch comedy's industrial flexibility bolstered many fledgling cable outlets' attempts to distinguish their brand identities and to target smaller audience segments than those of established broadcast networks. Over the course of the 1980s and 1990s, cable networks like MTV, Comedy Central, and HBO were among the most aggressive in using sketch comedy to experiment with programming and differentiate themselves from comparatively staid broadcast fare. More broadly, this period broke with network era practices, particularly in its drastic increase in viewing options and technologies that allowed audiences more control over these new channels.[41] Cable and satellite outlets eroded the long-held dominance of television's three-network oligopoly, home video devices provided time-shifting capabilities for viewers outside of broadcast schedules, and niche content increasingly supplemented mass-market mainstays.

Although cable operators were eager to counterprogram broadcast television and brand themselves as edgy, they "maintained, above all, a strong resemblance to and dependence on broadcast television—featuring a large number of broadcast reruns, old movies, and other inexpensive fare."[42] Indeed, cable networks saw the production of original programming as cost prohibitive early on, devoting much of their financial resources to carriage and distribution expenses. As they recovered start-up costs and gained more and more access to American homes, cost-efficiency and distinction remained goals of their original programming efforts. Such a viewing environment naturally accommodated the quick, cheap experimentation provided by sketch comedy, and many sketch shows would figure prominently in new channels' attempts to try on and discard various industrial identities over the course of the multichannel transition.

Michael Curtin suggests that, although driven by technology, the broader cultural, regulatory, and economic shifts that informed television practices during the multichannel transition resulted in a curious dialectical tension.[43] On the one hand, broadcast networks continued to produce apolitical, widely appealing programs aimed at national audiences. On the other hand, newer outlets on cable sought out comparatively smaller audience niches that would be intensely invested in their edgy, provocative content. Since the same handful of media conglomerates often owned both national broadcast and niche cable channels, though, their parent companies could flexibly deploy these strategies. The result, Curtin argues, was a shift away from media firms seeking centralized control of television distribution to an emphasis on the aesthetic and audience appeal of television programs themselves.

The edgy FOX sketch comedy *In Living Color*, for instance, courted young urban viewers with its transgressive black identity politics but was ultimately situated within the broader conservative agenda of Rupert Murdoch's News Corp. The coolly ironic sketch comedy *The Ben Stiller Show* (MTV 1989–1990, FOX 1992) fit MTV's appeal to Generation X, but it also needed to conform to the broader industrial mandates of parent company Viacom. Conglomerates' flexible corporate structures allowed for the quick movement of the oppositional audiences courted by these edgy sketch shows from niche to mainstream, as was the case with *In Living Color*'s role in the broader mainstreaming of black culture to white audiences in the 1990s. "One of the consequences of this new environment," Curtin suggests, "is that groups that were at one time oppositional or outside the mainstream have become increasingly attractive . . . the oppositional has become more commercially viable and, in some measure, more closely tied to the mainstream."[44]

The flexibility between oppositional and mainstream impulses on television at the time played out in the discursive domains of not only race and gender but also—given cable's focus on narrowly defined demographic categories—generation. For most of the twentieth century, baby boomers (Americans born between 1943 and 1960) exercised a sort of unquestioned cultural dominance. Joseph Turow points to panic in the advertising industry in the 1990s, however, as boomers slipped out of the prized 18- to 49-year-old demographic particularly coveted by television networks.[45] In their place as the newly and increasingly desirable young adult demographic was Generation X (born between 1961 and 1981). Generation Xers, for their part, defined themselves in ways directly opposed to their attempted co-option by advertisers and television programmers.

In chapter 3, I consider how MTV's sketch comedy *The State* (1993–1995) ambivalently manifested the era's oppositional-versus-mainstream tensions in humor centered on generation, identity, and commercialism. Using original archival material from the show, I examine how television industry discourses constructed Generation X as an identity based in consumerism, circumscribing its oppositional impulses and directing them to market-based expressions. Of course, this is not to say that there were no truly oppositional elements on the show. When directed by MTV to develop recurring characters that could be spun off into a movie, for instance, cast members of *The State* reflexively responded by creating a character whose catchphrase was too crude and simplistic to function in a feature-length narrative. However, these small gestures of defiance were ultimately folded into MTV's (and parent company Viacom's) imperatives to flexibly leverage edgy shows like *The State* beyond television. Indeed, *The State* would attempt the very movement described by Curtin—from oppositional to mainstream—in a failed jump to the broadcast network CBS in 1995. A closer look at the show's trenchant comedic critiques and later failure in the mainstream further illustrates the fraught flexibility of sketch comedy's power to express cultural identities.

Post-network Television: 2000s–Present

In many ways, sketch comedy's reflexive flexibility mirrors the industrial discourses of post-network television. Its short running time, amenability to cross-media movement, and cost efficiency make it ideal for today's digitally driven mediascape. Indeed, the industrial practices of television's multichannel transition—channel choice and viewer control—have only accelerated in the twenty-first century. Television content now lives not only on myriad broadcast and cable television channels but also on websites, streaming networks, mobile applications, and on-demand options from service providers. Accordingly, audiences now possess more means and devices for accessing programs than ever before. What distinguishes the contemporary post-network era of television is an ever-increasing "erosion of [networks'] control over how and when viewers watch particular programs."[46] Specifically, the digitization of media content, as well as the integration of internet-based interfaces with television technology, have created a broad range of interpretations and sites of meaning-creation perfect for sketch comedy's flexible industrial uses.

Consider post-network television's convergence with the internet through an example: "This is the missing link moment where TV and Internet finally merge. It will change the way we as human beings perceive and interact with reality," former *Saturday Night Live* cast member Will Ferrell proclaimed in June 2008, roughly a year into both the Great Recession in the

United States and the emergence of his viral video and sketch comedy website, Funny or Die.⁴⁷ The two events are not as unrelated as they might seem. The late-2000s financial crisis catalyzed growing instability in the American television industry and incentivized stars like Ferrell to venture online into the so-called "new media" world. Ferrell's statement—referring to the premium television network HBO's purchase of a small stake in Funny or Die—is tongue in cheek, but it highlights both the wild-eyed optimism and anxiety permeating television as it transitioned to the post-network era.

Faced with dwindling audience shares and the challenges of converging with digital platforms, networks like HBO increasingly took risks centered on short-form content like sketch comedy. HBO's interest in a website specializing in viral videos and sketch comedy bolstered the cable network's brand as something distinct from conventional television—after all, "It's not TV. It's HBO." Around the same time, old-guard broadcasters like NBC launched internet-specific comedy production and distribution companies, only to shutter them shortly thereafter. Meanwhile, internet comedy teams like The Lonely Island rocketed to success on *Saturday Night Live* with their social media–friendly digital sketches. Again and again in the post-network era, in debates among creators, executives, and viewers about the state of television, short-form content like sketch comedy has loomed large.

One useful way for conceptualizing the industrial role of sketch comedy in the post-network era is Curtin's description of television today as "matrix media." In light of increased audience fragmentation, user-controlled and digital distribution technologies, and a surge in entertainment options, he suggests, television networks are embracing "interactive exchanges, multiple sites of productivity, and diverse modes of interpretation and use."⁴⁸ Central to these processes are television programs or bits of digital content themselves, which networks, outlets, and their corporate parents use to build a brand and make it accessible to viewers at their convenience and on their terms. The accumulated media platforms and times at which audiences might engage with a program represent for advertisers a flexible way to target consumers in an increasingly fragmented mediascape.

Matrix media dynamics are particularly prominent in the increasingly fluid movement of sketch comedy between internet-based platforms and conventional cable or broadcast television. In some cases, internet-original sketch comedy shorts are available side by side with repurposed sitcoms on the various websites or streaming partners of established media firms like Sony, Viacom, and Time Warner. In other cases, the major media conglomerates have launched their own digital production and distribution platforms distinct from their television holdings, ones often driven by short-form comedic content. Although many original comedy websites like Funny or Die have since faltered in the face of competition on social media, new partnerships between established industry powers and online sketch comedy sites continue to crop up regularly.

Elsewhere, television networks and their corporate parents are continually experimenting with ways to bring sketch comedy made outside their purview into their financial fold, and they have created infrastructures for sifting through amateur comedy on sites like YouTube, Instagram, and other content aggregators. Sketch comedians often aim for success online and for the chance to write for network sitcoms or feature films, while networks have also found it advantageous to take low-cost ownership stakes in many online comedy outlets. As executives increasingly see the internet as a complement, rather than a rival, to their offline properties, the flexible movement of sketch comedy works in both directions. HBO's ownership stake in Funny or Die, for instance, represents one example of an established television power distinguishing its brand with edgy internet comedy, while comedy podcasts and digital platforms from the likes of former *Mr. Show* writer Scott Aukerman have spun off into successful sketch comedy television programs (e.g., *Comedy Bang! Bang!*, 2012–2016). Sketch comedy—at all levels of media industries—serves as a key site for examining the myriad movements that both performers and programs must make in order to survive in the post-network era.

The mobility of sketch comedy and comedy sketches—both within programs and across media—has long been key for Comedy Central. Its industrial identity as *the* television (then digital) home for sketch comedy, moreover, comes with important implications about the cultural identities of its presumed audience too. I examine the role of sketch comedy on Comedy Central in chapter 4, utilizing interviews with the network's founders to highlight how, even early on, Comedy Central sought to connect sketch shows and transmedia viewing habits to its targeted audience of young white men. Then, I consider Comedy Central's recent turn to post-politics humor in its sketch comedies, ones that appear to bolster the cultural identities of women and racial/ethnic minorities—identities decidedly outside its historically preferred audience. In case studies of the sketch comedies *Inside Amy Schumer* (2013–present) and *Key & Peele*, I argue that Comedy Central's industrial practices of promotion and distribution—ones driven by the cross-media mobility of television in the post-network era—actually undermine the shows' progressive, post-politics representational strategies. In the end, Comedy Central's myriad uses of sketch comedy for complex, sometimes contradictory, industrial ends highlight sketch's continued power of reflexive flexibility in the post-network era.

Conclusion

At each point in the survey of television's industrial history above, a variety of forces have flexibly utilized sketch comedy in efforts to redirect entrenched industrial practices or experiment with textual conventions. Many of the reasons for this are apparent enough. Sketch comedy—whether as an atomized, individual sketch or an aggregation of sketches into a show conforming to television's longstanding scheduling and distribution practices—is cheaper, edgier, and more tractable than many other television genres. These characteristics make the format an attractive option for media executives, programmers, and performers testing the aesthetic boundaries of television in its early days, or ones seeking a break with the past during the network era. Sketch comedy is malleable and mobile, able to fit into a variety of exhibition contexts—as interstitial material between programs, as a modular unit of a feature film narrative, or as a media "snack" while a viewer has a short viewing window. These conditions align the format with industrial logics of the multichannel and post-network eras privileging content that can be shared across media quickly, efficiently, and profitably.

The case studies in the ensuing chapters proceed in chronological order, for the most part, beginning with an overview of sketch comedy antecedents in the first chapter through to a consideration of the present environment of digital convergence in the last chapter. Just as this book does not cover sketch comedy programs comprehensively, I do not intend for it to be a definitive examination of any one historical period. Instead, I strive throughout the subsequent chapters to rely on scholarly research in broadcasting history and television industry economics, weaving the specifics of sketch comedy's reflexive flexibility among these established bodies of knowledge. Each case study highlights specific moments of tension between dominant television industry practices and the impulses of innovation and differentiation that figure so prominently in industrial growth.

Sketch comedy is attractive for the television industry because of the new performative modes or viewing groups it can marshal, yet risky and volatile because of the unpredictability inherent in deviating from past successes. Examining sketch comedy from the present, with a careful eye on its myriad sociohistorical contexts, provides a greater understanding of how popular media products serve both cultural and economic goals. Moreover, this approach demonstrates how media are open to uses and interpretations that constantly revise the practices through which those goals are achieved.

Notes

1. Michaels quoted in Itzkoff, "The All Too Ready for Prime Time Players."
2. I am deliberately borrowing Newcomb and Hirsch's vocabulary—"cultural forum"—here in order to invoke television sketch comedy's ritualistic function. Like them, I strive throughout this book to analyze sketch comedy "as process rather than as product," drawing attention to how competing cultural forces struggle over the terms of meaning creation rather than on the discreteness of the meanings themselves. See Newcomb and Hirsch, "Television as a Cultural Forum," 45–55.
3. See, among many others, D'Acci, "Cultural Studies, Television Studies, and the Crisis in the Humanities"; and Fiske, *Television Culture*.
4. I am working here off of Mittell's definition of television genres as cultural categories, ones whose meanings cannot be solely based in textual analysis. For more see Mittell, *Genre and Television: From Cop Shows to Cartoons in American Culture*.
5. Neale, "Sketch Comedy," 62. One of the more productive attempts to survey sketch and its relationship to other comedic genres comes from Neale's coauthored (with Krutnik) work *Popular Film and Television Comedy*.
6. Simons, "The Strange Persistence of Sketch Comedy."
7. Bourdieu, *The Rules of Art*, 167.
8. Bourdieu, *The Field of Cultural Production*, 78.
9. Friedman, "The Cultural Currency of a 'Good' Sense of Humour,"; Weaver, *The Rhetoric of Racist Humour,*; Claessens and Dhoest, "Comedy Taste,"; Kuipers, "Television and Taste Hierarchy,"; Smith, Eve, "Selling Terry Pratchett's Discworld,".
10. Bourdieu, *The Field of Cultural Production*, 164.
11. Deveau, *English Canadian Stand-Up Comedy*, 10.
12. Hesmondhalgh, "Bourdieu, The Media, and Cultural Production," 216.
13. Bourdieu, *The Field of Cultural Production*, 46.
14. Hesmondhalgh, 222.
15. Hesmondhalgh, 216.
16. Hesmondhalgh, 216.
17. Michaels quoted in Bauder, "Lack of Black Women."
18. See Gray, Jones, and Thompson, *Satire TV*, for extensive thoughts on this.
19. Hall, "Who Needs Identity?"
20. Ibid., 5–6.
21. Ibid., 4–5.
22. Ibid., 5.
23. Medhurst, *A National Joke*, 39.

24. Ibid., 19.
25. Carter, "In the Tastes of Young Men, Humor Is Most Prized, a Survey Finds."
26. Gray, *Watching Race*, 130–146.
27. Haggins, *Laughing Mad*, 207.
28. Ibid., 11.
29. Ibid., 187.
30. For the most part, I base these four historical eras on Amanda Lotz's periodization in *The Television Will Be Revolutionized*. Though she includes what I call "early television" as part of the subsequent "network era," I believe a separate discussion of television's formative years as a primarily live, New York–based medium bolsters the book's examination of sketch comedy and formal experimentation in chapter 1.
31. See Hilmes, *Radio Voices*.
32. See Wertheim, *Radio Comedy*. Television's first two decades or so are also commonly referred to as its first "golden age." See Everett, "Golden Age of Television Drama."
33. Quoted in Newcomb, *Encyclopedia of Television*, 2nd edition, 1002.
34. Jenkins, *What Made Pistachio Nuts?*, 5.
35. I'm here glossing Murray, *Hitch Your Antenna to the Stars*, which gets much more detail later in chapter 1.
36. Lotz, *The Television Will Be Revolutionized*, 9.
37. Kompare, *Rerun Nation*, xi–xv.
38. Minow, "Television and the Public Interest."
39. Marc, *Comic Visions*, 84–120.
40. Bodroghkozy, "*The Smothers Brothers Comedy Hour* and the Youth Rebellion."
41. Lotz, *The Television Will Be Revolutionized*, 12–15.
42. Mullen, *The Rise of Cable Programming in the United States*, 1.
43. Curtin, "On Edge: Culture Industries in the Neo-Network Era."
44. Ibid., 197.
45. Turow, *Breaking Up America*, 76–79.
46. Lotz, *The Television Will Be Revolutionized*, 15.
47. Quoted in Kane, "HBO Invests in Will Ferrell's FunnyorDie.com."
48. Curtin, "Matrix Media," 13.

1

FROM RADIO VOICES TO VARIETY CHOICES

The Colgate Comedy Hour *and* Sketch Comedy in Early Television

This chapter investigates television sketch comedy's key historical antecedents, as well as its iterations in early American television. It begins with a consideration of how media and cultural studies scholars have analyzed mediated comedy as a site of identity formation based in race/ethnicity, gender, and class. These studies characterize comedy, at least insofar as television sketch comedy is concerned, as a form of low culture with the potential to challenge dominant conceptions of taste and cultural power. As commercial mass media industries in the United States grew in the first half of the twentieth century, long-form comedy with recurring situations became the preferred norm. The vestiges of low culture often operated at a secondary level in sketch-like bits based in vaudeville, radio, and early sound film.

This dynamic would continue into early television vaudeo programs—sketch comedy's forerunners—where the traditions of vaudeville conflicted with the weekly production demands of live television. In a case study of the vaudeo program *The Colgate Comedy Hour*, I explore the stakes of the competing ideas producers, performers, and advertisers had for the program's comedy sketches. Although heavily reliant on former vaudeville stars like Eddie Cantor and Jerry Lewis, *Colgate* producers reflexively used sketches to mitigate the extent to which its star comedian hosts dictated the creative direction of the show. In doing so, *Colgate* contributed to the television industry's subsequent privileging of comedies based in representational performances and recurring, sitcom scenarios in the network era.

In exploring sketch comedy's various functions for early television, then, this chapter outlines the parameters of sketch comedy as a field of cultural production, one in which various agents struggled for the cultural resources to consecrate their particular interpretation of the nascent genre. The forms of social and cultural capital pursued by the stars and producers of programs like *Colgate* helped define the types of positions later sketch comedians would take—and react against—within the field. This chapter, then, establishes many of the key concepts—performative modes, cultural identities, and industrial pressures—on which this book's subsequent case studies will build. The influences of vaudeo television programs and atomistic comedy within long-form comedic texts figure prominently in how later sketch comedy shows on network and cable television, on the internet, and in feature films would negotiate their own reflexive flexibilities. Indeed, part of this chapter's goal is to demonstrate how sketch comedy is not necessarily unique to a particular time period but is part of a long tradition of mediated comedy that offers a way to see industrial and cultural changes over time. Examining how the format has historically worked against and within industry routines further highlights the constructed nature of how and why so many have used sketch comedy's malleability and modularity for a variety of purposes.

Television Sketch Comedy Antecedents in Vaudeville, Film, and Radio

The most relevant study to begin a survey of television sketch comedy antecedents is Robert Allen's analysis of taste and the commodification of burlesque in the late nineteenth century.[1] In examinations of the bawdy comedy and overt sexuality of women stage performers like Lydia Thompson, Allen describes how burlesque entered the American theatrical scene and upset the tastes of legitimate theatergoers. Rather than dismissing burlesque simply as low culture, Allen argues the opposite, suggesting that the form retained much of its transgressive potential *because* of its differentiation as less than other art forms. As such, Allen's work suggests that cultural distinctions—such as those based in comedic taste—need not be framed in strictly binary terms, but as providing a fluid framework that variously negotiates, privileges, and/or subordinates myriad cultural and industrial discourses.

The flexible nature of taste and comedy would play out again in burlesque and vaudeville theaters of the early twentieth century, as well as vaudeville comedians' transition into sound film. As Henry Jenkins notes, the Progressive middle class of the era spurned the indecorous pleasures of vaudeville and espoused a more sophisticated form of comedy based not in carnal laughter but social change.[2] Despite, or perhaps because of, Progressives' distaste, ribald humor became ubiquitous at the vaudeville theaters populated by a lower class seeking a quick release from the drudgeries of their work. Invoking French sociologist Pierre Bourdieu's framework for the social stratification of taste, Jenkins details the role of middle-class leisure time and how it led to an institutionalization of morality- and story-centric forms of comedy, increasingly marginalizing vaudevillian comedy as low.

In those cultural margins of the early twentieth century, peep shows providing minutes-long spectacles and titillation thrived in ramshackle nickelodeon movie theaters. But with the rise of the vertically integrated Hollywood studio system, cinema also moved into respectable downtown theaters and began to favor longer narrative formats. However, the move threw this industrial norm into flux in the early 1930s with Hollywood film's incorporation of sound, a transition in which sketch-like comedic bits would play a crucial role. A subset of comedy films attempted to integrate the self-contained sketches of vaudevillian comedic spectacle with Hollywood's preferred storytelling norms of linear causality and goal-driven characters.[3] Jenkins calls these films "anarchistic," a label referring both to the aesthetic boundaries they broke and to what the breaking of those boundaries meant in their sociocultural milieu. In anarchistic comedies, mainstream and low comedy existed side by side, thereby highlighting the constructed nature of the respective class distinctions of their intended audiences.

Jenkins investigates this dynamic via a case study of the early sound films of comedian Eddie Cantor, who would later become a regular on NBC's vaudeo program *The Colgate Comedy Hour* in the 1950s.[4] Cantor, then a wildly popular Jewish vaudevillian, found himself negotiating the conflicting demands of two moviegoing audiences in the early sound era—coastal audiences in sound-equipped theaters for whom vaudeville was a familiar aesthetic, and hinterland audiences catching up to the unfamiliar sound technologies. Cantor's comedic persona would gradually undergo a de-Semitization, one manifest in his later films' privileging of conventional romantic plots over vaudevillian sketch-like comedy bits. Cantor reluctantly adjusted his humor in order to play to what was becoming a national cinema audience, downplaying his Jewish identity and sexually charged jokes. Although early sound cinema utilized sketch-like comedy in attempts to build uniform viewing experiences, flexible, ambiguously expressed ethnic identities persisted in Cantor's work.

In a similar vein, radio comedian Fanny Brice devised clever ways to use bit-driven comedy both to speak to broad audiences and to maintain a sense of cultural specificity for women. Using what Michele Hilmes calls the "Schnooks strategy," Brice's routines relied on a recurring baby character named Schnooks who feigned infantilized innocence as a way to slip in double-entendre and sexual puns.[5] Like Cantor's dual address, Brice's Schnooks was not a mere gag. The character voiced critiques of patriarchal authority and bolstered feminine cultural identities, while at the same time providing an early template for a sketch convention—the recurring character.

Many comedians used sketches and characters from their vaudeville acts to experiment with what would and would not work in film, radio, and television during the first half of the twentieth century. Some particularly struggled to adapt to commercial broadcast media's advertising demands. One common method, as seen in the Schnooks strategy, was to take an initially one-note character and stretch it out over several appearances of a given program. Indeed, this recurring character approach naturally lent itself, on the one hand, to the recurring narratives—and all of the production routines they entailed—of the situation comedy. On the other hand, the device provided comedians with room to experiment with a unique cultural voice or critique and to discard it if it did not work. Given the flexibility of this sketch comedy device, many worked in some version of the format across the social and cultural realms of mid-century America.

In many cases, however, the mandates of a broadcasting industry seeking predictable production routines mitigated sketch comedy's early experimental impulses, a dynamic with cultural consequences. Women viewers and discourses of femininity, as Lynn Spigel has noted, were the primary sites through which radio and television sought to tame comedy's vaudevillian impulses and domesticate them, a process governed by dominant ideologies of ethnicity, suburbanization, and consumerism.[6] Television's centrality in the living rooms of post–World War II suburban houses created a seamless overlap between the roles of wife and mother, leisure and domestic labor for women, with consumption as its nexus point. As a result, Americans increasingly left behind their ethnic roots in favor of the cultural logic of consumption more commonly seen in situation comedies.[7]

In other words, more than just the industry's desire for production stability fueled its eventual move from the sketch-fueled vaudeo programs of early television to the stability of domestic sitcoms that would dominate the subsequent network era. Just as Cantor toned down his Yiddish in-jokes for broader sound film audiences, so too did scores of other vaudevillians adapt their transgressive comedic personas to meet television's mass audience demands. Lucille Ball's domestic sitcom *I Love Lucy* (1951–1957), for example, retained much of the bawdiness of her vaudeville humor, but in ways ultimately deferential to the patriarchal logic of television's national appeal.[8] Those who didn't adapt to the rigors of filmed sitcoms—and all their implicit privileging of whiteness, domesticity, and consumption—largely fell by the wayside, a historical process privileging long-form comedy traditions that subtly overrode sketch-like comedy traditions in early television.

As this brief sampling of sketch antecedents indicates, sketch in the early twentieth century was not yet the coherent entertainment genre we largely identify with television today. Its clearest forebear was the minutes-long comedy bit that entertainers of all stripes had been honing for decades in vaudeville theaters. It is no accident, then, that when mass media like film, radio, and television started or faced technological changes, producers looked to comedians with a stockpile of successful sketches and bits from their stage shows in order to help soothe any growing pains. It is this formal malleability and openness to experimentation that provides sketch comedy its most salient power—the flexibility for performers and producers to figure out just what the hell they are (supposed to be) doing with a given medium. In other words, perhaps sketch's earliest function for television was helping the medium determine what it could and could not be. As I discuss below, this debate informed many discussions about the creative direction of vaudeo shows like *The Colgate Comedy Hour*, as it became clear comedy sketches were not enough to sustain it week in and week out. On a larger scale, sketch's emergence as one thing in early television and reemergence as something else in later eras would have long-term implications for the kinds of programs and audiences television would privilege for decades.

Variety, Vaudeo, and Sketch Distinctions in Early Television

So far I have been reluctant to define sketch comedy's closest generic kin, the variety show. Generally speaking, we might think of variety simply as the broader parent genre of which sketch comedies are a part. As I discuss below in the case of *Colgate* and other programs like it, just about all vaudeville comedians on early television worked in variety shows, but not all variety shows were vaudeo programs. A variety show is any mixture of short entertainment segments such as music, comedy, magic, monologues, and/or dance "whose unity lies solely in a time span, a distinctive structure, or in the recurrence of a particular performer or performers across otherwise separate acts and items."[9] A grade school holiday pageant might be considered a variety show organized around a Christmas theme, just as the celebrity host and the Academy of Motion Picture Arts and Sciences serve as the aegis for the variety structure of the annual Oscars broadcast. One manner of understanding a comedy sketch, particularly for early television, is as an "act," one of many entertainment segments contained within the variety program that is likely unrelated to others.

Where the distinction between sketch and other generic categories matters for early television is in how sketches created short, self-contained narrative units that would, on the one hand, provide building blocks for later sketch comedy programs, and, on the other hand, form the backbone for dozens of longer-form sitcoms. Before becoming one of the most beloved sitcoms of all time, *The Honeymooners* (1955–1956), for example, ran as a recurring sketch for several years on various variety programs hosted by Jackie Gleason. Producers quickly saw the advantage of borrowing vaudevillians' sketches for vaudeo, repeating those sketches in vaudeo, and then using that logic as the template for the weekly plot scenarios of sitcoms. The key at each step in this process, particularly as it marked the comedian's work as distinct from film or radio, was how his or her comedic persona supported television's broader economic imperatives of consumption. Star comedians carrying over their stage personas from vaudeville to vaudeo provided early television, as Susan Murray's work has shown, with one of its most important markers of distinction from film—intimacy.[10] In contrast to the larger-than-life conceptions of film stardom that drove audiences to movie theaters, television brought stars right into viewers' homes. By opening up their performances of one-note bits and repeating sketches across episodes, rather than occasionally performing unconnected bits and songs more commonly seen in variety, vaudeo stars humanized themselves for home viewers. Eventually, this performative mode would align with television's growing industrial imperative of routinizing production practices, one that would increasingly favor sitcom stability over the live, weekly grind of vaudeo.

Vaudeo placed its star comedians in a tricky bind that both relied on and drastically departed from their work in vaudeville theaters. On the one hand, they had built theatrical careers on intimate, direct interaction with in-person audiences. Many continued these presentational practices on television by reflexively addressing both the studio audience and home audience through the camera.[11] Moreover, many television vaudeo programs made little effort at establishing any fictional diegesis for their stars due to the nascent medium's advertising model, one in which performers served as trusted spokespeople for myriad consumer goods in America's booming postwar economy. On the other hand, vaudeo as a mass-consumed mode of comedy presented performers with a new host of problems they did not have in vaudeville theaters. Live broadcasts to massive national audiences meant comedians could not as easily repeat material as viewers might tire of their repetitive, presentational shtick. The result, Murray maintains, was a flexible approach that created comedy "fluid in its relation both to narrative and to constructions of authenticity and performance."[12] Often, this meant shows that bounced between narrative sketches in which star comedians would play thinly fictionalized characters, alternated with presentational monologues or musical numbers in which they would play themselves—an aesthetic tendency that remains strong in sketch comedies to this day.

Vaudeo programs thus present an ideal case study for examining the role of comedy sketches for the early television industry as it negotiated the competing demands of producers, star comedians, and external economic pressures. One of these, NBC's *The Colgate Comedy Hour*, saw terrific success early on in its run from 1950 to 1955, led by a rotating cast of former vaudevillian stars such as Eddie Cantor, Dean Martin and Jerry Lewis, Donald O'Connor, Bud Abbott and Lou Costello, and Jimmy Durante. By the show's final seasons, however, it became clear that its mix of sketch and variety acts was unsustainable. The original production documents and correspondences I analyze below highlight competing demands between those wanting to maintain (and even bolster) original sketches and those wishing to remove them altogether. At the same time, *Colgate*'s star hosts succumbed to the demands of live television production and began dropping

From Radio Voices to Variety Choices | 47

Fig. 1.1. The title card for *The Colgate Comedy Hour* in its early seasons.

out for, among other things, more lucrative film opportunities. Program content came to be less and less focused on original comedy sketches and more on the variety mix of musical revues, gimmicky spectaculars (such as a broadcast from Mexico), and promotional segments for stars' films, books, and theatrical appearances. By 1955, *The Colgate Comedy Hour* had been renamed *The Colgate Variety Hour* to reflect a shift away from original comedy sketches. Interrogating *Colgate*'s creative process in these later seasons can help us better understand how television comedians—and even the industry writ large—saw comedy sketches as a flexible tool for meeting the medium's evolving creative and economic demands.

"'We wish we could've finished the show, but that's television'": NBC's *The Colgate Comedy Hour* and Comedy Sketches in Early Television

The Colgate Comedy Hour was born of NBC's desire to be a comedy leader in early television, a plan that began in earnest with the hiring of executive Sylvester "Pat" Weaver in 1949. By the 1950–1951 television season, Weaver's comedy plan began to bear fruit with vaudeo and variety hits like Milton Berle's *Texaco Star Theatre* (1948–1956), Sid Caesar and Imogene Coca's *Your Show of Shows*, and *The Colgate Comedy Hour*, the latter of which was programmed opposite Ed Sullivan's *Toast of the Town* on CBS. Weaver's pursuit of star comedian talent paid dividends in the ratings, but it came at a financial cost. With Jackie Gleason hosting its second season premiere, *The Colgate Comedy Hour* was the highest budgeted, single-sponsor program on television. At that point, sponsor Colgate-Palmolive-Peet was funding it at $3 million per year. By the following season, that figure ballooned to more than $6 million.[13]

One method that *Colgate* producers used to try to control the cost of rotating so many hosts was to rewrite the comedians' star personas as fictional characters in sketches. As Murray notes, the narrative expansion of sketches within and across episodes helped focus audience attention on comedians' television work, rather than allow viewers to think of them as singular stars. This de-emphasized star hosts as the primary point of audience identification and returned authority of program content back to producers and advertisers: "Recurring characters and settings helped standardize production practices and enable the program to rely on plot and character to attract an audience, rather than being completely dependent on the personality of a sole vaudeo comic."[14]

As the show progressed, *Colgate* producers began focusing less on acquiring high-priced star comedian talent who would exercise near-total creative control over their episodes. Instead, producers focused more on how they could use talent most profitably and efficiently. Somewhat paradoxically, this shift meant acquiring existing entertainment properties for the show that catered to the comedian's star persona, without granting him or her ultimate creative control (as original material often did). At the same time, *Colgate* producers began exploiting their star comedians' careers beyond the confines of the show by increasingly incorporating film clips, re-creations of musical numbers, and one-off spectaculars.

Sketches, then, were the fulcrum on which many of *Colgate*'s other variety elements balanced with the appeal of its star hosts. In a typical episode from February 1952, for example, hosts Dean Martin and Jerry Lewis open the show with a sketch called "Mayhem Inc. Annual Awards Dinner," in which the duo bungles multiple attempts to entertain a group of mobsters at a banquet. Lewis predictably breaks out of character several times in the sketch before Martin joins him at the front of the proscenium to introduce the evening's lineup. The two then separate to individually play up their respective comic personas—Lewis mugs and improvises by ducking in and out of frame for several minutes before throwing over to Martin who croons the standard, "When You're Smiling." Several song-and-dance routines from other performers follow, but nearly half of the episode's running time is devoted to two sketches in which Martin and Lewis play thinly fictionalized characters. "Next-Door Neighbors" satirizes *Colgate* stars' diminished status on the show, as Martin haggles with an actor portraying Weaver over the terms of their appearance ("This time we want the writers working for us!" he shouts) while Lewis interferes. "Soda Jerk" later sees Martin playing straight man to Lewis's spectacularly messy comic set-pieces, ones that would have been right at home in a purely theatrical setting.

The episode's final segment has Martin and Lewis back at the proscenium, covered in sweat, to close out the show and preview the following week's episode hosted by Eddie Cantor. They are exhausted from an evening of intense, physical performance on live television, but they are also clearly perturbed, half-jokingly acknowledging signals to wrap up from producers and writers off-camera. They make several mentions of having to cut segments for time. "We wish we could've finished the show, but that's television," Lewis wryly says. Although it is unclear what these segments were, it is safe to say that Martin and Lewis are unhappy about their exclusion. Aside from plugs for upcoming club appearances and for Lewis's work with the Muscular Dystrophy Association, there is little explicit in the episode to suggest that Martin and Lewis are the larger-than-life, multimedia stars that led them to be hosts in the first place. Although just a snapshot of the series, this episode's curious coda highlights *Colgate*'s move away from having star hosts dictate the creative direction of an episode, as well as producers' use of sketches as a mechanism to maintain creative control.

Behind the scenes, this dynamic played out in the show's final seasons in struggles among its creative personnel over how best to utilize hosts' increasingly marginalized status for the program's overall economic aim. Although many writers for the show wanted to continue using sketches as a way to keep star comedians in check, external forces increasingly drove the show away from original sketches and toward more non narrative variety acts. The late winter months of 1954 proved to be a turning point in *Colgate*'s evolution as it finished up its fourth season and made plans to recapture declining audience shares in its fifth season. In January 1954, NBC and *Colgate* producer Fred Wile brought in an independent consultant to offer her appraisal of the show's situation at the time and the direction it might take. She noted: "The *Comedy Hour* is basically a variety type revue, sans any story line. Occasionally a thin thread continues on for a sketch or two, but more often it is a series of specialties with an opening production number, a sketch or two, and another production number.... Novelty acts should be employed to great advantage.... The argument [stars] become stale the next day, etc., shouldn't stand up, otherwise we couldn't have legitimate shows where performers are given nightly."[15] NBC executive director of programming Thomas McAvity followed up the consultant's diagnosis with similar sentiments. He informed the program's creative personnel to lean away from the star system and place emphasis on novelty acts more akin to what Ed Sullivan was doing, rather than on crafting expensive and time-consuming original sketches for the program's star comedians: "It is believed that comedy can be achieved through using comedians and comedy acts with already prepared and tested material, minimizing the need for new and high priced sketches to be written each week."[16] *Colgate*'s various writers, directors, and producers set to the task of brainstorming exactly how they could continue the comedic tradition of *The Colgate Comedy Hour* without aping Sullivan's variety stylings too much. Director Pete Barnum was one of the program's only creative personnel who concurred with McAvity. Barnum sought to "keep change constant," each week importing some spectacle (such as the Barnum & Bailey circus and rodeo) in lieu of original comedy sketches crafted around the host's comedic persona.[17]

Crucially, though, Barnum raised the idea that would guide *The Colgate Comedy Hour* through its final season: base an episode's original sketches on its star comedians' work outside of television, thereby providing quick content while at the same time affording any given host a marketing platform. In the following weeks, Barnum sought out the rights to, for example, Fred Astaire's *Top Hat* (1935) for host Donald O'Connor. This shift in strategy highlights how the economic conditions surrounding the show exerted pressure on the creative processes happening within the narrower field of sketch comedy production. A live, weekly broadcast of new material with little continuity from one sketch to the next proved unsustainable in meeting demands for textual consistency and reliability in meeting advertiser and audience expectations. It also provides an early instance of content sharing across media (one already common for decades among radio comedians) at a time not commonly associated with the practice. Certainly, early television and network era producers routinely reached outside television for ideas and promotional opportunities, but it is important to note this practice's specific relationship to sketch comedy in the case of *The Colgate Comedy Hour*. Namely, producers viewed sketch comedy's erratic and costly flexibility as something to be normalized and made more predictable as a profit-centered commercial product.

Following the directive to ease *The Colgate Comedy Hour*'s production routine in anticipation of its final full season in 1954–1955, executive producer Fred Wile Jr. took Barnum's cue. He instructed program personnel to create a list of vehicles—adaptations of motion pictures, Broadway musicals, or farces—that the program could musicalize as well as use as the basis for sketches that would not have to be written from scratch.[18] In February 1954, Wile, Barnum, New York executive producer Sam Fuller, and several newly hired writers and directors (among them, famed animator Frank Tashlin) convened to discuss exactly how this new creative direction would manifest. Tashlin warned that the current lineup of comics was "dangerously repetitive" and that creating each episode as an "idea show, more even in the direction of doing a movie, would be better."[19] Others were keen to adapt more Broadway musicals, such as those of Cole Porter.[20] All were in favor of increased characterization of any given host, slotting them into fictionalized sketch scenarios that minimized presentationalism, while at the same time using the host's star persona to exploit marketing opportunities for his or her film and theater vehicles.

In his own appraisal of the proceedings, Wile saw drastic change as necessary and inevitable:

> None of these alternatives seems to offer the hope and opportunity of staying with the hour and keeping the star dominated rotating pattern but doing it much better, with more imagination, scope, resourcefulness and guts than we have in the past.... By refusing to hew closely to the revue line and encouraging the producing directing writing folk to cut loose, not only in ideas themes stories books etc., original as well as adaptive, but also with respect to backgrounds and locales, real and functional, we have a chance to be real funny and certainly different, and at the very minimum to be talked about.[21]

The premiere of *The Colgate Comedy Hour*'s fifth season on September 19, 1954, began with a very tangible departure from shows past—it was the first ever television program to be broadcast from the Hollywood Bowl in Los Angeles, California. Subsequent episodes would continue to exploit this newly fortified bond with Hollywood in explicit ways. Promotional film clips, including ones for Mamie Van Doren's *Ain't Misbehavin'* (1955) and

Ray Milland's *A Man Alone* (1955), constituted regular blocks of content week by week. In a May 15, 1955 episode originating from March Air Force Base in Riverside, California, in honor of Armed Forces Day, Bud Abbott and Lou Costello re-created a scene from their early motion picture hit, *Buck Privates* (1941).[22] In fact, *The Colgate Comedy Hour*'s explicit aping of film and theater material increasingly drove its promotional strategies too. According to memos, producers asked that a weekly promotion for the upcoming episode with Jimmy Durante be rewritten in order to highlight elements of the show beyond the star's name. Instead, the ad repeatedly mentions Durante as performing a number from "his hit opera *Inka Dinka Doo*," suggesting that even promotional material move away from publicizing potentially unique elements of sketch comedy on the show in order to emphasize the existing projects of imported singers and film stars.[23]

Due to both internal tensions and external pressures, *The Colgate Comedy Hour* struggled to recapture the creative identity that drove its early popularity. More broadly, the program fell victim to larger industrial trends that saw vaudeo star comedians falling out of favor. As a result, Murray notes, the vaudeo format "was either altered to suit the needs of the amateur program or to include longer sitcom style sketches, thereby fostering little-known performers and lessening the focus on any single vaudeo personality."[24] The program reflected this shift under its new name, *The Colgate Variety Hour*, midway through 1955, in an episode not coincidentally hosted by a feuding Dean Martin and Jerry Lewis. Despite these last-ditch attempts to salvage the show, it continued to struggle against stiff competition provided by Ed Sullivan.

Of course, when *Colgate* and its ilk faded away or shifted creative focus, the bawdy, presentationalist aesthetic of vaudeo did not disappear from television entirely. Indeed, it lived (if in somewhat mutated form) in the performances of actors like Lucille Ball on *I Love Lucy* and Jackie Gleason on *The Honeymooners*. What was clear by the end of the 1950s, though, was that original comedy sketches, while providing early television comedy with quick, easily translatable material for its live broadcasts, were ill-suited to fit the medium's sustainable, long-term economic aims. Nonetheless, the case of *Colgate* highlights sketch's centrality in the efforts of numerous competing forces—star comedians, producers, network executives, writers—to define the aesthetic sensibilities of early television comedy.

As the television industry transitioned away from liveness as its primary production mode, short-form comedic formats like sketch would increasingly drift to dayparts outside of prime time and give way to long-form narratives in television genres like the situation comedy. Filmed television sitcoms afforded television in the subsequent network era many of the same economic benefits as product standardization did for film's studio system. Production shifted from the chaotic proscenia of New York to the soundstages of Los Angeles, which were sometimes the same facilities left underutilized by the collapse of the Hollywood studio system. Vaudeo stars found their comedic stylings supplanted by advertisers' and networks' efforts to create and sell to American audiences (presumed to be) composed of suburban families. Networks developed renewable, episodic narrative formulas to satisfy television's voracious appetite for content. They exploited not only the sitcom's reliability in regularly delivering viewers but also the newfound sense of intimacy fostered by idealized TV families sharing audiences' living rooms each evening.

Sketch Comedy and Variety into Television's Network Era

Of course, sketch-like comedy formats existed outside of prime-time vaudeo and variety too, in ways that experimented with early television's unique aesthetic capabilities. Such programs provided precedent for many of the televisually obsessed sketch comedies of the later multichannel and post-network eras. One instructive example for understanding how sketch comedy would move away from vaudeo and embrace televisuality is in the work of Ernie Kovacs.[25] Across a number of different programs and time slots, Kovacs displayed a completely unorthodox style that explored the possibilities of the young medium. "While his contemporaries were treating TV as an extension of vaudeville stages," writes one historian, "Kovacs was expanding the visible confines of the studio. His skits incorporated areas previously considered taboo, including dialogue with the camera crew, the audience, and forays into the studio corridor."[26]

Perhaps Kovacs's most audacious experiment was the January 19, 1957, half-hour "Silent Show" in which he starred as the mute, Chaplinesque Eugene and performed entirely in pantomime, accompanied only by sound effects and music. Kovacs reveled in brazenly breaking with television conventions in general, particularly those of his vaudeo and variety contemporaries.[27] Instead of pandering to celebrity guest stars, for example, Kovacs often roamed the aisles of his television studios for impromptu interviews with audience members or for demonstrations on the innards of a television set. As a critic of the time noted of Kovacs, "He enjoyed a remarkable rapport with his audience, who by some strange chemistry seem to feel they are a part of what is going on."[28]

In the recurring character of Percy Dovetonsils, an effete poet in a smoking jacket, Kovacs frequently broke from the script for asides to the audience or crew. In one segment from a 1954 episode of *The Ernie Kovacs Show* (1952–1962), Percy stops the recitation of a poem and comments on his cameraman's muscular legs with an affected lisp. Studio audience members and crew alike break out in laughter. Kovacs at times utilized these exaggerated parodies of ethnic or sexual stereotypes as recurring characters not necessarily as overt political commentary, but in an effort to demystify the nascent medium for his audience and to offer it as a point of engagement with him.

Kovacs's mode of sketch humor was rooted in the specific technological affordances of television as a distinct aesthetic medium, and it would greatly inform later programs such as *Late Night with David Letterman* (1982–1993) and sketch shows like *Mr. Show*. Despite critical adulation and a small but loyal fan base, however, Kovacs's unique brand of experimentation was too far afield from contemporaneous vaudeo and variety programs to be incorporated into them, and it was too avant-garde to find a sustainable sponsor and time slot on network television. Moreover, the turbulent sociopolitical climate of the 1960s, along with FCC chairman Newton Minow's infamous indictment of network television as a "vast wasteland," mandated a more socially responsive and responsible brand of programming that precluded many of the first wave of sketch-fueled vaudeo and variety shows from television's early days.[29] In the subsequent network era, broadcasters, with a vertically integrated stranglehold on the industry, sought to create mass-appeal programming that would maintain their robust profitability and, at the same time, speak to the burgeoning baby boomer generation.[30]

NBC attempted this strategy with its creation of the variety program satire *The Bob Newhart Show* (1961–1962). In his study of NBC and satire, Jeffery S. Miller details the unique relationship to the Kennedy administration (and Kennedy appointee Minow) that expedited NBC's risky plunge into prime-time satire.[31] The show ended after one season, Miller notes, due to the "identity crisis" brought about by NBC's desire to explicitly market it as satire and Newhart's reluctance to "go for the idea that comics should be social critics."[32] While Newhart incorporated topical satire into the show's sketches, he often utilized it as a gag line and not as source material that structured the program's overarching themes. Newhart's case is particularly notable because it marks a rare occasion wherein the network, seeking to distinguish itself from competitors and to placate regulators, attempted to push potentially subversive sketch content on to resistant talent. Many subsequent sketch and variety programs structuring their humor around explicitly satiric content found themselves in the opposite scenario, wishing to appease networks and regulators with youth-courting fare, yet not wanting it to be too risqué for fear that it would not be appropriate to air.

No show of the 1960s better embodies this tension than CBS's *The Smothers Brothers Comedy Hour* (1967–1969), a variety program that, at least initially, delicately wove Tom and Dick Smothers's left-wing sensibilities into sketches alongside their conservative-friendly, wholesome personas. The recurring character of Goldie O'Keefe provides a particularly salient example of this balancing act.[33] Parodying afternoon TV advice shows for housewives, spacey hippie-chick O'Keefe dispensed anecdotal advice in sketches laced with druggy slang, instructing viewers in one episode on how to get rid of "unsightly roaches." Much of the material was cleared for broadcast thanks to the writers' savvy use of double entendres that likely went over censors' heads.[34] However, as the brothers sought to respond more explicitly to the increasingly tumultuous social climate of the late 1960s, their battles with network censors over controversial musical guests and inflammatory sketches reached a boiling point, and CBS cancelled the show in April 1969.

Despite its short run, the show highlights the extent to which comedy sketches largely remained at the level of component bits in variety shows during the network era. Similarly, *Rowan and Martin's Laugh-In* (1968–1973) on NBC incorporated sketches not as its focal point but as a minor element of the show's scattershot, "anything goes" variety aesthetic. "If *The Smothers Brothers Comedy Hour* captured the political earnestness and moral conscience of the 1960s counterculture," Jenkins notes, "*Laugh-in* snared its flamboyance, its anarchic energy, and its pop aesthetic, combining the black-out comedy of the vaudeville tradition with a 1960s-style 'happening.'"[35] Hosts Dan Rowan and Dick Martin, who cut their teeth in the boozy nightclubs of Las Vegas, did not see sketches as comprising the core comedic identity of the show but as brief punchline options on par with physical gags or sexual puns. Nonetheless, what distinguished the show's use of sketch from others was *Laugh-In*'s use of rapid-fire one-liners and quick-cuts in place of "laboriously overwritten sketches and overproduced

Fig. 1.2. *Rowan & Martin's Laugh-In* captured the visual aesthetic of 1960s counterculture but little of its political critique.

musical numbers."[36] The overall effect of *Laugh-In*'s sketch aesthetic was an attempted deconstruction of the variety genre, one often muddled by the show's ham-fisted and awkward attempts at social commentary.

A sketch from September 1968 illuminates how Rowan and Martin approached sketch from a greater critical distance than the Smothers Brothers did, utilizing it more to pander to youth culture as part of a something-for-everyone approach than for any salient cultural critique. The sketch begins with the camera moving in to a swinging party scene adorned with psychedelic art, with all of *Laugh-In*'s regular cast members chatting and dancing to the music. Every several seconds, the music and commotion stop, the camera frames one or two characters, and a short bit ensues. A young Goldie Hawn, characterized as a sweetly naïve ditz, opens the sketch by saying, "I'm so glad the new TV season has started. It gives us a chance to see next year's reruns early."

Several bits follow in a similar manner, punning and musing on everything from fall fashion to segregationist Alabama governor George

Wallace. Toward the end of the sketch, the camera stops on host Dan Rowan and cast member Arte Johnson, who plays a Soviet expatriate named Mr. Rosemenko. Rowan asks him how he likes America, to which Mr. Rosemenko awkwardly replies, "Well it's, uh, very excitational for to be immigrationated. But it's one thing with all the criticalizations from the people, if they don't like it here, why don't they go fly a boat?" While *Smothers* sought to use sketches within the variety format for political commentary, the critique contained in Rosemenko's character is largely undermined by *Laugh-In*'s quick cuts to silly sight gags. *Laugh-In* thus brought sketch comedy to align more closely with network era imperatives mandating content for mass appeal.

Considered more broadly, *The Smothers Brothers Comedy Hour* and *Laugh-In* pointed just as much to 1960s programming practices as it did to shifting audience demographics. Many older viewers of the same generation as vaudeville stars like Eddie Cantor and Jimmy Durante comprised the mass audience prized by networks less and less. Baby boomer comedians who grew up watching the elder vaudeo stars used sketch comedy to define the format their own way, mixing sociocultural commentary with innovative comedic performances that explored the unique aesthetic qualities of television. We see this generational negotiation at work in the contrast between *Smothers* and *Laugh-In*. The former hailed emergent baby boomer audiences with its oppositionally oriented references to drugs and counterculture, while the latter attempted to incorporate young boomer viewers into a vaudevillian, bit-driven approach to sketch comedy that was becoming increasingly unfashionable. Although the social satire of *Laugh-In* may have seemed toothless in comparison to that of *The Smothers Brothers Comedy Hour*, aesthetically, it distinguished *Laugh-In* from contemporaries and previewed some of the formal playfulness that would characterize later sketch comedies. As Jenkins notes, "Not until *Saturday Night Live* would another television variety show ensemble leave such a firm imprint on the evolution of American comedy."[37]

Many performers on *Saturday Night Live* viewed sketch comedy as a way to experiment with televisual conventions, win screen time over fellow cast mates, and reject previous vaudeo-variety traditions en route to bigger and better things beyond television. The variability of sketches on the show granted performers ample screen time to demonstrate their versatility in a number of different performative contexts. At the same time, however, performers who found the most success beyond the show were often ones who aggressively inscribed their own personalities across their various characters, a dynamic I explore more in chapter 2. The reflexive flexibility of performers on *SNL* was closely tied both to the broader, baby boomer generational identity and to the economic logic of the television industry in the network era. The program's contribution to the format, then, came not only in its many memorable characters and catchphrases, but also in its pursuit of a new form of cultural consecration, one taken up by a number of later comedians and viewers across television, film, and the internet.

Conclusion

In surveying historical antecedents for sketch comedy in film, radio, theater, and early television vaudeo and variety, I have established many of the format's key early manifestations of reflexive flexibility. Indeed, for the sketch comedies I discuss in subsequent chapters, this dynamic is not simply a matter of exploring television's comedic possibilities but reacting against them. The generation of sketch performers who came of age across the 1970s, 1980s, and 1990s grew up under the influence of many of the texts and performers analyzed in this chapter. They sought symbolic and cultural capital just as much by breaking from previous traditions as they did from demonstrating an understanding of how those previous traditions worked.

Saturday Night Live represents the longest-running and most influential program that bridged the gap between the vaudeo programs before and the many sketch comedies after it. It did so by creating a forum that gave voice to the cultural identities of the emerging baby boomer generation, one that defined itself in direct opposition to the comedic traditions of vaudeo and variety before it. In this chapter, I have primarily provided an overview of historical constructions of sketch comedy, noting how they have aligned or not aligned with dominant industrial and sociohistorical discourses along the way. Implicit in these analyses are the ways in which early television assumed certain viewer types. In early versions of mediated sketch comedy, while television was still centered in urban areas on the east coast, vaudeo reflected the presumed sensibilities of a generation that had matured under live vaudeville and presentational performances as the dominant comedic aesthetic. When the industry refocused on filmed long-form sitcoms in the network era, sketch comedy conflicted more explicitly with network attempts to hail broad audiences. The young adult audience addressed in coded, layered terms by programs like *The Smothers Brothers Comedy Hour* found themselves directly hailed as new and different by *Saturday Night Live*. The program's aggressive aesthetic both spoke to and helped create in its baby boomer audience a sense of separation from the comedy of previous generations. *SNL* would go on to become such a dominant presence in sketch comedy across the network era and beyond that, inevitably, its original boomer audience no longer found itself clearly defined as the courted young adult audience. In chapter 2, I explore *SNL*'s many reflexive addresses to comedians, industry personnel, and viewers variously defining themselves as different from what came before, eager to explore what lies beyond television.

Notes

1. Allen, *Horrible Prettiness*.
2. Jenkins, *What Made Pistachio Nuts?*, 26–58.
3. Ibid.
4. Ibid., 153–184.
5. Hilmes, "Fanny Brice and the Schnooks Strategy," 11–25.
6. Spigel, *Make Room for TV*, 1–10.
7. Ibid., 99–135.
8. Murray, *Hitch Your Antenna to the Stars*, 170–178.
9. Neale and Krutnik, *Popular Film and Television Comedy*, 179.
10. Murray, *Hitch Your Antenna to the Stars*, 9–10.
11. Ibid., 1–40.
12. Ibid., 73.
13. Sternberg, "The *Colgate Comedy Hour*."
14. Murray, *Hitch Your Antenna to the Stars*, 115.
15. Greshler, "Memo to Fred Wile Jr., January 19, 1954."
16. McAvity, "Memo to *Colgate Comedy Hour* staff, January 25, 1954."
17. Barnum, "Interdepartment Correspondence to Sam Fuller: *Colgate Comedy Hour*, February 2, 1954."
18. Wile, "Memo: *Colgate Comedy Hour*, February 2, 1954."
19. Wile, "Memo: *Colgate Comedy Hour* Proposal, February 11, 1954."
20. Ibid.
21. Ibid.
22. Promotional Materials, Broadcast Publicity Files, Box 133, Folder 61, NBC Archives.
23. Douglass, "Letter to Sam Fuller, March 2, 1955."
24. Murray, *Hitch Your Antenna to the Stars*, 109.
25. See Thompson, *Parody and Taste in Postwar American Television Culture*, 98–124.
26. Chorba, "Ernie Kovacs."
27. Weinstein, *The Forgotten Network: Dumont and the Birth of American Television*, 175–208.
28. *New York Daily News* critic Sid Shalit quoted in Weinstein, *The Forgotten Network: Dumont and the Birth of American Television*, 180.
29. Hilmes is careful to note that "the set of social phenomena we think of as the sixties didn't really get started until after 1965" (*Only Connect*, 218). I include Minow's 1961 speech as

part of this time period because of its relevance to Jeffery S. Miller's later discussion of NBC and satire.

30. In the introduction to their anthology on the period, *The Revolution Wasn't Televised: Sixties Television and Social Conflict*, Spigel and Curtin note that "the networks presented social movements of the 1960s less as a break with television's general entertainment logic than as part of the flow of its 'something for everyone' programming philosophy," 2.

31. Miller, "What Closes on Saturday Night: NBC and Satire," 192–208.

32. Ibid., 194.

33. Bodroghkozy, "*The Smothers Brothers Comedy Hour* and the Youth Rebellion," 205.

34. Ibid.

35. Jenkins, "Rowan and Martin's Laugh-in."

36. Miller, "What Closes on Saturday Night," 200.

37. Jenkins, "Rowan and Martin's Laugh-In."

2

"... AND YOU'RE NOT"

Saturday Night Live *in the* Network Era and Beyond

From the moment *Saturday Night Live* premiered in the fall of 1975, its creator, Lorne Michaels, sought to distinguish his sketch comedy show from the many vaudeo and variety shows before it. As Michaels notes of his thinking during *SNL*'s inaugural season: "We wanted to redefine comedy the way the Beatles redefined what being a pop star was. That required not pandering, and it also required removing neediness, the need to please. It was like, we're only going to please those people who are like us. The presumption was there were a lot of people like us. And that turned out to be so."[1]

His desire to "redefine comedy" indicated a rejection of the presumed pandering characteristic of vaudevillian-influenced comedians and aesthetics that populated those programs. Early on, it was not entirely clear how his Not Ready for Prime Time Players would do so, particularly from their positions as relative unknowns toiling in a late night time slot. Quickly enough, though, the program's unique comedic sensibility successfully played to the desire of the baby boomer generation—"people who are like us"—for cultural identities distinct from those of its elders. As "the cult NBC sketch show *Saturday Night Live*" approaches nearly half a century on air, the program has grown into a comedy empire, "the single most influential showcase for filtering comedians into the mainstream" beyond television.[2]

The characterization of *SNL* as a cult show somehow separate from the mainstream provides a good entry point for understanding the reflexive flexibility of both its onscreen humor and subsequent decades of growth across media. Indeed, the show's aggressive humor catering to young boomer viewers distinguished it from the staid style of contemporaneous network comedies meant for broader audiences. Early on, this often took the form of cast members like John Belushi and Chevy Chase commandeering screen time and playing versions of themselves even when in character. Chase's greeting at the top of "Weekend Update" segments—"I'm Chevy Chase, and you're not"—was thus not only a boastful and selfish power grab but also a tacit endorsement of Michaels's mission to set *SNL* apart. Chase's departure for Hollywood after his first and only season created a model that many others would follow over the years, so much so that, as frequent host Buck Henry joked, *SNL* came to be seen simply as a "launching pad . . . which leads to making bad movies."[3]

As the longest running sketch comedy in American television history, *SNL* has been the subject of countless reviews, interviews, and retrospectives. These resources, particularly Tom Shales and James Andrew Miller's infamous oral history *Live From New York*, provide titillating details of cast members struggling with one another for screen time so that they can eventually move on to bigger and better things. Such a narrative supports the broader framing in this book of sketch comedy as a field of cultural production, one in which cast members jockey for consecration in the form of a star persona that transcends the show. Henry's "launching pad" metaphor also highlights how *SNL* refracts external economic discourses through its own peculiar logic, compelling comedians both to compete with one another within and position themselves in cultural fields beyond *SNL*. Rather than rehash dishy anecdotes about the show, this chapter seeks to complicate the mythology of *SNL* in two separate but related ways. First, I examine how *SNL*'s aggressive comedy early on was not based simply on cast members' vying for consecration by proving their knowledge of and rejecting previous comedy traditions. Instead, I suggest, this competition was centered on a flexible play with identity politics, one that again and again privileged humor constructed around comedians who were straight, white men like Chase. Although much popular commentary on the show has grappled with this issue, I provide industrial and cultural context for why Michaels's presumption that "there were a lot of people like us" marginalized cast members and, by extension, viewers, who were women and/or nonwhite.

Second, I consider how the early individuation of *SNL*'s stars (most of whom were men) en route to film careers has contributed to ongoing critical debates about the ill fit between sketch comedy and movies. The aggressive, reflexive identity work of *SNL*'s early years has, over the years, become grounded in comedy that is more dialogic. As cast members have continued to graduate from the show and this more communal sketch aesthetic has filtered into the mainstream, critics often decry the distracting improvisations, non sequitur narrative units, and general sketchy-ness of former *SNL* stars' films. While sketch comedy's formal malleability has led to experimentation and innovations on television, in film this impulse is often seen as a bad thing. In the second part of this chapter, I explore how sketchlike comedy scenes in film today provide additional, complementary pleasures for viewers and possibilities for performers, not distractions. By pairing this diachronic view of *SNL* stars' transition to film with the synchronic view of *SNL*'s early identity work, I hope to further fill in the already immense footprint the show has left on sketch comedy, television, and American culture.

Gender and the Cultural Politics of Looking Past Saturday Night

In the summer of 1974, NBC's king of late night, Johnny Carson, informed the network that he no longer wished to have *The Tonight Show* rerun on weekends. NBC president Herb Schlosser gave the task of filling the timeslot to newly appointed head of late night weekend programming Dick Ebersol, who in turn tabbed former *Laugh-In* writer Lorne Michaels to produce what would become *Saturday Night Live*.[4] The young Michaels quickly sought to set his show apart from the tradition of comedy in network variety programs before *SNL*, specifically citing his desire to emulate the newly imported BBC sketch comedy program *Monty Python's Flying Circus*.[5] Steve Neale describes *Python* as distinctive from other television comedies because it "encompassed a much wider range of 'thought' than had hitherto been the norm . . . while persistently playing with the formats and forms of traditional variety and its sketches, of popular culture and popular film, and most notably, of TV itself."[6] The program found success in both the UK and United States by appealing to the young, often college-educated TV generation of baby boomers, one receptive to *Python*'s surreal comic attacks on institutional authority and television tropes. Indeed, many variety shows (e.g., *The Smothers Brothers*) had made appeals to the same viewing audience but ultimately tempered their risqué content in response to prime-time censorship standards and sponsor demands. The American broadcast of *Python* eschewed these problems on the commercial-free PBS, and *SNL* used its late-night time slot similarly to push the formal and aesthetic boundaries of sketch comedy.

No sketch better encapsulates early *SNL*'s aggressive and edgy aesthetic better than its very first ("Wolverines," October 11, 1975), one provided as a cold open without any contextual credits or introduction. In it, writer Michael O'Donoghue plays the role of a teacher instructing a vaguely Eastern European immigrant (played by John Belushi) in the finer points of the English language. Belushi haltingly repeats each of O'Donoghue's increasingly bizarre sentences, such as "I would like to feed your fingertips to the wolverines." He mimics the teacher's final lesson—collapsing of a heart attack—and punctuates the bizarre moment announcing the arrival of a new American comedic sensibility. At the same time that it departs from contemporaneous television comedy, the sketch's epilogue features Chevy Chase calling out the first iteration of *SNL*'s pretitle introduction—"Live, from New York! It's Saturday Night!" The introduction reflexively marks the program's live, late-night industrial identity, the one clear holdover from the many vaudeo and variety shows before it.

SNL was not an instant success in securing the massive viewing numbers mandated by network era practices, but it did succeed with demographically desirable young adult audiences, a dynamic that presaged television's governing logic in ensuing decades. "Overall ratings for the first few shows were nothing more than what *Best of Carson* had provided, and for a lot more money; the demographic breakdown, however, showed that *Saturday Night* was attracting a higher percentage of viewers in the all-important eighteen-to-forty-nine age group—the "television generation"—than any other program on the air."[7] While the show treaded water in the ratings and struggled to return on NBC's investment, it did capture the emergent comedic voice of baby boomers and won six Emmys in its first five years.

The new comedy aesthetic advanced by early *SNL* was an overtly egotistical, often aggressively presentational style, one embodied most explicitly in *SNL*'s first season by Chevy Chase. Tall, handsome, and carrying himself with an arrogant swagger that alienated his cast mates, Chase quickly became the face of the show by consciously positioning himself as its star. As a wheelchair-bound character in the opening sketch on October 25, 1975, Chase drew riotous laughter after taking a hard fall. In the opening sketch the next week, Chase took an identical tumble in his bumbling impression of President Gerald Ford. Without makeup that would allow him to better approximate Ford physically, the resultant impersonation accommodated a dual reading of both presidential parody and star performance. It lampooned Ford's clumsiness at the same time that it reflexively foregrounded

Chase's comedic persona. Soon thereafter, a *New York* magazine cover story called Chase "the funniest man in America,"[8] and Chase would continue to play an exaggerated version of himself in subsequent sketches that year, his only on the show.

Chase was not lacking for offers from Hollywood after his departure from *SNL*. Producers of the frat-house comedy *Animal House* (1978) crafted the lead role of Otter for Chase, a move director John Landis adamantly opposed. Landis convinced Chase to opt instead for the lead in the romantic comedy *Foul Play* (1978), explaining to him: "'Chevy, if you take *Foul Play*, you're then like Cary Grant; you're opposite Goldie Hawn, a major sex star, you're like Cary Grant. But if you take *Animal House*, you're a top banana in an ensemble, like *SNL*.'"[9] Landis's comments echo what many film directors and critics would reiterate over the years: *SNL*'s sketch comedy aesthetics were best suited for television, not feature film. The expectation was for Chase to continue playing himself in much the same way he had on *SNL*, but the move would get Chase's film career off to a sputtering start. To be sure, Chase's presence starring as himself would not necessarily guarantee the film's success, but it fit with industrial discourses that embraced his *SNL* identity while they attempted to distance him from it. Aggressive individuation distinguished Chase from the *SNL* ensemble on television and, at the very least, provided him with enough familiarity among audiences to attempt the next step in film. For a similar shot at film stardom, it quickly became clear to fellow cast members that Chase's model was the most direct route to notoriety and subsequent capitalization on the cultural cachet the show was building.

Of course, Landis's career advice to Chase turned out to be misguided, as *Animal House* went on to huge box office success. The film's notoriety was due thanks in part to the carnivalesque performance of another *SNL* star, John Belushi. Film scholar William Paul has connected the aggressive aesthetics of *SNL*'s early years to the films its alumni went on to make as part of a larger trend in 1970s film comedy called "animal comedy."[10] This cycle of films, further embodied by non-*SNL*-related movies like *Bachelor Party* (1984) and *Porky's* (1982), foregrounded an "insistent emphasis on animality," "physicality," and the notion that "physical comedy generally receives pride of place over verbal comedy."[11] With this theoretical framework, we can see how the comedic persona Chevy Chase honed on *SNL* might fit uneasily within the context of animal comedy. "A lot of the comedy in Chase's performances," Paul claims, "comes from his own conception of himself as suave and debonair while events around him conspire to puncture holes in that image. Ultimately, though, the image proves real."[12] In other words, the comedic persona that bolstered Chase's success on *SNL* did not align closely enough with the aesthetic of animal comedy. Therefore, he was ultimately ill-suited for the type of sustained success in film comedy as other *SNL* alumni. Chase was ultimately consumed with the maintenance of his own laid-back image, and his shtick—from "I'm Chevy Chase, and you're not," to the quick rebound from his pratfalls, to his cool detachment from the news on "Weekend Update"—articulated a generalized indifference that insufficiently addressed the industrial imperatives driving animal comedy's success at the box office.

Whether it launched them to successful film careers or not, many subsequent *SNL* cast members emulated Chase's presentational mode of performance on the show. However, *SNL*'s early aesthetic, despite distinguishing the show from variety predecessors, warrants additional consideration in the context of the program's early climate of institutionalized sexism. Caryn Murphy notes that although *SNL* was born of countercultural impulses, ones that manifested in a comedic voice distinct from others on television, "advancing gender equality was not a shared goal."[13] The show's men subjected women writers, performers, and producers early on to a range of maltreatment. The generally hostile environment toward women meant that screen time for them was less meaningful and their comedic voices factored into the program less than those of men. This hostility created "pressure on the few women involved in the creative process to disprove a generally accepted notion about gender and comedy, as compared with the men on the staff, who were presumably attempting to prove their own individual talent."[14] While popular histories of the show highlight the more egregious instances of sexism (such as Belushi's infamous proclamation shared with many *SNL* cast mates that "women aren't funny"[15]), the environment clearly influenced softer forms of power wielded by above-the-line personnel like Michaels too. According to original cast member Laraine Newman:

> Lorne urged me to repeat characters. I refused to do it because I wanted to, you know, dazzle everybody with my versatility. And that kept me anonymous. That was the same pitfall for Danny [Aykroyd]. He was much more comfortable doing characters, and I think that it made him less recognizable than John, who was always John even when he was the Samurai. And Billy [Murray] was Billy. He did Todd in the Nerds but basically he was Billy. So even though I loved the kind of work that I did, and still do—I love the character work—I think it keeps you more anonymous than people who play themselves.[16]

Fig. 2.1. *SNL* cast member Gilda Radner invited audiences to form an intimate bond with her through recurring characters like Roseanne Rosannadanna.

Newman's comments speak directly to the central contradiction of *SNL*'s reflexive flexibility in its early seasons. Effacement of one's personality via recurring character work meant more screen time but without the individuation that could lead to film opportunities beyond *SNL*. Performers who only played themselves, conversely, minimized their chances to appear often in varied roles on the show in the hope that their comedic personas would click with writers, cast mates, and audiences. Clearly, the divide between the two is not absolute, but Newman's comments suggest a gendered bias toward men in the latter mode.

The original woman cast member that most approximated Chase's presentational style was Gilda Radner, yet even her case highlights how sketch comedy performance modes on *SNL* could articulate gendered biases that marginalized women and propelled the show's men into film stardom. Radner thrived in the representational performance modes of recurring character work in her five-year tenure on the show, creating such memorable roles as Roseanne Roseannadanna, the crotchety "Weekend Update" commentator Emily Litella, and the Barbara Walters parody Baba Wawa. She often appeared in presentational monologues and backstage segments as herself too, interstitial bits that formed a major component of the original cast's efforts to form rapport with its boomer audience and reflexively invite them in on the joke of television's constructedness and artificiality.[17]

While Chase imbued these segments with an aloofness that maintained distance between himself and audiences (and thus implicitly positioned himself as star), Radner formed an intimate bond with viewers in ways that reinforced the program's gendered hierarchy. In a scene from *SNL*'s fourth episode (November 8, 1975), Radner chats onstage with host Candice Bergen about everything from the stresses of dating to the proposed Equal Rights Amendment. In a monologue entitled "What Gilda Ate" from the program's third episode (October 25, 1975), Radner playfully rattles off a lengthy list of her day's diet before host Rob Reiner cuts her off. While they lightheartedly lampoon some of the problems faced by many American women, the sketches take on additional significance in light of Radner's struggles with her self-image and bulimia at the time. Her vulnerability in sketches humanizes her and offers a point of identification for viewers, particularly women. Yet the fact that her femininity provides the basis for this identification and figures so prominently into her presentational comedic persona closes the gap between Gilda and "Gilda." The blueprint laid out by Chase for TV-to-film stardom required this gap, allowing audiences to get close to him, yet keeping them far enough away so that he could position himself as star.

If the egotistical aesthetic *SNL* used to distinguish itself from network era contemporaries was primarily masculine, so too did it privilege whiteness. Unlike the contentious gendered dynamic alluded to by Newman and other women cast members, though, *SNL*'s early racial identity politics are not as legible in commentary from those who have worked on the show. Some of this illegibility has to do with the paucity of nonwhite writers and cast members over the years, many of whom the show relegated to supporting roles instead of ones foregrounding their racial identities. Much more has to do with television's complex relationship with blackness, in particular, during the network era, as I explore more below. Although sketches based in transgressive racial politics would seem to have bolstered *SNL*'s edgy aesthetic early on, the show marginalized black identities by privileging those of white men.

Race and Reflexivity on Early *SNL*

Garrett Morris was *SNL*'s sole nonwhite cast member for the show's first five years until Eddie Murphy's arrival in 1980. As a classically trained vocalist, Morris occasionally got the opportunity to sing on the show both as himself and in character, an acknowledgment of the enduring influence of variety on *SNL*. More often, though, the show typecast Morris as one-dimensional black characters, assigned him to celebrity impersonations of Sammy Davis Jr. and Tina Turner, or simply deployed him as the nonwhite utility player. Morris's most memorable role was perhaps the recurring character Chico Escuela, a fictional Dominican baseball player whose primary comedic appeal was in delivering the heavily accented catchphrase, "Baseball been berra berra good to me."

Clearly, there was little room for Morris to pursue the type of self-centered, presentational performances that would launch Chase and others to stardom beyond the show, a situation Morris has at least partially blamed on his own off-screen tendencies to be withdrawn. At the same time, he was on the receiving end of the same hostility with which white men treated women in the cast: "Either it's that they were all niggers with me or I was a woman with them—because I got the same raw deal."[18] Even though he was an established playwright, Morris claims to have been "relieved of [his] writing duties" upon joining the cast, a fact that undoubtedly exacerbated the lack of diversity among creative voices shaping *SNL*'s early sketches.[19] Despite these challenges over the course of his five-year tenure as a cast member, Morris succeeded in getting on air several sketches that directly engaged black identity and black televisual representations. These sketches' critiques were often constrained, however, by *SNL*'s privileging of comedy grounded in the identities of white men, as well as by television's ambivalent politics of representing blackness in the network era.

The best example of this dynamic is "Black Perspective," recurring sketches with Morris as host of a mock talk show interviewing *SNL*'s guest of the week about race relations. Much like Chase on "Weekend Update," Morris plays (an exaggerated version of) himself. Each sketch's premise centers on Morris's guest making polite conversation initially before stating something outlandish about race, gender, or stereotyping. The format allowed Morris not only to indulge briefly in a presentational performance as himself but also to speak directly to issues of race relations. In the sketch's first iteration (January 29, 1977), strangely enough, Morris chats with white NFL star quarterback Fran Tarkenton about the stereotype that black athletes are ill-suited for the position. Tarkenton gamely baits Morris with outlandish claims—"Every black I know has trouble with area codes, let alone numbers of plays. . . . If you were on the offensive line, would you turn your back on a black guy standing behind you? Especially during a night game?"—before Morris concedes that Tarkenton is right. In the sketch's second installment later that season (April 9, 1977), Morris interviews black politician and civil rights activist Julian Bond about "the myth that whites are inherently more intelligent than blacks." They joke about the racial bias of IQ tests before Bond tells Morris about his theory that "light-skinned blacks are smarter than dark-skinned blacks." The dark-skinned Morris, flustered by the assertion from the light-skinned Bond, rushes to wrap up the segment to avoid further embarrassment.

In the sketch's final iteration on February 10, 1979, Morris interviews Academy Award–nominated black actress Cicely Tyson. Following the same beats of the previous sketches, Morris and Tyson chat initially about Hollywood's discrimination against women of color. Their banter is breezy, but they make explicit references throughout to systematic inequalities in media industries. When Morris presses Tyson on her thoughts about the lack of positive film roles for black women, the following exchange ensues:

TYSON: Well . . . I think . . . Garrett, I think until recently, this was a man's society.

MORRIS: Mm-hm.

TYSON: And, um, an ethnic group or race was really judged by its men.

MORRIS: Mm.

TYSON: So what I think happened was that . . . the black woman . . . has just gotten a raw deal because black man has always been such a loser.

[MORRIS GLARES ICILY AT HER.]

MORRIS: Say what?

TYSON: I mean, you are all so shiftless, and lazy—I mean, just too shiftless and too lazy to get anywhere!

MORRIS: Wait-wait-wait-wait-wait-wait a minute, uh, Tyson, I'm not sure I understand what you're sayin', now. Could you. . . .

TYSON: It's not complicated at all, Garrett. It is very simple.

MORRIS: Well, break it down for me, will you?

TYSON: I mean, it's very simple. Black men just ruined it for black women. I mean, you were always busy gettin' high, pimpin', tryin' to prove your manhood by fightin', and stealin', and wheelin', and dealin', instead of studying like the Jewish men!

MORRIS: Uhhhhhhhhhhhhhh . . . uhhhhhhhhh. . . .

TYSON: I mean, do you think that Barbra Streisand has any difficulty getting parts?

MORRIS: Well, now, listen, bitch. Uh. . . .

TYSON: [enraged] Garrett! [starts to rise from chair] I mean, that's what's wrong with you black men!!

MORRIS: [holds up hands] Joke! Joke!

TYSON: I don't talk that way!

MORRIS: Tyson, you have the most beautiful eyes I have ever seen in my life!

TYSON: Oh, man, don't give me that!

MORRIS: The avenues for the white man. . . .

TYSON: I don't need you to tell me about my eyes!

MORRIS: . . . have been traditionally closed to black men, now, you know that!

TYSON: Hey, listen! You all fall back on that old story all the time! It's old, it's clichéd—forget it! The black man just never got himself together—and that's all there is to it! I mean, look what you all did to Detroit! That used to be a nice town!

Tyson's reframing of their initial discussion about structural inequalities as an intraracial tension between black men and women undermines the sketch's transgressive potential. Indeed, it is the same comedic pattern as the previous sketch starring Bond, one that turned a critique of cultural assumptions about race and intelligence into a squabble between light- and dark-skinned blacks. Both sketches diminish their critiques, moreover, by distilling the complex targets of their commentaries to an individual wrongdoer—Morris—whose personal peccadilloes comprise most of the sketches' punchlines.

Cultural conservatives have commonly used this strategy to absolve whites' guilt for their continued complicity in racial inequality, and Tyson's word choice echoes it comedically. Black men, for Tyson, are not working within a system that limits their opportunities for success, as she indicates in their earlier discussion about Hollywood casting processes. Instead, individual black men are to blame for their bad choices—they are "always busy gettin' high, pimpin', tryin' to prove [their] manhood by fightin', and stealin', and wheelin', and dealin'. . . . The black man just never got himself together." In the same vein, Bond's explanation of intelligence in light- versus dark-skinned blacks centers on Morris simply not understanding the fundamental difference between them, telling him, "There's very little to explain—it's just like I told you."

In all three iterations of "Black Perspective," potentially transgressive dialogue devolves into an indulgence of racial stereotypes and blaming of racial inequality on individuals. *SNL*'s treatment of Morris and racial politics in the sketches bolsters the broader construction of its primary identity for "people who are like us" (to borrow Michaels's turn of phrase) as white. Of course, this is not to discount the possibility of "Black Perspective" utilizing racial stereotypes and racist discourses in order to deconstruct and critique those racist stereotypes. Such a decoding of the sketches is certainly available and apparent but secondary to the one I have described above.

SNL's compromised racial identity politics take on additional significance when considered alongside the work of other black sketch comedians during the 1960s and 1970s. Christine Acham has written compellingly about network era television's conflicting impulses to represent blackness as having achieved integrationist ideals on the one hand but remain authentic to heterogeneous post–civil rights black identities on the other. In describing the former tendency on *The Flip Wilson Show* (1970–1974), for instance, Acham suggests that despite his use of "hidden transcripts" to address black audiences, Wilson's success came from "his unthreatening appeal and his ability to quell any white angst over the state of blackness. Here, mainstream Americans could sit back and laugh with a black man who had clearly made it. Indeed, Flip Wilson was used as a token at a time when many African Americans struggled for basic rights. Wilson's success indicated that the problems of black society were the fault not of racism but of the individual's lack of effort."[20] Acham's observations about Wilson echo the comedically framed views of Tyson in the "Black Perspective" sketch. Although one might decode empowering critiques hidden in the sketch's various beats, it, like Wilson, ultimately serves to "quell any white angst over the state of blackness" by blaming "the individual's lack of effort."

If Flip Wilson articulated race within the sketch/variety format in accordance with network era mandates to serve broad, mainstream audiences, Richard Pryor took the opposite tack. Already a highly successful stand-up comedian due in no small part to his incendiary discussions of race relations, Pryor's short-lived sketch series *The Richard Pryor Show* (1977) directly confronted African Americans' political, cultural, and economic realities from a variety of critical perspectives. In detailed analyses of each of *The Richard Pryor Show*'s four episodes, Acham gestures both to sketch comedy's power to create resonant, raced identities, as well as the industrial discourses that constrain them. In the end, she suggests, Pryor's comedic critique was simply too much for network era television to sustain a multiple season run. Rather than reproduce those analyses, though, I'd like to use them to reconsider Pryor's December 13, 1975, turn as an *SNL* host, particularly his much-lauded "Racist Word Association Interview" sketch opposite Chevy Chase. Doing so highlights how, despite its avowal of racial tension, the sketch ultimately participates in the same affirmation of identities based in whiteness as the "Black Perspective" sketches and others on early *SNL*.

Over the years, "Racist Word Association Interview" has taken on a sort of totemic significance, with former cast members and critics touting it as evidence of the show's era-defying edginess. Frequent guest filmmaker Albert Brooks claims that "nobody had seen that kind of thing before they did it,"[21] while *Entertainment Weekly* calls it "one of the most audacious two-minute segments in TV history."[22] Chroniclers of the show return to the sketch again and again to counterbalance criticism that "the show has a history of either downplaying, ignoring, or not realizing how important it is to have people of color represented in the cast."[23] Many of these plaudits gesture to the sketch's shockingly explicit use of racial epithets, ones that have since become so taboo that revisiting them now creates the immediate impression of transgression. However, "Racist Word Association Interview"—as well as the episode of which it is a part—belie broader efforts by *SNL* at the time to contain Pryor's volatility and the transgressive blackness he represented.

These efforts began with NBC executives demanding that the episode be broadcast with a five-second delay, a fact that was kept secret from its star host. Despite Pryor managing to bring frequent collaborator Paul Mooney into the writers' room that week, sketches often settled on, as Scott Saul notes in his biography of Pryor, "splitting the difference."[24] In the episode's reflexive first sketch, for example, Chase and Morris stage a fight over who gets to open the show, one rife with implied tension about race and stardom on *SNL*. "Richard Pryor's here tonight, and I thought that I would open the show, I mean, do the fall," Morris tells Chase. Chase replies with self-seriousness, "I *always* open the show. Is it understood?" The sketch moves through several beats before giving both a starring moment—Chase performs his signature pratfall, and Morris says the show's signature line, "Live from New York! It's Saturday Night!"

Mooney and Chase also clashed over credit for the conception of "Racist Word Association Interview." The former used the sketch to channel subtly racist treatment he and Pryor had felt from Michaels and NBC that week, while the latter saw the sketch's creation as a collaborative effort between like-minded artists. As Saul notes of Pryor's ambivalent role in the sketch's conception, "Mooney saw Richard as an artist who weaponized comedy to an unprecedented degree, while Chase saw him as an artist who, by nature, did not reach for arms."[25] Chase's deference to Pryor at the writing stage of the sketch stood in stark contrast to his aggressive self-figuration elsewhere on the show. Importantly, though, this deference seemed to neutralize the possibly transgressive, race-based identity work so clearly at the core of Pryor's comedic persona.

Despite its contested creation, "Racist Word Association Interview" eschews the "hidden transcripts" of Wilson's comedy for an aggressive confrontation of post–civil rights racial tension. Indeed, the sketch is among the most fondly remembered of *SNL*'s early years precisely *because* of its frank use of racial slurs. The sketch begins innocuously enough: An employer played by Chase interviews Pryor's Mr. Wilson, a prospective employee, asking him to respond to his one-word prompts with "anything that comes to your mind." "Tree," "dog," their exchange begins, before quickly escalating:

INTERVIEWER (CHASE): [casually] "Negro."

MR. WILSON (PRYOR): "Whitey."

INTERVIEWER: "Tarbaby."

MR. WILSON: [silent, sure he didn't hear what he thinks he heard] What'd you say?

INTERVIEWER: [repeating] "Tarbaby."

MR. WILSON: "Ofay."

INTERVIEWER: "Colored."

MR. WILSON: "Redneck."

INTERVIEWER: "Junglebunny."

MR. WILSON: [starting to get angry] "Peckerwood!"

INTERVIEWER: "Burrhead."

MR. WILSON: [defensive] "Cracker!"

INTERVIEWER: [aggressive] "Spearchucker."

MR. WILSON: "White trash!"

INTERVIEWER: "Jungle Bunny!"

MR. WILSON: [upset] "Honky!"

INTERVIEWER: "Spade!

Fig. 2.2. Richard Pryor scowls at Chevy Chase after exchanging racial epithets with him in an infamous *SNL* sketch from 1975.

Mr. Wilson: [really upset] "Honky Honky!"
Interviewer: [relentless] "Nigger!"
Mr. Wilson: [immediate] "*Dead* honky!" [face starts to flinch]

Clearly, by the end of the sketch, Pryor's Mr. Wilson has gained the upper hand on Chase's Interviewer, meeting every strike in their semiotic war with a more powerful weapon of his own. When the sketch's climax ("Nigger!," "*Dead* honky!") escalates from a war of words to the threat of bodily harm, we can read an articulation of a range of strategies for black oppositionality—from resentful protest to violent revolt—in Pryor's flinching face. As Mooney indicates, the sketch was "like an H-bomb that Richard and I toss[ed] into America's consciousness . . . the N-word as a weapon, turned back against those who use it."[26]

Situated within the broader context of network era television's representational strategies, however, the sketch's searing critique becomes muddled in ways that bolster the cultural politics of whiteness on early *SNL*. Although Pryor's resistance to racism and reassertion of blackness are the sketch's most salient messages, it is impossible to ignore Chase's complicating role in the sketch. On the one hand, his flippant, then antagonistic, use of racial slurs provides the same deconstruction of racist humor as "Black Perspective" does, ironically using racism to critique racism. On the other hand, we can interpret Chase as voicing the sort of unambiguously bigoted sentiments characteristic of contemporaneous television characters like *All in the Family*'s Archie Bunker. That sitcom "was far more open and polysemic" than the progressive politics of creator Norman Lear—and his liberal mouthpiece on the show, Mike Stivic—might indicate, so that "both hard hats and longhairs could find discursive room to maneuver."[27] Academic studies of viewer affiliations revealed that older, conservative viewers sympathized with Archie's bigotry, while younger, liberal viewers aligned with Mike's embodiment of boomer rebellion.[28] *All in the Family* was born of the same industrial moment as *SNL*, one prizing a focus on baby boomers couched within broad audience appeal. Chase's seemingly ironic racism, then, also participates in the same dual address as *All in the Family* does, one that encodes his performance with the same normative white masculinity as Archie Bunker. As Saul notes of the sketch's contested creation and interpretation, "The different fractions of Richard [Pryor]'s audience could come together at the crossroads where Richard stood, even if they couldn't agree on where to travel afterward."[29]

Admittedly, the examples and commentary from Morris and Pryor above provide just a sample from the show's early years of how the sheen of flexible identity politics ultimately privileged whiteness. The show's next cast member of color would not come until 1980 with Eddie Murphy, whose tenure (despite producing such memorable sketches as "White Like Me") was wracked with contention, as producers, according to Murphy, "tried to 'Garrett Morris' me, turn me into the little token nigger."[30] It is tempting to see the years after Murphy's *SNL* tenure as making steady improvement in racial diversity, though even as recently as 2014, *SNL* confronted a chorus of protest for its lack of black women cast members and writers. In response, the show conducted a high-profile search that resulted in the hiring of Sasheer Zamata, LaKendra Tookes, and Leslie Jones. In response, none other than Julian Bond would pen an editorial expressing support for the new hires and, not coincidentally, regret for the insensitive tone of his 1977 appearance on "Black Perspective" with Morris.[31]

The identity politics that relegated many black and women *SNL* cast members to one-dimensional and supporting roles also inhibited them, for the most part, from breaking out beyond the show. Indeed, in *SNL*'s first decade, only Murphy "became the exception to the rule: an African American performer that used the show as a launching pad to superstardom."[32] But as the show grew into a brand in subsequent years spanning home video, movies, merchandising, and internet video, so too did the possibilities for performers seeking to parlay their time on *SNL* into other opportunities. Of course, this did not eliminate the persistent power imbalance between white men and minority cast members on the show, as I explore below. It did, however, present a more aesthetically oriented challenge as more and more cast members graduated from *SNL*: critics and audiences reading the post-*SNL* work of former cast members as somehow sullied by the show. In the next section, I examine the implications of sketch comedy's reflexive flexibility for *SNL* beyond television, particularly in the film work of former cast members.

A Degree from the *Saturday Night Live* Graduate School: The Pleasures and Possibilities of Sketch Comedy in Film

Exhaustion, turmoil, and opportunities in Hollywood led to massive turnover on *Saturday Night Live*, with John Belushi, Dan Aykroyd, and Lorne Michaels all leaving by the end of the fifth season in 1980, marking the end of what many consider the show's classic years. The respective reigns of executive producers Jean Doumanian (1980–1981) and Dick Ebersol (1981–1985) are often seen as a blight on the proud legacy of the show in many popular histories. "*Saturday Night Live* was competing against the memory of itself. And losing," Shales and Miller muse of the post-Michaels years in their oral history of the program.[33] Internal strife and further tumbles in the ratings created real doubt about *SNL*'s viability in the minds of viewers and NBC executives alike. A number of overhauls of the cast moved its style away from that of its original members, many of whom had worked together in comedy troupes before television. The new casts drew heavily from the 1980s stand-up comedy boom, incorporating the likes of Gilbert Gottfried and Joe Piscopo with underwhelming results. The era is perhaps best remembered for introducing America to Murphy, followed by Billy Crystal, Martin Short, and Christopher Guest. As the 1980s wore on, the influence of the Canadian sketch comedy *Second City Television* (1976–1981) became apparent in *SNL*'s increasing incorporation of filmed segments, ones that took a more *Python*esque approach to lampooning television conventions and institutional authority than anything else. Ebersol attempted to make recorded material an increasingly integral part of the show, but NBC refused to allow him to shut down live production for a period in order to tape segments. The 1984–1985 season drew critical raves, but change was on the horizon once again.

Michaels returned as executive producer in 1985 and installed a curious collection of film stars and young actors such as Randy Quaid, Robert Downey Jr., and the teenaged Anthony Michael Hall. Michaels was also coming off the critical and financial failure of another NBC sketch comedy, *The New Show* (1984), the previous year, into which Michaels had sunk much of his own money. The experience speaks less to a direct cause for his return to *SNL*—though it certainly contributed—than it does to an indication of how *SNL* would fit in television's shifting industrial landscape toward the end of the network era. Michaels had created his own production and distribution company, Broadway Video, in 1979 originally to assist in postproduction duties for *SNL*. By the late 1980s, though, the company was deeply invested in the creation and circulation of all things *SNL* beyond the moment of its original broadcast on NBC.

In addition to releasing now-ubiquitous, home video "Best of" collections for cast members such as Chase, Belushi, Radner, Aykroyd, and Chris Farley, Broadway retained most of *SNL*'s lucrative distribution rights as it was syndicated across cable outlets and internationally. This "regime of repetition" served two key functions for the program.[34] Reruns served to reinforce *SNL*'s already-robust mythology of distinctive, envelope-pushing comedy, further solidifying its legacy in the minds of viewers and driving their interest back to the live broadcasts. At the same time, reruns established *SNL* as a cross-media authorial voice, helping it stake a claim in the later film successes of stars who would move on from the show. Michaels expanded what could begin to be called *SNL*'s brand beyond the program itself, producing several movies based on characters from the show, such as *The Blues Brothers* (1980) and *Coneheads* (1993).

Indeed, the seed of this multimedia mindset is present in many *SNL* episodes from the late 1980s through the early 1990s seasons. Cast members such as Phil Hartman, Mike Myers, and Dana Carvey effortlessly impersonated pop culture and political figures with the same deftness as they developed original recurring characters. In doing so, *SNL* prompted viewers to think of the program not only as a once-weekly diversion but also as a repository for catch phrases and cultural commentary they could use and reinterpret in their day-to-day lives. As former cast member David Spade notes, "It's never been the case, in any sketch that's worked in history, to leave it at one. It's usually 'leave it at thirty.'"[35] Shales and Miller suggest that Michaels was under pressure from NBC to develop recurring characters that could be spun off into sitcoms for the network, and the program responded in kind with Julia Sweeney's Pat and Al Franken's Stuart Smalley, among others. Television projects for various SNL characters fizzled, however, and movies of both Pat and Stuart Smalley flopped. Michaels's greatest financial success came in the 1992 spin-off of Mike Myers and Dana Carvey's popular "Wayne's World" sketches, as the film would go on to earn over $180 million worldwide.

The expansion of SNL's sketch sensibilities beyond television would continue in movies that were not direct spinoffs of characters from the show too, but not without manifesting many of the same gender inequalities that plagued the program early on. Cast members like Adam Sandler and Chris Farley released successful movies and comedy albums outside of SNL's production cycle, and they were often foregrounded as stars on the show in support of their side projects. The rise of these casts dominated by men in the 1990s, however, troubled other cast members and critics alike, who saw the show in this era as representing a particularly sophomoric brand of humor. Janeane Garofalo, for instance, described her only season on SNL (1994–1995) as "the year of fag-bashing and using the words 'bitch' and 'whore' in a sketch."[36] A widely discussed 1995 New York magazine piece entitled "Comedy Isn't Funny: Saturday Night Live at Twenty—How the Show That Transformed TV Became a Grim Joke" chronicles the SNL workplace as "obsessed with maintaining its internal pecking order" and compares the viewing experience of that season to "watching late-period Elvis—embarrassing and poignant."[37] Clearly, close competition among cast members continued to play out through an identity politics that reinforced, rather than undermined, broader power dynamics outside the show.

To be sure, the article—like many others at the time invoking the now-familiar "Saturday Night Dead" trope—wistfully yearns for the generation-defining humor of the original Not Ready for Prime Time Players at the same time that it glosses over the problems created by that cast's chaotic, misogynistic, and drug-addled working habits. It also points to tensions surrounding the show's growing cultural footprint, suggesting that—just as in the show's early years—cast members only saw it as a stepping stone to film careers. Indeed, popular press coverage of *SNL* since the 1990s commonly refers to the program as the "graduate school" of comedy.[38] Some of the biggest box office draws in film comedy over the last several decades—Mike Myers, Adam Sandler, Chris Farley, Tina Fey, Will Ferrell, Amy Poehler, and Kristen Wiig to name a few—have all honed their skills for comedic performance on *SNL* before moving on to the higher profile platform of feature film.

Although the show has produced some of the biggest film comedy stars of recent memory, critics nonetheless tend to see the same strategies of reflexive flexibility that drove the show's early popularity as a nuisance on the big screen. Some critics lament the tendency of *SNL* alumni to play "the same character[s] seen on *SNL*"[39] or question whether or not this performative mode can "carry a whole movie."[40] Others see an ill fit between *SNL*'s sketch comedy sensibility and the structural demands of feature-length film narratives. Reviewers noted of Ferrell's *Anchorman* (2004), for example, that it felt "like an extended skit stretched and stretched"[41] or "loosely strung-together *SNL* skits;"[42] of Fey and Poehler's *Baby Mama* (2008) that it "plays out like a very long and very mediocre sketch on 'SNL';"[43] and of Sandler's *Jack & Jill* (2011) that the actor appears "caught in an abysmal *Saturday Night Live* sketch."[44]

Saturday Night Live, according to critics, has no business being in the movie business, a sentiment further bolstered by universally panned flops like *It's Pat!* (1994), *Stuart Saves His Family* (1995), *Blues Brothers 2000* (1998), *Superstar* (1999), and *MacGruber* (2010). Though these movies were spun off directly from *SNL* sketches in a relatively transparent effort to capitalize on their fleeting popularity, they also highlight the same critique levied at the other films of *SNL* alumni: former *SNL* stars are too closely tied to their reflexive sketch comedy personas, ones that disrupt conventionally representational film performances and long-form, goal-driven film narratives. Chase's smug gadabout in *Fletch* (1985) is therefore too much like the anchor he played on *SNL*'s "Weekend Update" segments. Myers buries his own personality among characters in *So I Married an Axe Murderer* (1993), the *Austin Powers* franchise (1997, 1999, 2002), and *The Love Guru* (2008) the same way he did in portraying Deiter, Linda Richman, and Simon on *SNL*.

These extra-fictional comedic personas, based in the reflexive sketch sensibilities of *SNL*, become the focus often at the expense of the film's narrative, according to critics. This tension is illustrated when *Anchorman*, for example, pauses for a silly street fight in which Ron (Ferrell) can spout his characteristically absurdist non sequiturs, and when *Tommy Boy* (1994) provides Tommy (Farley) time to perform a song and dance in which he ruins a tiny sport coat with his famously fat frame. Although this relationship between *SNL* stardom and film performance is certainly not unique in the history of popular comedy, it has been repeatedly encoded in reviews, publicity materials, and fan activity surrounding performers as they move from small to big screen. However, popular and critical commentary rarely account for how the reflexive flexibility of television sketch comedy and film narrative can interact to provide pleasures unavailable in each medium by itself.

In the case of recent *SNL* stars' transition to film, then, sketch comedy's malleability actually works to complement, not detract from, film comedy aesthetics. The film performances of Ferrell, Fey, and others explicitly invite viewers to make connections back to their television work, a dynamic reflective of a contemporary industrial context in which comedic stardom operates intertextually and across media. In exploring this dynamic, I read against the above critical trope of sketch comedy as incompatible with film narrative. As Philip Drake has argued, contemporary comedic performance invokes "multiple semantic frames—of fictional character, of star persona, and of generic codes and conventions."[45] My analyses below thus explore the textual possibilities of contemporary comedic performance and suggest probable interpretations of its many frames by viewers. Former *SNL* stars' performance can certainly be read as disruptive to conventional film narrative, yet it is one of many possible layers of intertextual meaning for many viewers today. As Drake notes, we may also enter into moments of more or less recognition of any one layer of meaning without detracting from our overall ability to comprehend their interaction in the aggregate.

Drake's conception of comedic performance is a useful updating of Steve Seidman's "comedian comedy," a film genre in which comedians like Charlie Chaplin and Jerry Lewis systematically undermined the representational strategies of classical Hollywood performance with a presentational style—not unlike that of many *SNL* alumni—that "parades the specialty performer *as* a performer rather than subjugating his or her presentation to the demands of character construction."[46] Seidman suggests that this tension also plays out at the thematic level of comedian comedy films, whose stories often develop around the eccentric comedian's rejection of and/or acquiescence to some normative environment.[47] Indeed, one can easily map this generic convention onto any number of films starring *SNL* alumni. John "Bluto" Blutarsky (Belushi) and his cohort overrun the institutional powers-that-be in *Animal House*, for example, while Billy Madison (Sandler) must abandon much of his immature behavior and accept some responsibility in order to graduate in *Billy Madison* (1995). Yet the tension between performance and narrative is not always clear-cut in constructing this theme, as each film speaks to a different sociohistorical and industrial context. Even in the films of Belushi and Sandler, for instance, intergenerational conflicts inform their narratives in different ways, ones that complicate Seidman's generic formulation.[48] Henry Jenkins has argued that comedian comedy assigns static meaning to comedic performance modes that vary greatly across decades, and he suggests more proximate causes—such as the influence of vaudeville and Hollywood's shift to sound—as guiding aesthetic forces in classical comedies.[49] Taking Jenkins's cue, I place the textual quirks of the films of *SNL* alumni into dialogue with their material conditions of production and reception. In doing so, I illustrate how sketch comedy can take its experimental impulses from one medium to flexibly fit into many other media.

Tina Fey, Will Ferrell, and Contemporary Sketch Comedy Aesthetics on Film and Beyond

For much of its history, *SNL* has privileged reflexive performance modes that foreground individual cast members as stars, and much of the abovementioned critical discourse about their films bears this out. Chase, Belushi, and Sandler, among others, distinguished themselves from the *SNL* ensemble by aggressively inscribing their own personalities onto the characters they played across sketches, a dynamic largely born of Lorne Michaels's efforts to distinguish the program itself from contemporaneous television comedies. The show's strategy catalyzed the varyingly successful film careers of a number of men on the show across the 1970s through to the 1990s at the same time that it marginalized women performers. However, as *SNL* has adapted to the contemporary media environment of cross-media mobility, so too has its preferred method of star-making shifted.

Today, the majority of *SNL* cast members hail from training grounds like the Groundlings, Second City, and the Upright Citizens Brigade, which emphasize group writing and performing skills. These impulses for communal performance often conflict with longstanding notions of individual expression on *SNL*, a dilemma further exacerbated by the show's tradition of privileging solo stardom as *the* way to break free of the show and make it in film or starring television projects. Recent cast members, as a result, have not entirely shied away from presentational star-making performances, but they have increasingly used them as complements to more dialogic, group-based modes. This dynamic aligns with *SNL* stars' increasing exposure across ever-proliferating media outlets, an environment more amenable to flexible articulations of a range of sketch comedy aesthetics than to the fixed identities of performers who merely "play themselves" all the time. The comedic personas of former cast members like Tina Fey and Will Ferrell, for example, equally accommodate the dialogic aesthetics of group performance *and* individual identities that develop from collaboration. This shift in *SNL* stars' formation requires a reframing in critical discourse about their films away from a medium-specific notion of performance toward one that acknowledges the many frames through which former *SNL* players encode meaning and audiences decode it. The graduate-school metaphor today no longer speaks to a singular performance mode placing individual *SNL* stars on a linear trajectory from television to film. Instead, it speaks to the reflexive flexibility required of those stars to accommodate the myriad cultural and industrial contexts of many media simultaneously.

Will Ferrell and Tina Fey are among the two biggest recent stars to use sketch comedy to graduate from *SNL* and move on to multimedia careers beyond the show. They have not followed precisely the same path, but the respective comedic personas they developed along the way are emblematic of the same contemporary industrial context in which sketch comedy flexibly moves across media boundaries. Their myriad appearances—in public forums and internet comedy shorts as themselves; on television and Broadway as prominent political figures like Sarah Palin and George W. Bush; and in any number of film roles—have utilized both presentational and representational performative modes, variously playing themselves and subsuming these bit-driven elements of their personalities to character construction. Given their shared background in improvisational troupes and overlapping time together at *SNL*, the major factors shaping their performances have accordingly been collaborative, dialogic, and therefore amenable to the contemporary transmedia climate. Critiques insisting their films too often invoke the aesthetics of other media, then, risk overlooking the extent to which they can and often do interact in complex and complementary ways. In analyses of films like *Date Night* (2010), *Anchorman*, and *Step Brothers* (2008) below, I offer strategies for reading Fey and Ferrell's films with the same flexibility that already frames their performances everywhere else.

Fey joined the *SNL* writing staff in 1997, headed at the time by frequent Ferrell-collaborator Adam McKay. Whereas Ferrell was one of the program's most popular onscreen presences for much of his tenure, Fey only occasionally appeared in sketches as a supporting player, focusing much of her creative output on writing. As a result, Fey cannot be said to have the same fully formed comedic persona as full-time cast members did, at least not until she joined Jimmy Fallon as coanchor of "Weekend Update" in 2000. She thrived there for six seasons, contrasting her witty, matriarchal charm with Fallon's impish antics and, after Fallon's departure, Poehler's volatile energy. It was during this mid- to late-2000s period alongside Poehler on "Update," writing for women cast members like Maya Rudolph, Rachel Dratch, and Kristen Wiig, and making guest appearances as vice presidential nominee Sarah Palin that publicity discourses made Fey the focal point of a newly ascendant feminine voice on *SNL*, despite it not being entirely clear what Fey's own voice was as a performer.

Though she has returned often to portray Palin and serve as host, Fey left *SNL* in 2006 to create NBC's mock-*SNL* sitcom, *30 Rock* (2006–2013). Her character Liz, a thinly veiled version of herself, is the hardscrabble showrunner for *The Girlie Show*, a fictional late-night sketch comedy program on NBC. In "Jack Gets in the Game" (2007), vain and neurotic cast member Jenna, seeing her popularity on the show decline, begins a new season of *The Girlie Show* grossly overweight. Audiences react favorably to her new "character," and offers pour in to Jenna for movie and merchandising deals. Instead of leaving the show for greener pastures, Jenna loses weight and stays not out of loyalty to *The Girlie Show* but because she doesn't want to be typecast as the fat girl. Through the character of Jenna, Fey expresses ambivalence in explicitly articulating a star persona as many of the *SNL* alumni (most of whom were men) before her had. Flexibly positioning *SNL*—by way of *The Girlie Show*—as a punchline in *30 Rock* allowed Fey both to acknowledge the importance of *SNL* in defining her comedic persona as well as ensure it isn't *the* defining characteristic.

Fey would often express this tension through the character of Jenna. In the episode "The Ballad of Kenneth Parcell" (2012), Liz attempts to bring

Jenna back down to earth by reminding her of a pact they made as struggling improv actors together in Chicago. "Liz, if I become famous, will you tell me if I start acting weird?" Jenna asks, to which Liz replies, "Definitely, and will you do the same for me?" Jenna bursts into laughter at the thought of Liz/Fey becoming famous. *SNL*-made fame, for Fey, is absurd, particularly when it is based on the type of antiquated, aggressively selfish mode of individuation represented by Jenna. Yet *SNL* persists as a star-making forum nonetheless, and Fey's critique of *SNL* suggests that this contradiction is a key aspect to the comedic personas of the show's alumni. Her performances on *30 Rock* vary among directly presentational moments that acknowledge the television audience with fourth-wall-breaking comments, as well as vaguely representational scenes as the character of Liz. Indeed, Fey is quite often simply playing herself on the show, but her performance is embedded in a deeper critique of and dialogic relationship with *SNL*, one most often satirically voiced through Jenna. By exposing the trappings of *SNL* stardom, as well as the comedically seedy underbelly of corporate-controlled network television comedy, Fey/Liz and *30 Rock* offer multiple points for considering how performative identity need not be defined by any given text or medium.

Fey's film performances contain obvious overlaps with her television work, particularly in their tendency to de-emphasize her individual comedic persona. Instead of Fey as a conventional, solo film star, her persona is more often flexibly integrated among coterminous layers of performance, narrative, and the variable amounts of knowledge about her sketch work brought by audiences to the moment of viewing. This layered interaction has been inflected not only broadly by the practices of the contemporary transmedia environment but also specifically by performance modes increasingly amenable to those practices. The skills for sketch improvisation and character work that many *SNL* cast members bring with them to the show, then take into feature films, are ideally suited for a contemporary mediascape that requires performers to wear many hats across many media. These skills also manifest in film narratives that, in Drake's terminology, enact "multiple semantic frames," allowing viewers both to see the extra-fictional sketch parts of comedic performance and how they function within the film's reality.[50]

In a scene from *Date Night* with Fey and fellow Second City alumnus Steve Carell, for instance, the actors play out a scene that simultaneously invokes their theater training, their respective star personas, and the generic tropes that integrate both into the film's narrative. Portraying a bored married couple out to dinner, their characters scan the restaurant and see a young couple on a date. In an effort to entertain one another, Phil Foster (Carell) prompts his wife Claire (Fey) to make up the couple's backstory. They decide the couple is having an unsuccessful third date and proceed to improvise their conversation from afar. Phil affects a groggy monotone for the man, and Claire adopts the personality of vapid ditz, responding that she is going to go home and "fart into a shoebox." After they chuckle to one another, Claire mutters to herself, "That's not . . . that doesn't make sense."

The scene mimics any number of improv games—in which actors on one side of the stage provide commentary for the pantomimes of actors on the other—Carell and Fey might have practiced in their time at Second City. It also invokes the dialogic rapport Fey developed with her "Update" coanchors at *SNL*, punctuated by her breaking and acknowledging the presentational performance to herself in the scene's final beat. Importantly, though, neither frame necessarily distracts from the scene's place in the narrative. Drake suggests that such self-contained moments function as motivated "narrative enclosures,"[51] accommodating sketch-like, reflexive performance without disrupting the verisimilitude of the film's diegetic world. Indeed, Phil and Claire—bored married couple—are performing for one another just as much as Carell and Fey—comedy stars—are performing for the film's audience. Reviews for the film frame these layers of performative signification as complementary too, suggesting that audiences look out for—and take pleasure in—such scenes of seeming distraction based in sketch comedy. The above-mentioned scene and others like it "create hilarious but accurate verbal portraits of contemporary types, while saying a great deal about the unsatisfactory lives that the Fosters themselves are living."[52] Another review advises audiences to "Stay for the outtakes—they're improv delights,"[53] and "funnier than screenwriter Josh Klausner's lines."[54]

In addition to suggesting that improvisations invoking Fey and Carell's comedic star personas work within the narrative, the reviews also point viewers beyond that narrative to material providing additional pleasures. The practice of tacking outtakes onto film end credits is not an uncommon one, particularly for contemporary comedies. Yet their inclusion and emphasis across a number of reviews highlights the multiple sites of meaning creation both within the film and in its ancillary material. Jonathan Gray has identified such paratextual material—reviews, film trailers, DVD extras, and merchandise—not simply as extensions of a primary text but as "filters through which we must pass on our way to the film or program, our first and formative encounters with the text."[55] Audiences likely arrive at comedies like *Date Night* with some sense of how a potentially disruptive performance mode like improvisation will affect their viewing experience, as well as how that mode functions in paratexts to characterize the film's stars. Audience activity among and with paratextual material, then, additionally informs layered constructions of comedic star performance and catalyzes their movement across platforms. And few *SNL*-alumni-turned-film-stars have thrived in this transmedia environment as Will Ferrell has.

Ferrell has undoubtedly been the most notable *SNL* alumnus to embrace—and become identified with—transmedia comedy practices. After leaving *SNL* in 2002 for starring film roles in *Elf* (2003), *Kicking and Screaming* (2005), and *Stranger Than Fiction* (2006), he cofounded with McKay the sketch comedy and viral video website Funny or Die in 2007. With the instantly viral success of the site's first short, "The Landlord," Ferrell established a middle ground between the aesthetics of user-generated content and Hollywood prestige that the industry has been attempting to replicate since then.[56] His film career has continued to be financially successful, yet he has often veered from conventional paths of publicity that would clearly position him as a star. Ferrell often shows up in friends' projects and coproductions like *Eastbound and Down* (2009–2012), *The Goods: Live Hard, Sell Hard* (2009), *Tim and Eric's Billion Dollar Movie* (2012), and *The Internship* (2013) buried deep in the persona of some bizarre character. Over the course of 2011–2012, he and McKay made several television advertisements for Old Milwaukee beer that aired only in local markets in the upper Midwest (one of which ran during the 2012 Super Bowl) but would later be shared across social networking sites the following weeks. The ads' lo-fi aesthetic and Ferrell's bumbling, faux-sincere demeanor work just as much to position him outside the Hollywood mainstream as they do to expand the boundaries of what's included in that mainstream. Because Ferrell's bit-driven comedic persona is so spread across roles and media, identifying a singular articulation of it within and among his films detracts from the many intertextual pleasures such flexibility offers.

In his seven-year tenure at *SNL*, Ferrell's comedic star persona was similarly flexible, anchored on the one hand in versions of himself—Will Ferrell, versatile everyman who could play any number of straight roles—and erratic, volatile characters with a tendency for the absurd on the other. No sketch better encapsulates this variability than "Get Off the Shed," his very first on *SNL* in the fall of 1995. Gazing over the heads of the audience while he unassumingly flips burgers on a grill, Ferrell as a plainly dressed suburban dad serenely and familiarly makes small-talk with neighbors. He intermittently interrupts the polite banter to gently implore his off-screen children to stop their horseplay atop the family's shed. He returns to his conversation with the neighbor. Suddenly, his tiny eyes narrow, and his gaze shifts back to the children: "Hey! There's gonna be a meeting between your ass and the palm of my hand, if you don't get off the shed! Now, get off the shed!" Without a beat, he continues his conversation with the neighbors, who are aghast at his verbal abuse of the children.

Ferrell honed this delicate balance between the familiar everyman and absurd, impulsive surrealist in many characters and impersonations over the years. As Neil Diamond, he gently cooed to his audience before inserting non sequiturs like "I'll smack you in the mouth, I'm Neil Diamond!," and as a drunken businessman telling tall tales of a recently deceased coworker like "He once scissor-kicked Angela Lansbury!" The abrupt and tangential aggression in Ferrell's comedic persona hewed closely to that of Chase, Belushi, and Murray before him, but with Ferrell, this aggression was purely performative and rarely part of some broader process of reflexive distinction. Instead, it more often functioned as the initial step in a dialogic give-and-take with a fellow performer, turning what might appear initially as a tangent into another performative layer. Ferrell would translate this aesthetic—like Fey did after him—into many of his film roles, ones accused of being disruptive and meandering by critics but ultimately built around this very disruptiveness.

Early in 2004's *Anchorman*, Ferrell, as the eponymous news anchor Ron Burgundy, warms up for the evening newscast by spouting comedic non sequiturs masquerading as preparatory vocal exercises, such as "The arsonist has oddly shaped feet." When the newscast begins, he looks into the camera and directly addresses the filmic audience, but only via the mediation of the fictional television audience to which he broadcasts, suggesting the same sort of dual registers of reality necessary for a narrative enclosure. This winking knowingness doubly frames both the Burgundy character performing for his studio/television audience and Ferrell's comedic performance of him, one invoking his *SNL* persona.

A similar dynamic plays out in several subsequent scenes. The day after sleeping with love interest Veronica Corningstone (played by Christina Applegate), Ron recounts his conquest to his news team. After each describes his idealized version of love to Ron only to have it questioned,

Fig. 2.3. From left to right, David Koechner, Paul Rudd, Steve Carell, and Will Ferrell provide a narrative enclosure in their performance of "Afternoon Delight" from *Anchorman*.

they collectively pause to ponder what a perfect version of love would look like. Suddenly, they break out into a minute-long rendition of Starland Vocal Band's "Afternoon Delight" (1976), replete with harmonizing and mimicry of the instruments. The sequence might be dismissed as yet another extended sketch stretched too far were it not for the many cues indicating it as one of many semantic frames through which we might process the scene. Ron sings the first line of the song alone, then in harmony with his compatriots. Upon finishing, sports anchor Champ Kind (David Koechner) claims that the model of love they have collectively expressed "sounds kinda dumb." This explicit acknowledgment of the performance serves to maintain it as integrated within the film's diegesis—nondiegetic scoring does not cue its beginning, a character's lead-in does; characters do not simply cordon off the musical number from their respective narrative roles, they acknowledge its relevance to them, performing simultaneously for one another and for the presumed audience of the film.

The improvisation-heavy 2008 film *Step Brothers* also provides a number of narrative enclosures that accommodate layered comedic performance by Ferrell. After several failed job interviews, forty-something halfwits Brennan (Ferrell) and Dale (John C. Reilly) solicit investments from family and friends for their entertainment company, Prestige Worldwide. Their pitch includes upbeat techno music, an amateurish slideshow, and Brennan frantically dancing and ad-libbing over Dale's composed recitation of talking points. The assembled audience is initially amused by the duo's promises of music, event planning, and management. Yet as the presentation drags on into its fifth minute, Brennan and Dale begin showing pictures that do not appear to have anything to do with the company, including one of Dale sitting on a toilet that Brennan "put in at the last second to mess with the flow a little bit, break it up a little bit." Here Ferrell presentationally acknowledges a scene that trails off into irrelevance for the film's narrative yet remains true to its established diegetic world. Brennan and Dale perform for their potential investors just as Ferrell and Reilly are performing for the film's audience. The layered frames for the scene take on extra significance in the context of the film's publicity campaign, which included Ferrell, Reilly, and director Adam McKay producing similarly scatological shorts like "Green Team" for Funny or Die. Critics, predictably, characterized the toilet humor as "pointless"[57] and "a bad *SNL* skit,"[58] yet both evaluations ignore how texts beyond the film reveal intertextual pleasures associated with it.

The *Step Brothers* scene, as well as seemingly disruptive scenes in the films of a number of recent *SNL* alumni, indicates the need for a mode of evaluation "where terms conventionally associated with realist performance—such as 'authenticity' and 'sincerity'—have very little explanatory force."[59] That is to say, the complaint that *SNL* films' meandering, sketch-like narratives and ostentatious, reflexive performances violate some prescribed norm misses the point. Given the abundance of extra-textual information about *SNL* stars, their respective performance backgrounds in sketch and improvisational comedy, and their work across media, audiences likely enter the moment of viewing their films with that norm as one of many available frames for decoding layered performative meanings. Just as sketch comedians flexibly perform across media, then, so too is it likely that audiences interpret their work outside of sketch comedy television with the same flexibility. Many of the most salient comedic moments—the ones so often bemoaned by critics as sketch-like or *SNL*esque in their characterization—provide ample justification for their place both within the world of the film and in the many media platforms beyond it. Indeed, one need only peruse YouTube for a sampling of scenes lifted from the films of *SNL* alumni that work just as well on their own as they do in the context of the movie. Not coincidentally, these scenes often exist in the same internet-based flow as sketches pulled from recent broadcasts of *SNL*. We can better understand these newly formed flows of sketch comedy by acknowledging their interconnectedness from the start.

Conclusion

This chapter closed by considering the interconnectedness of sketch comedy aesthetics across media, but it opened with an exploration of the idea that sketch comedy's performative possibilities are not available to everyone equally. This negotiation might be most usefully seen in comparing the sensibilities of two performers, bookending the chapter, Radner and Fey. Both comedians share similarly idiosyncratic and brazen takes on femininity, but the gender politics of *SNL* at the time circumscribed Radner's views. Fey, by contrast, works in a moment with myriad outlets for the gender identity work of her humor, inspiring a range of performances that are at the same time anchored in the comedic persona she developed on *SNL*. Despite the newfound freedom afforded to a range of sketch comedy performers and audiences today, though, many dominant conceptions of what works and what does not still persist. These conceptions continue to be structured around the identity politics of *SNL*'s early days that privileged comedians who were white men. While Fey has found her own niche in sketch comedy performance modes beyond *SNL*, for instance, her success is still commonly framed around the aspirational idea of a woman making it in a comedy world dominated by men. Although such discourses can indeed be empowering, they obfuscate the underlying, assumed norm—that sketch comedy is and should be predominantly masculine and that success by a woman is inherently transgressive. In other words, although the sociocultural contexts of feminine identities have changed from Radner's to Fey's time on *SNL*, the fact that men are the baseline identity group from which both must distinguish themselves has not.

On an industrial level, *Saturday Night Live*'s bold comedic style—however problematic—has had important implications for how sketch shows would self-identify in the increasingly competitive landscape of television in the multichannel transition. Many of these we take for granted now, such as *SNL*'s reclamation of the late-night weekend time block, long an afterthought for networks that simply dumped reruns and dusty movies of the week during these low viewership hours. *SNL*'s status as appointment television in the network era habituated viewers to staying in and staying up late to see the next big thing in comedy, music, and culture. Today, the late night and after-midnight hours remain a playground for experimental and transgressive sketch comedy on programming blocks like Cartoon Network's Adult Swim. The implications of *SNL*'s other industrial innovations, though, require more exploration, such as its complicated relationship with generations and their shifting cultural identities. In the next chapter, the consecrated comedy of *SNL* looms large in the cultural and industrial struggles of multichannel transition sketch comedies like *The State*.

Notes

1. Michaels quoted in Shales and Miller, *Live from New York*, 69.
2. Krutnik, "Introduction Part Five: Post-Classical Comedian Comedy," 169.
3. Henry quoted in Shales and Miller, *Live from New York*, 168.
4. *NBC's Saturday Night* would not take on the now-familiar *Live* part of its name until the January 1976 cancellation of ABC's prime-time variety show *Saturday Night Live with Howard Cosell*.
5. Hill and Weingrad, *Saturday Night: A Backstage History of Saturday Night Live*, 33–40.
6. Neale, *Monty Python's Flying Circus* sidebar in "Comedy" in *The Television Genre Book*.
7. Miller, "What Closes on Saturday Night: NBC and Satire," 202.
8. Shales and Miller, *Live from New York*, 59.
9. Landis quoted in Shales and Miller, *Live from New York*, 90.
10. Paul, *Laughing Screaming*, 85-87.
11. Ibid., 86.
12. Ibid., 156.
13. Murphy, "'Is This the Era of the Woman?'," 176.
14. Ibid., 177.
15. Hill and Weingrad, *Saturday Night: A Backstage History of Saturday Night Live*, 233.
16. Newman quoted in Shales and Miller, *Live from New York*, 124.
17. Whalley, *Saturday Night Live, Hollywood Comedy, and American Culture*, 35–39.
18. Morris quoted in Shales and Miller, *Live from New York*, 144.
19. Morris quoted in Harris, "Garrett Morris on *SNL*."
20. Acham, *Revolution Televised*, 71–72.
21. Brooks quoted in *Rolling Stone*, "My Favorite 'Saturday Night Live' Sketch."
22. Busis, "'Saturday Night Live': Each Season's Best Sketch."
23. Deggans quoted in Shedd, "Diversity in the Spotlight on *SNL*: From Pryor to Zamata."
24. Saul, *Becoming Richard Pryor*, 376.
25. Ibid., 379.
26. Mooney quoted in Saul, *Becoming Richard Pryor*, 379.
27. Bodroghkozy, *Groove Tube*, 229–230.
28. Ibid.
29. Saul, *Becoming Richard Pryor*, 380.
30. Hill and Weingrad, *Saturday Night: A Backstage History of Saturday Night Live*, 484.
31. Bond, "Civil Rights Leader Julian Bond's *SNL* Hosting Regret."
32. Shedd, "Diversity in the Spotlight on *SNL*: From Pryor to Zamata."
33. Shales and Miller, *Live from New York*, 192.

34. Kompare, *Rerun Nation*, xi–xv.
35. Spade quoted in Shales and Miller, *Live from New York*, 379.
36. Garofalo quoted in Shales and Miller, *Live from New York*, 389.
37. Smith, "Comedy Isn't Funny."
38. See, among others, Connelly, "'Comedy at the Edge' Looks at '70s Standup Explosion" and Poniewozik, "All-Time 100 TV Shows."
39. Silver, "YouTube HOF: Great Moments in Selling Out."
40. Dominus, "Can Kristen Wiig Turn On the Charm?"
41. LaSalle, "Flip the Channel on 'Anchorman,' a Comedy Sketch Stretched Too Far."
42. Travers, "Anchorman: The Legend of Ron Burgundy."
43. *Richmond Times-Dispatch* Staff, "'Baby Mama' Seems Like a Long, Bad 'SNL' sketch."
44. Setoodeh, "Movie Review: Adam Sandler's 'Jack and Jill' Is the Worst Movie Ever Made."
45. Drake, "Low Blows?," 188.
46. Krutnik, "General Introduction," 7.
47. Ibid.
48. See Whalley, *Saturday Night Live, Hollywood Comedy, and American Culture* for a deeper exploration of generational dynamics across the films of *SNL* alumni.
49. Jenkins, *What Made Pistachio Nuts?*, 1–25.
50. Drake, "Low Blows?," 188.
51. Ibid., 190–192.
52. Bogle, "*Date Night* and *City Island*: One Comedy That Knows Where It's Going, Another That Can't Seem to Decide."
53. Peter Travers, "*Date Night*."
54. Phillips, "Steve Carell, Tina Fey Deserve a Better 'Date Night.'"
55. Gray, *Show Sold Separately*, 3.
56. See N. Marx, "'The Missing Link Moment,'" 14–23.
57. "Movie Review: 'Step Brothers' is Men Behaving Badly."
58. Berardinelli, "Step Brothers."
59. Drake, "Low Blows?," 192.

3

BRAND X

MTV's The State and Generation X in the Multichannel Transition

As *Saturday Night Live* increasingly led American television sketch comedy away from the vaudeo and variety traditions, a number of new outlets provided ample opportunity for even more innovative takes on the format during the multichannel transition. FOX's *In Living Color*, HBO's *Mr. Show*, and MTV's *The State* all explored the unique aesthetic properties of television while hailing various pockets of underserved audiences, experimentation made possible by television industry practices during this time that favored edgy content for small viewing segments throughout the 1990s. As *SNL* continued its success into the multichannel transition, it became the predominant tastemaker in American sketch comedy, one whose style—although highly influential—replaced variety as the new consecrated comedy from which the later cable sketch shows sought to distinguish themselves.

However, the basis for this differentiation transcended mere comedic tastes, a dynamic that I explore throughout this chapter in examining the emerging cultural identity of Generation X and its expression in sketch comedy. Just like their boomer predecessors on early *SNL* before them, Generation X comedians used sketch to speak to smaller audiences and distance themselves from previous comedic traditions. Unlike early *SNL*, though, television industry practices increasingly sought to guide sketch comedy's niche appeal toward mainstream, profitable ends over the course of the 1990s. In the case of *The State*, the result was a comedic voice both angry and ambivalent, framed by contradictory mandates from MTV to create edgy, niche-oriented comedy that could transcend television to reach broader audiences in film, audio recording, merchandising, and beyond. In a general sense, sketch comedy of the era reflected a growing unease by Generation Xers in grunge, hip hop, and independent cinema about mainstream commercial tastes co-opting their culture. But even discussions centered on "oppositional versus mainstream" in cultural trends of the 1990s are constructions, ones whose meanings television networks, comedians, and viewers alike fought over. Looking more closely at programs like *The State* can help us better understand the terms and implications of sketch comedy as a continued site of struggles for meaning.

I do so in this chapter first by examining generation, a concept that has hovered in the background of this book thus far but receives critical consideration here. Just as the baby boomers of *SNL* did to their sketch predecessors, Generation X used sketch comedies like *The State* to demonstrate both knowledge of and opposition to the consecrated humor of its elders. However, this opposition was largely a product of the broader industrial discourses of the multichannel transition. Increasing competition incentivized television networks to appropriate cultural objects (perceived to be) outside of the mainstream as a way to differentiate themselves from competitors. Cable television networks like MTV, for example, programmed sketch comedy in attempts to develop an industrial identity distinct from that of broadcasters. The result of these two competing forces—young Xer artists expressing anger through sketch comedy versus television industry practices seeking to profit from that anger—was an ambivalent articulation of oppositionality on the part of Generation X cultural producers. While performers on *The State* attempted to resist the commercial impulses of their working conditions by satirically attacking them, MTV strove to incorporate these attacks into the production and publicity of the show. This dynamic bled out into broader portrayals of the MTV audience as well, one that the network framed as edgy, dynamic, and culturally savvy. Ultimately, though, MTV's efforts at both the programming and publicity levels only served to reinforce the importance of already-dominant commodity audience categories.

The State aired on MTV from 1993 to 1995 before attempting a move to the broadcast network CBS in the fall of 1995, but the program's run on MTV served as a key site of struggle in negotiating the nuances of cultural production within the field of sketch comedy and its broader economic contexts. The case of *The State* and MTV highlights a clearly hegemonic pull by the network to identify, extract, and commodify cast members' various forms of symbolic and cultural capital. MTV applied this logic across its programming lineup in the early 1990s, scouring the cultural peripheries for marginal figures in fashion, music, and comedy, then mainstreaming them to viewers who were young, white men. It saw programs like *The State* as especially appealing to that demographic, even though the network and the cast tussled over exactly what that appeal was. By the end of *The State*'s tenure on MTV, broadcast networks like CBS were making similar attempts to appeal to a young adult audience (though one more broadly defined). In the end, *The State* turned out to be a much worse fit at CBS, falling victim to the network's ill-conceived rebranding efforts. Through analyses of its episodes, promotional content, reviews, trade reports, and original correspondences from cocreator Steven Starr, MTV and *The State* provide key cases for understanding how the cultural and economic struggles implicit in sketch comedy's reflexive flexibility can often end up without a clear winner.

"The Purple-Haired People": Generation, Cultural Identity, and Brand(ing) Generation X

While boomer nostalgia thrived in the 1990s, the cultural products of that decade have, fittingly enough, also seen their own recent resurgence. Over the course of the late 2000s and 2010s, various pockets of the American commercial media industries have resurrected and repackaged television programs, music, and movies of the 1990s for reconsumption by a post–baby boomer populace presumed to be nostalgic for its childhood. Teen-Nick, a part of Nickelodeon's stable of cable channels, reaired episodes of 1990s comedies such as *Clarissa Explains It All* (1991–1994), *Doug* (1991–1994), and *Kenan & Kel* (1996–2000). The programming block was called "The '90s Are All That," after the long-running sketch comedy originally shown on Nickelodeon from 1994 to 2005, *All That*.[1] Bands like My Bloody Valentine, Pavement, and Hole all reunited in the late 2000s in an effort to recapture their 1990s appeal. The 2012 Sundance Film Festival even offered *Reality Bites* (1994) as part of its "From the Collection" series, either oblivious to the film's mordant critique of corporate media's co-option of indie sensibilities, or eager to indulge in that very practice.[2] The nostalgic ploys were, on one level, a way for these outlets to extract additional revenue from recycling their archived content. But on another level, the 1990s nostalgia cycle played into what George Lipsitz describes as evoking "the experiences of the past to lend legitimacy to the dominant ideology of the present."[3]

Rather than reinforce narratives of national unity and social cohesion, however, this dominant ideology sought to balkanize media consumers. The commodification of 1990s nostalgia served as a way to assure millennial and Generation X audiences—as they age their way through television's prized demographic of eighteen- to forty-nine-year-olds—that they too have their own cultural heritage distinct from, and just as important as, that of baby boomers.

Perhaps the most notorious purveyor of 1990s nostalgia has been, fittingly, MTV, the cable network that became its own self-perpetuating zeitgeist across the decade by appropriating Generation X's "barely formed narratives" and selling them back at young viewers.[4] Its stock of music videos and original programming from the era provided an ample source of material to feed the nostalgia wave and exploit its own televisual legacy. In the late 2000s, MTV and its subchannels relaunched 1990s staples like *Headbangers Ball* (1987–1995; MTV2, 2003–2012), borrowed *Ren & Stimpy* (1991–1995) reruns from Nickelodeon (also owned by Viacom), and ordered new episodes of *Beavis and Butt-Head* (1993–1997, 2011). The rebooted *Beavis and Butt-Head*, in which the eponymous characters crack more jokes about MTV's pandering reality fare than they do about Ween and Blind Melon videos, suggests that the network is trying to have it both ways, inviting millennials—now the network's preferred young adult audience—to laugh at *Teen Mom* (2009–2012, 2015–) and *The Hills* (2006–2010) through an ironic decoding that is decidedly not of their time. Indeed, MTV's 2010 rebranding as simply MTV (and no longer "Music Television") accompanied a bizarre proclamation from MTV Networks vice president Van Toffler that it was "pushing Generation X out. We're slaves to our different audiences, for MTV that's millennials, who are vastly different than Generation X; they're definitely less cynical—they're more civic minded."[5] MTV told the viewers who first defined the aesthetic and comedic sensibilities of its original programming not only that they were no longer welcome there but also that those sensibilities shifted to fit a more attractive commodity audience.

Popular press and television industry trade papers are awash with talk of age groups, since they are ostensibly the currency used by networks and advertisers to buy and sell commercials, programming, and carriage on cable providers. Age is one of the primary demographic categories that "correlate with behavioral patterns pertaining to product-purchasing and media consumption habits."[6] Advertisers believe young viewers possess spending and taste-making power, while they view older viewers as savers and thus less desirable targets. While age groupings provide shorthand for many in the industry, they often belie much more complexity within any given demographic and require further description. When trade analyses extend to the identities and tastes of age groups, then, generational terms often become defining cultural categories: baby boomers (born, roughly, between 1943 and 1960), Generation X (1961–1981), and millennials (children of boomers born between 1982 through the early 2000s).[7]

Media scholarship, however, has a spotty history of using generation as a category for analyzing broader processes of identity formation and cultural consecration, and the reasons for this are readily apparent. The very notion of investigating diverse groups of people according to whether or not they fall within the same two decades of birth seems, at first glance, short-sighted. It elides much more salient identity categories like race and ethnicity, nationality, gender, and class, lumping them together without a concrete framework for suggesting how they might interact. For instance, though it is coterminous with many of the temporal and aesthetic developments of punk and grunge music, hip-hop culture is often absent from popular histories of Generation X, implicitly privileging whiteness in that generation's popular conception.[8] Television trade discourses similarly tend to flatten the many identities comprising a generation. To be sure, a number of racial and gender categories matter to television executives and advertisers, if only as ways to organize their various commodity audiences. Yet these identities inevitably intersect with age and generation, requiring critical work dissecting how the television industry powerfully and systematically uses those guiding concepts to describe its audiences, as well as the ways audiences can defy, negotiate, or comply with industry discourses. Like other cultural categories of analysis, then, generation must be understood as a construction, one in which myriad social and industrial discourses intersect but are nonetheless structured in specific ways.

Advertisers aggressively participated in the construction of a Generation X cultural identity early on. In a widely discussed address to the Magazine Publishers Association late in 1992, Karen Ritchie, a senior vice president at the advertising agency McCann-Erickson Worldwide, notoriously referred to Generation X with thinly veiled derision as "the purple-haired people."[9] In the speech, Ritchie spoke in broad strokes about the emergence of a generation of young people whose political, cultural, and economic sensibilities did not align with hers or with members of the baby boomer generation. These young people were crude, disengaged, and unreceptive to the advertising and marketing ploys that had long formed the backbone of the American commercial media industries. More importantly, the image provided a powerful signifier for a collective of millions of young Americans that countless popular and trade publications picked up and reiterated. Generation X was different, these pieces often pondered, but what was the best way to turn this difference into financial gain?

Of course, Ritchie's commentary was also meant to be tongue in cheek, expressing admiration of Gen X's cultural savvy at the same time that it sought to exploit that savvy. The ambivalence in her characterization of Generation X seeped into the cultural products created by and for young people across the 1990s, as well. As myriad industrial and cultural forces tussled over the meaning of the term, it began to lose any clear meaning altogether. As an analytic tool, however, the polysemy contained in the Generation X label provides a powerful way to organize the various discourses that sought to construct, constrain, and circulate the media production and consumption patterns of young people in specific ways. Generation X as a cultural identity, then, is shot through with contradiction, indicating powerfully oppositional sensibilities on the one hand but also cultural practices structured according to the hegemonic pull of commercial media on the other.

The media produced by and targeted at members of Generation X represented this contradiction in a number of ways. Throughout the 1990s, artists, consumers, and media executives alike debated the extent to which Generation X constituted a true cultural identity. While many qualities of the media—the sneering resentment of Nirvana; the ruminative demurral of *Slacker* (1991)—associated with Xers expressed angst about their social status throughout the 1990s, it remains difficult to identify a coherent center of resistance expressed through these cultural products. Of course, across many generations of Americans, cultural practices resistant to dominant power have often been centered in and around youth.[10] But unlike the world wars, economic depression, and social upheavals of generations of youth before it, Xers were "free of any defining event or experience," with no "powerful touchstone for group identity."[11] Critics lamented "the age of increasing despair" of the 1990s, and demographic studies abounded with details of the difficult socioeconomic conditions into which Xers were born.[12] There were fewer of them, with the national birth rate declining in 1965 for the first time since the start of the baby boom in the mid-1940s.[13]

They grew up with less parental guidance than prior generations, as the number of latchkey children left alone after school doubled in the 1970s.[14] When Xers did enter the workforce by the early 1990s, they earned less: with "the median income of families headed by someone under 30 . . . 13% lower than such families earned in 1973."[15] As one report cynically put it at the time, they "read less, know less, care less, vote less and are less critical of almost all institutions than any previous generation."[16]

One of the more widely discussed conceptions of Generation X came from historians William Strauss and Neil Howe, who in a 1992 article outlined what they viewed as fundamental differences between Xers and baby boomers, ones resulting from the cyclical nature of birth patterns that every century brought two generations into conflict.[17] In the authors' view, Xers defining feature was the fact that they were not boomers, with no distinct cultural identity of their own except that which positioned them in opposition to the elder generation. "Since Xers grew up in the leviathan shadow of the boomers, a sense of apartness played a role in forming our identity from the start," Jeff Gordinier, editor-at-large for the Xer-oriented *Details* magazine, would later concede.[18] But other responses broadened Strauss and Howe's account, arguing that discursive formations of Generation X were created, circulated, and reinforced by a boomer-controlled "propaganda campaign intended to . . . [slow] the next generation's succession to power."[19] Some accounts suggested more insidious mechanisms at work in the boomer-controlled media industries, ones that fabricated a Generation X identity as a way to prevent anything more authentic from emerging: "Today a generic youth culture has been assembled from above precisely because it doesn't exist down below. . . . The twentysomething generation is indeed a myth—an imaginary resolution of real contradictions. . . . But these characteristics don't cohere into a shared identity. . . . [Generation X's] true cultural legacy is to have been disunited by the very experiences it has had in common."[20]

Douglas Coupland's 1991 novel about sardonic, shiftless youths living in southern California, *Generation X: Tales for an Accelerated Generation*, popularized the concept Generation X.[21] One often-quoted line from the book ("I am not a target market") underlines the common thread among the above-mentioned popular commentaries and from young people elsewhere to the pejorative label—it was not theirs. Not only was it not theirs, but it was also a label crafted according to the logic and language of consumer culture. This tie to commercial culture, more than anything, seemed to be the implicit object of Xers' resistance. They recognized that Generation X was little more than a category constructed by the converging efforts of advertisers and media industries seeking to organize increasingly fragmented consumption practices around a shared identity. Indeed, young people voiced objection to these efforts throughout the late 1980s and 1990s, and much of the scholarship about Generation X and youth culture insightfully examines the aesthetics and identity politics in music of the time.[22] But as television shifted from the three-network oligopoly structure of the network era to a multichannel landscape thanks to cable, the medium negotiated generational cultural identity in ways reflexive of its unique, industrial fragmentation.

The proliferation of new channels across the 1980s and 1990s recontextualized familiar fears about the deleterious effect of television, ones that expressed a heightened sense of disillusionment and disunity among youth. A report about young people's voting patterns in the 1992 presidential election, for instance, stated, "This generation, after all, has been raised on the distancing and isolating medium of television, in an age when many of the traditional mediating institutions that once brought the young into social action have weakened or collapsed."[23] Blaming television as a tool of modern alienation was not necessarily a new idea, but the sheer abundance of texts generated by the expanding industry complicated attempts to characterize its effects monolithically. One program that embodied this ambiguity was MTV's *Beavis and Butt-Head*, the crudely animated meta-comedy in which two teenagers crack (not-so-)wise about music videos and popular culture. When a five-year-old boy, after having viewed the eponymous characters playing with fire, burned down his family's mobile home in 1993, critics, media watchdogs, and parent groups vociferously attacked *Beavis and Butt-Head*. Even accounts that recognized the program's parodies of authority figures conceded that, in the end, its "social defiance is extremely limited and highly problematical."[24]

Conflating *Beavis and Butt-Head*'s satiric strategies with how they did or did not effect social change, however, overlooks the ways in which they also created meaning in subtler ways. The characters' imbecilic chuckling and inane observations, for instance, were also vehicles for a subversive and smart mode of televisual humor, part of "a growing crowd of characters who have found a magic formula: nothing cuts through the clutter like a slap of bracing crudity. . . . Stupidity, served with a knowing intelligence, has become the next best thing to smarts."[25] Concerned parents and interest groups may have been inclined to decode the program in a straightforward way, seeing only its overtly silly aesthetic. But young viewers additionally saw it as reflexive of their own thoughts and experiences and as a satire of conventionally literal readings. The appeal of Xer comedies like *Beavis and Butt-Head*, *Mr. Show*, and *The State* was partly based—indeed, thrived—on ambiguous, multivalent modes of addressing its small, targeted young adult audience, often laying bare the seemingly straightforward, dominantly encoded ideologies of mass audience–courting fare. As I explore below, this distinction—between risqué cable sensibilities and mainstream broadcast safeness—is what ultimately brought *The State* from modest success on MTV to collapse on CBS. Regardless of network, though, the generational identity struggles between Xers and boomers drove conversations across television about what audiences were most desirable and how best to program for them across the 1990s.

Industrial Identities on MTV and in the Multichannel Transition

Young adult audiences have served as one of the primary testing grounds for cable television's experimentation with original programming in the last several decades. Beginning with the introduction of Nielsen's people meter in 1987 and through the rise of database-driven marketing in the 1990s and 2000s, media industries have gained more and more information about exactly who is watching and consuming what products and when. The ensuing shift away from practices that courted an undifferentiated, mass television audience coincided with new ways of understanding demographics by American advertising agencies.[26] The abundance of new outlets on cable—in well over half of American homes by 1990—provided ideal venues for demographic-specific programs and advertising directed at particular segments of the population.[27] Advertisers promised their clients campaigns that could foster in desired audiences feelings of intense loyalty toward the program, network, and products of any given viewing experience.[28] As advertisers saw baby boomers slip out of the prized eighteen-to-forty-nine demographic, they came to embrace the taste-making capabilities and spending power of the so-called "forgotten generation" of youth that followed—Generation X.[29]

This is not to say, however, that targeting niche and young adult audiences became the predominant industrial logic of the multichannel transition. The Big Three broadcast networks of ABC, NBC, and CBS still brought in exponentially more advertising revenue than their relatively new competitors on cable did, and as a result they were reluctant to risk alienating long-held and still-robust boomer audiences to pursue Generation X fully. Moreover, because cable outlets increasingly became part of the same media conglomerates as broadcast networks, we can instead view mass and niche audience targeting practices as complementary, allowing the shared corporate parents of broadcast and cable outlets to pursue viewers with flexibility. In the merger mania of the 1980s and 1990s, Michael Curtin notes, large media firms created both apolitical content aimed at national/global markets that required low audience involvement, as well as niche products designed to inspire intense loyalty in viewers from smaller market segments.[30]

The hope for media conglomerates was that their niche content might eventually catch on and become mass-market fare. As a part of the Viacom conglomerate, for example, MTV sought young viewers intensely loyal to the cool irony of sketch comedies like *The State*. At the same time, MTV functioned under the same corporate umbrella as mass-market companies like the film studio Paramount, producer of such blockbusters as *Ghost* (1990), *Forrest Gump* (1994), and *Titanic* (1997). Over the course of its MTV run, as I explore below, cast members of *The State* bristled at the prospect of catering their edgy sketch sensibilities to mainstream tastes, unless it was on their terms.

Elsewhere, the FOX network infamously embodied the edge strategy as a way to counterprogram against its competitors, bringing black and Generation X subcultural elements into the mainstream with sketch comedies like *In Living Color* and *The Ben Stiller Show* in the early 1990s. Although the network's programming was comparatively oppositional to that of much broadcast television, it would eventually trade up to the even bigger mass audiences of NFL football and fold its niche elements into the more conservative News Corporation conglomerate. Grunge music followed a similar path from regional subculture to international, multimillion dollar phenomenon, as bands like Nirvana and Pearl Jam topped record charts across the early 1990s. The genre became the most ubiquitous signifier of Generation X culture, and the more it filtered into the mainstream, the riper it became for parody.

One of the more memorable sketches from *The Ben Stiller Show*, which had an initial run on MTV before moving to FOX, lampooned a fictional band called "The Grungies" by using the wacky tone and stylistics of *The Monkees* (1966–1968). The sketch's theme song ("We're not trying to be friendly / We just want money and fame / We're the X generation / We just

Fig. 3.1. *The Ben Stiller Show* sketch "The Grungies" parodies both baby boomer television like *The Monkees* and the Generation X cultural identity.

like to complain") explicated the conflicted feelings grunge musicians had about their authenticity versus their commercial viability. Certainly, such a dilemma was not unique to grunge music, or even to musicians in general. Yet the cultural and industrial context of grunge's appropriation by commercial media institutions amplified the uniqueness of this particular artistic dilemma. Coming on the heels of the boomer-dominated rock generation, and with exposure across ever-proliferating media outlets, grunge became a crucible for the new youth culture of the 1990s.

On television, MTV seized on the grunge music zeitgeist as a steady resource for content and for its highly reflexive appeals for young adult audiences. Yet in doing so, MTV was continuing its decade-old strategy of building a brand around product differentiation and niche targeting.[31] Since the network's launch in 1981, MTV (with record labels bearing much of the financial burden for production) offered music videos found nowhere else on television and delivered a highly desirable demographic to advertisers with them. In doing so, it also created a unique visual identity for its own interstitial content based on the now-familiar pastiche of music videos' quick cutting and hyper-stylized aesthetics, differentiating the network further from cable competitors that relied on familiar syndication packages and cheap knockoffs of broadcast fare. As important as music videos were for MTV early on, though, it gradually began filling out its schedule with original programming in the late 1980s and into the early 1990s, just as oppositionally oriented grunge and hip-hop music ascended to mainstream awareness. Here, the discourses of Generation X identity formation and MTV's pursuit of profitable growth would meet in the form of original programs like *The State* but not without some contention in how to find a comfortable meeting point between the two impulses.

As Lauren Rabinovitz has noted, MTV was not yet profitable by 1984—three years after launching—due to considerable start-up costs.[32] In the face of financial pressures and brief competition from Ted Turner's Cable Music Channel, MTV increased efforts to consolidate its power over cable's music video market. The network negotiated with cable companies for long-term carriage and with record labels for exclusive rights to previously free videos, streamlining "its on-air formula for success" accordingly.[33] After being sold to Viacom International in 1986, MTV again revamped its programming flow, further narrowing its focus on heavy metal artists that would hail a desired audience of young, white men. The move kept in line with MTV's spotty history of airing videos by black artists, further reifying the same commodity audience—middle-class, white viewers aged eighteen to forty-nine—that broadcast television prized, but concentrated on a younger segment. The strategy also corresponded with other measures by the network to please advertisers, many of which involved moving further away from an undifferentiated flow of music videos and closer toward the half-hour and hour-long scheduling conventions of broadcast television. But in order to hold on to some vestige of the edgy aesthetic that defined its early identity based on music videos, MTV introduced short, animated, identification segments and logos in between them: "The logos could provide a structural link that would address a presumed audience desire for the flow of images signifying Postmodernism while identifying MTV as the purveyor of that desire. Since MTV had made a name for itself with both viewers and advertisers as a Postmodern-styled channel, it still needed to maintain its own identity/product differentiation in order to keep its audience and advertisers."[34]

This characterization of MTV suggests its embodiment of the "superficiality, stylistic jumbling"[35] and "neutral practice"[36] of postmodern pastiche.

Indeed, MTV provided a number of scholars at the time with evidence of a purely stylistic, uniquely ever-contemporary postmodern condition unmoored from the power relations of the past.[37] Yet Rabinovitz's analysis argues for an understanding of MTV and the logos as products of a particular industrial and historical context. MTV's style was not simply an unqualified separation from the dominant aesthetic norms and ideologies of the time, enabling either escape from domains of political engagement altogether or radical new modes of occupying them. Instead, the network served as a site for the ongoing negotiation of these discourses, one informed by the material conditions of its production, distribution, and viewing contexts.

Any perceived break with these contexts had just as much to do with postmodernism's abandonment of grand narratives as it did with buying into the smaller ones that would replace them. As Andrew Goodwin notes, "It isn't just that MTV must be seen as hip and irreverent, but that it must seem always to be hip and irreverent in *new* ways."[38] A self-perpetuating, reflexive awareness of its newness, then, became intentional industrial strategies for MTV, performances of differentiation based on their prospective appeal to desired demographics.[39] As MTV's first format evolution took shape, the stylized look of the promotional logos increasingly pervaded across the network as it diversified beyond music videos. What's more, the interstitial bits primed audiences for the sort of eclectic, sketch-like content that would proliferate across the network in the multichannel transition. *Remote Control* (1987–1990), for example, departed from the staid game show genre with a set cluttered by pop culture artifacts in tune with trivia questions that plumbed the depths of contestants' music, television, and movie knowledge. Another one of its original programs, the short-lived sketch comedy show *The Idiot Box* (1990–1991), frenetically mixed short comedic bits in between music video segments. As seen in the promotional logos and in these programs, MTV's stylization at both the program and network level was less an attempt to hold onto a purely postmodern past and more an adaptation of its defining characteristic—the music video—to the normalizing schedule demands of audiences, advertisers, and network executives.

John Caldwell has described the relationship between this self-conscious performance of style and the industrial discourses that informed it "televisuality."[40] Over the course of the 1980s, programs across television's range of expanding outlets embraced exhibitionism, privileging style as their subject instead of as a vessel for transmitting narrative and informational content. A number of converging factors motivated this move, including networks' need to self-identify and differentiate from one another amid growing competition, advances in video technology, and increased media literacy on the part of viewers. Though televisuality would manifest in a number of ways, MTV fare like *Remote Control* and *Beavis and Butt-Head* represented a "trash" aesthetic that played into worries about its effect on vulnerable young viewers. But, as Caldwell notes, "the spatial and temporal excesses that define trash television, also inevitably flood the viewer with knowing references. The accumulation of junk and gestural marks swirling around the performers in these shows is matched only by the thickened flood of smart cultural codes given off by the very same objects."[41] The televisuality of MTV's original programming thus bore the effects of contemporaneous industrial and cultural discourses just as much as its (supposedly purely) postmodern music videos and promotional segments had.

On the one hand, then, MTV foregrounded televisual style in order to self-identify as edgy in a cluttered cable marketplace. On the other hand, this style increasingly manifested within established programming practices and genres elsewhere on cable that also sought out the audience of young, white, men desired by MTV. Megan Mullen notes that MTV's early negotiations of music video and half-hour formats catalyzed the spread of "video bites" on cable networks such as CNN and Comedy Central. The attention-grabbing aesthetic and affordability of minutes-long programming "buttressed the notion that audiovisual meaning can be conveyed in much shorter spans of time than the traditional half-hour or hour scheduling slots . . . increasing recyclability while creating new meanings."[42] The flow of MTV's early days may have been aesthetically innovative compared to broadcast shows, but the network was also motivated to find equally innovative ways to subsume this style to growing financial pressures. As its cultural codes proliferated beyond its own programming and into advertising and press, MTV invariably attempted to claim ownership of them and structure their meanings around the perceived tastes of the Generation X identity.

MTV executive vice president Sara Levinson, for instance, said in 1993, "We're definitely seeing an increase in the number of programs targeted to the younger demographic, but I think MTV is the only place that really has as its mission to serve this audience all day, every day. . . . We have a long-term commitment to this audience."[43] That same year Taco Bell hired Bill

Plympton, the animator responsible for many of MTV's promotional shorts in the late 1980s, for an Xer-targeting ad campaign. A Taco Bell marketing representative called the ads "very edgy stuff with multiple messages.... It's constant visual change and challenge. The boomers are just not going to get this one."[44] Efforts to brand a particular cultural commodity as Gen X often came with a corresponding implication of how baby boomers did or did not figure into the equation, a dynamic that played out as MTV positioned itself among a crowded field of cable outlets.

When the music channel VH1 launched in 1985, for instance, it and MTV both courted a broadly conceived young adult audience for much of the remainder of the decade. VH1 often made more direct appeals to boomers with nostalgic retrospectives like footage from the 1969 Woodstock music festival repackaged as "Woodstock Minutes," in which "bite-sized chunks of history cascade[d] along with the rest of the network's 'flow.'"[45] The network aggressively embraced the "growing 'cult' of the past in popular music" and exploited the "generational narcissism" of baby boomers, though both MTV and VH1 would make use of the past with direct generational appeals as their respective forays into original programming evolved.[46] But while VH1 packaged the past in a flattering light, MTV came increasingly to use it ironically, appealing to the emerging aesthetics of Generation X. MTV, before coming to focus eventually on Xers, packaged boomer-friendly fare (such as cheap syndication runs of *Speed Racer* [1967–1968] and *Monty Python's Flying Circus*) alongside the likes of *Beavis and Butt-Head* and *Liquid Television* (1991–1994). The strategy had the purpose of solidifying its core young adult audience—twelve-to-twenty-five-year-old Gen Xers—while also hailing aging boomers toward the twenty-five-to-thirty-four-year-old end of the young adult demographic. But if both VH1 and MTV sought young adult audiences through the late 1980s, "The strategy behind this targeting seems to have changed somewhat in 1994. Whereas VH-1 defined itself as 'The difference between you and your parents,' by late 1994 the network was targeting 'graduates' of MTV. The aim is still to flatter the viewer into feeling young, but now with music video itself (MTV) as an explicit frame of reference."[47] Here again the language of MTV as a referent occurs not as a postmodern signifier but as a branded commodity using another reflexively (VH1) to self-identify. The industrial logic of this distinction becomes even more apparent considering that both MTV and VH1 were subsidiaries of the same parent company, Viacom. Segmenting its audience in this way allowed the conglomerate to create the illusion of differentiated taste cultures so crucial to pitching the networks to advertisers and cable carriers. At the same time, revenues from both stayed within the same corporate structure.[48]

In a more recent setting, as older Xers have gradually slipped out of television's eighteen-to-forty-nine-year-old demographic, cable outlets have once again looked to the relationship between generations and the American television heritage as a way to frame their programming practices. While Nick at Nite and TV Land, for instance, have programmed for boomer nostalgia in much the same way VH1 did, they shifted focus in the 2000s to reruns of 1980s hits like *Cheers* (1983–1993) and *The Cosby Show* (1984–1992)—"the TV neverland of Generation X parents."[49] As the industry has treated generations with such disposability, it would be tempting to see the idea as little more than a sound-bite friendly manner of expressing the same information contained in dry demographic numbers. Yet that does not mean that generation-based cultural identities are not meaningful. Even if it were and would continue to be primarily, as Coupland worried, "a target market," Generation X expressed opposition to cultural hegemonic forces not as the boomers before them did, but in ambiguous ways that made their critique seem less salient. Nowhere was this balance more explicitly engaged than in sketch comedies like *The State*.

"I Don't Have a Problem, That's My Problem!": *The State* on MTV

By early 1993, 85 percent of MTV's programming was music videos, but the channel began relying on original comedy programming as a cost-efficient way to fill time and develop talent.[50] Among its efforts at the time were the above-mentioned *Remote Control*, *The Idiot Box*, *Liquid Television*, *The Ben Stiller Show*, and *You Wrote It, You Watch It* (1992–1993). Hosted by Jon Stewart, *You Wrote It* solicited humorous anecdotes from viewers, which comedy troupe The State then re-enacted in exaggeratedly parodic ways. Though crude in its execution, the program highlighted many of the absurdist tendencies for which *The State* would later be known. Moreover, the program functioned as a pilot of sorts for the troupe, and it also aligned with MTV's broader shift toward original reality and comedy programming. Seeking to further develop and retain in-house comedy and reality talent, Viacom launched the production unit MTV Prods. in May 1993, headed by future Viacom wunderkind Doug Herzog.[51] Though initially focused on shepherding MTV television properties such as *Joe's Apartment* (1992) and

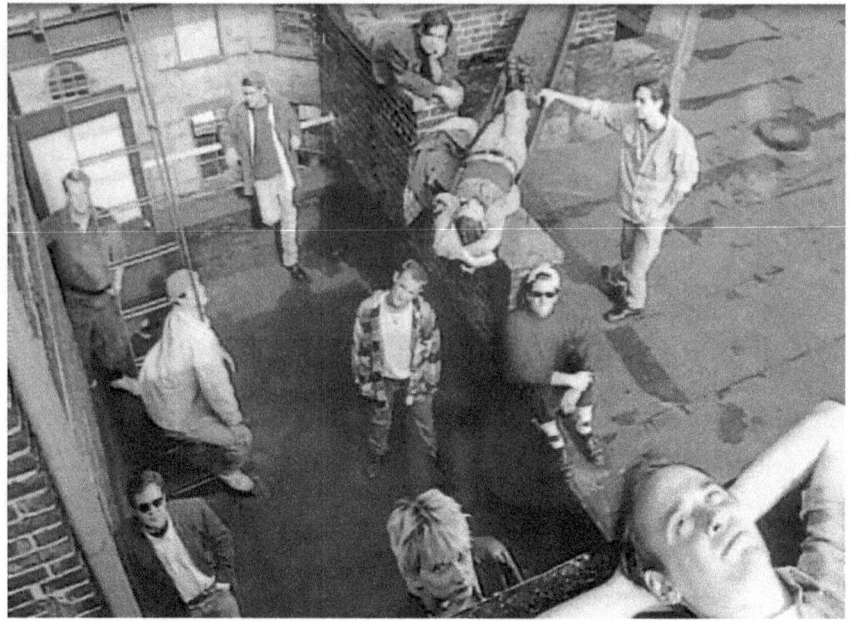

Fig. 3.2. The eleven cast members of MTV's *The State* from the show's opening.

Beavis and Butt-Head through to film production, MTV Prods. sought to develop original ideas that could flexibly travel across media platforms.[52]

Before arriving at MTV, The State had already had a successful run as a sketch and improvisation troupe as undergraduates at New York University in the late 1980s. The eleven members of the comedy troupe, then known as The State: Full Frontal Comedy, performed in an off-Broadway show coproduced by Steven Starr (and fellow *State* cocreator Jonathan Bendis) in October 1992. Soon thereafter, the group dropped "Full Frontal Comedy" from its name and starred in *You Wrote It, You Watch It*. In April 1993, troupe members Kevin Allison, Michael Ian Black, Robert Ben Garant, Todd Holoubek, Michael Jann, Kerri Kenney, Thomas Lennon, Joe Lo Truglio, Ken Marino, Michael Showalter, and David Wain and producers Bendis and Starr signed a development deal with MTV's Remote Productions Inc. The initial agreement was for a six-episode cycle and included a list of "pre-existing characters."[53] While a standard development practice at the time, the explication of preexisting characters in the case of *The State* would prove to be a site of tension between the cast and the network later on. MTV continuously pressured *The State* to showcase recurring characters and catchphrases in order to familiarize viewers with the unwieldy eleven-member cast. Given cable's appetite for new content and the thriving home video markets, moreover, MTV likely envisioned *The State* as a bountiful source for spinning off recurring characters onto new merchandising, television, and film platforms.

The State defiantly responded to these pressures in the form of the recurring sketch character Louie, an obnoxious, catchphrase-spewing boor who simultaneously appeased and flew in the face of MTV's demands. Before the character even appears onscreen for the first time in the series' second episode (1993), a title card with spotlights and bombastic voiceover announces his forthcoming appearance: "And now . . . Louie! The guy who comes in and says his catchphrase over and over again!" Inside an apartment party, the entire cast mills around looking bored. Louie (played by Ken Marino) enters and the partygoers perk up. "Who's got something to drink?" he asks. After accepting an orange juice, Louie exclaims, "I wanna dip my balls in it!" and gestures suggestively towards his crotch. Though it is not readily apparent until a couple of repetitions of the gag, Louie is holding two white golf balls in his hand, a bit of business possibly required of Marino by MTV standards and practices personnel. From the network's perspective, the move allowed Marino to skate by with a bit of edgy, envelope-pushing comedy. *The State* was seemingly able to capitulate to MTV's demands for catchphrase-friendly characters while also undermining the ultimate purpose for them. Clearly, MTV would not be able to develop further such an offensive and crude character for spin-offs and films. At the same time, the gag proved immensely popular and resonated with Generation X audiences' distrust of authority, and the character would go on to appear in two more sketches over the series' run.

While Louie embodied both resentment toward MTV and fodder for *State* fans hungry for dumbed-down humor, another recurring character would express the Generation X cultural identity with much more ambivalence. In his first appearance on the series (also in episode two), the teen-aged slacker Doug (played by Michael Showalter) confronts his boomer father (played by Thomas Lennon) while his friends stand slack-jawed in the background. Exchanges parodying after-school-special-type problems ensue—Doug's father wants to know why his son has condoms and cigarettes, accusing him of being on drugs as well. Doug grows increasingly agitated with each new charge, storming out (with the catchphrase "I'm outta heeeeeere!") only to return and indignantly justify his life choices. The central joke of the sketch hinges on Doug's father not actually being angry with him, but indulging his transgressive behavior. Instead of worrying about Doug's promiscuity and smoking habit, he asks Doug for a cigarette and invites him and his girlfriend to have sex at their house. After shouting down his dad's attempts at offering an "easy solution that's gonna bridge the generation gap between you and me," the following exchange occurs:

Dad: Doug, your mother and I think you're on drugs.
Doug: Drugs?! Hey, I'm Doug, man, not Bob Dylan.
Dad: Doug, do you even know who Bob Dylan is?
Doug: No, but I know he died of drugs.
Dad: Doug, Bob Dylan is alive and well. I produced his last three albums.
Doug: Oh, you mean Uncle Robert?

The exchange fittingly centers on music in portraying a generational clash, with Dad enlightening his Xer son about the boomer icon Dylan. But the clash turns out to be manufactured, one resolved within the context of a commercial media exchange. Dad declines to give Doug an oral history of the 1960s and its attendant lessons about speaking truth to power. For Doug—and, by extension, Generation X—Dylan and recreational drug use are evidence that commodity culture has co-opted boomer counterculture. Doug looks silly for not realizing this and for not embracing the prospect of this assimilation happening to Generation X's iconoclasts too.

The sketch climaxes with Doug's dad growing impossible to hate no matter the provocation, further underlining the extent to which Xers resented the simultaneous marginalization and misdirection of their oppositional impulses toward their elders. "Doug, what is your problem?" his father asks. "I don't have a problem, that's my problem!" Doug responds, parodically inverting Johnny Strabler's flippant retort of teenaged insouciance ("Whadda you got?") from *The Wild One* (1953). By the sketch's end, Doug has angrily rebelled and Dad has calmly riposted, and neither has conceded any power as Doug barges out past his friends for the last time. In the sketch's final beat, Doug's friends decide to stay behind with his dad to have some drinks, punctuating one more time Generation X's various fluctuations among oppositional anger, ambivalence, and eventual complicity with the cultural hegemony of boomers and the media industries they controlled.

Fig. 3.3. Michael Showalter, as the teenaged slacker Doug (center), engages in an intergenerational feud.

The muddled nature of this push back against paternalistic forces carried over to *The State* cast members' relationship with MTV as well. On the one hand, sketches like "Louie" and "Doug and Dad" articulate their explicit oppositionality through satiric attacks on dominant cultural discourses. On the other hand, this oppositionality is often aimless, directed just as much at the troupe itself as it is at external forces. Commentary tracks from *The State*'s 2009 complete series DVDs suggest as much, with the tone of cast members' anecdotes vacillating between lingering resentment toward MTV and embarrassment for their own immaturity and insubordination.[54] Yet at the time of the series' initial run, cast members voiced their dissatisfaction in a number of venues, a move that, at least early on, MTV attempted to contextualize as irony for its Generation X demographic.

In a promotional spot for *The State*'s second season alongside *The Jon Stewart Show* (1993–1995) and *Dead at 21* (1994), for instance, the cast appears onstage in a mostly empty auditorium, pitching their show to a bored-looking producer. Cast member Thomas Lennon rattles off a quick tagline: "*The State*: we're twenty-something postmodern sketch comedy whores."

Backing cast members echo Lennon's sentiments: "Yeah, we're whores, definitely whores." In another promo, graphics display several excerpts of particularly vitriolic reviews of *The State*'s first season—"So terrible it deserves to be studied"; "Every MTV executive who gave a thumbs up to *The State* should be given a urine test." The latter review may have been a subtle jab at Eileen Katz, MTV's vice president for series development, who, according to a contentious *New York Times* profile, handed the troupe a list of suggested pop culture ephemera to parody early in the show's run.[55] Katz and MTV vetoed content they deemed to be too intelligent and esoteric, such as references to the novel *Catcher in the Rye* (1951). When cast members complied with a parody of *Beverly Hills 90210* (1990–2000) only to have a gag about Bob Dylan removed for fear that viewers wouldn't know who Dylan was, the joke would resurface in the "Doug & Dad" sketch.

MTV's strategic attempts to control *The State*'s humor according to demographically driven market mandates and the show's tactical evasions of them highlight the highly reflexive flexibility of sketch comedy and generational identities. The dumbed-down humor of *Beavis and Butt-Head* had worked well for MTV, yet trying to map that same sensibility onto *The State* overlooked how it could function flexibly—a silly Bob Dylan joke suppressed in one sketch appeared in another with arguably more resonance. From Katz's perspective, though, structuring the content of MTV programming according to perceived audience tastes was straightforward: "The State is doing what MTV does when it does things well, which is bringing our audience their experience in their own language and their own terms. . . . The State was the first generation weaned on MTV. They are savvy. They know the music and the lingo and television, and so does their audience. It's a direct connection."[56] *The State* cast members, for their part, bristled not only at the network notes but also at the notion that it and its generational cohort could be so easily targeted. "It's interesting MTV has a very low opinion of their audience," cast member Showalter remarked in the same *Times* piece.[57] The article ran on the eve of *The State*'s third season premiere in January 1995, where it would compete in the Saturday late-night slot just before NBC's *Saturday Night Live* and go on to hold its own at a respectable 1.4 rating/3 share.[58] Yet tensions between MTV and the troupe would soon boil over.

The day after the *Times* article ran, MTV senior vice president Doug Herzog sent *The State* cocreators Starr and Bendis a memo admonishing the cast for their insolent remarks.[59] The incident may have been the last straw for *The State* at MTV, one exacerbated by MTV's "problem holding on to talent. They'd discover Ben Stiller and Jon Stewart, but couldn't do talent-holding deals, because the budgets were so small, and talent would eventually leave."[60] Starr and Bendis began planning a more lucrative move to CBS, which had had a recent run of success importing the Canadian sketch comedy program *The Kids in the Hall* and sought to compete with NBC on Saturday nights. In March, Starr informed Herzog that *The State* would not return after its contract expired in August (with thanks to "Eileen Katz in particular for her commitment on our behalf").[61] Throughout the summer of 1995, the troupe planned a Halloween special for CBS that, if successful, might have meant a regular, Saturday late-night series competing against the consecrated sketch comedy of *Saturday Night Live*. However, things did not go as planned.

"I'm Outta Heeeeeeere": *The State* on CBS

Although Doug's catch-phrase—"I'm outta heeeeeere!"—may have indicated their excitement at the prospect of leaving MTV for CBS, *The State* cast members faced a dilemma: How did a program coming from basic cable retain the edgy, generational identity that made it popular among a narrowly targeted audience and, at the same time, create a comedic sensibility appropriate for a broader broadcast audience? In June 1995—a full month before production for the final cycle of MTV episodes had wrapped—Starr broached the subject with head of CBS late-night programming John Pike, noting that "Our MTV show, as good as it looks, needs to look better if we are going to attract and impress a network audience."[62] In its MTV iteration, *The State* mixed in-studio live-to-tape segments with video shorts shot on location. In addition to wanting to shoot the remote segments on 16mm film, Starr laid out other requests to enhance the look of the show and bring it up to perceived network standards: "Sets, props, materials must be upgraded. [Production designer] Ruth Amon is a miracle worker, but her crew has been ill-equipped and we need to give them the means to make us all look fabulous in the network circumstance.... For the first time, we are inviting non-State talent to guest on our shows. This costs money.... Also, let's not overlook all the free music that MTV was able to make available to us."[63] One key point of distinction in the working conditions between MTV and CBS, Starr noted, was *The State*'s ability to appeal to young adult viewers with music of the moment, done at no cost to the troupe and producers.

Music from grunge groups like the Smashing Pumpkins regularly provided the soundtrack to *The State* sketches, and without easy access to the music, CBS would be taking on extra cost to license it. Additionally, using music from groups with young fan bases might have been antithetical to CBS's goal of delivering a broader age range of young viewers, fearing that such music would alienate older viewers.

In addition to wanting to create a successful Halloween special, Starr stated his intentions to build the long-term viability of *The State* as "a franchise that will serve all parties for years."[64] The sentiment echoed the struggle over recurring characters and catchphrases between MTV executives and the troupe years earlier. Starr's emphasis in memos on budgeting concerns may have indicated a desire to hold to *The State*'s edgy, ironic humor in the content of sketches but upgrade the *look* of those sketches in order to broaden their appeal beyond young adult viewers.

By August, production for the special was already well underway, yet Starr and Bendis felt neglected and underserved by the considerable financial and promotional resources at CBS's disposal. In August, Starr contacted James Dixon, the troupe's manager at the William Morris Agency, asking him to lobby CBS on *The State*'s behalf, noting that the special had yet to receive the promised financial and promotional support from the network. Starr complained, "We are the only MTV show to move to a network, and critically considered the best sketch show on television. I've heard nothing. No interest generated anywhere."[65] Clearly, *The State* sought to build on and carry over the momentum generated from its MTV run, yet Pike and CBS were reluctant to commit to anything beyond the special.

The documents in Starr's collection do not detail the exact nature of these exchanges with CBS executives, but we might infer more about the network's thinking by examining broadcast television's broader industrial climate at the time. As Ron Becker notes, the then-looming 1995–1996 season represented an important shift in programming practice by CBS that sought to replicate NBC's success in winning broadcast's key eighteen-to-forty-nine-year-old demographic.[66] These socially liberal, urban-minded professionals—or "slumpies" as Becker calls them—gravitated toward edgy content that was not the stock-in-trade of CBS hits at the time like *Murder, She Wrote* (1984–1996). After leading the networks in overall viewers in the 1993–1994 season, CBS tumbled in the ratings the following year and initiated a high-profile effort to court the slumpy audience for the 1995–1996 season. It focused its efforts primarily on primetime with the likes of *Cybill*

(1995–1998) and *New York News* (1995), but one can see how the cutting-edge humor of a late-night program such as *The State* could be molded into this demographically driven model for CBS's fall 1995 schedule.

While these issues played out on one level, the troupe members set to the onerous task of producing a one-time special that would ostensibly decide their collective future on broadcast television. In a 1996 postmortem article for *Details*, journalist David Lipsky describes the uncomfortable feelings shared among cast members of *The State* and how the lack of a vote of confidence from CBS began to wear on their democratic decision-making processes. In one infamous anecdote, Pike expressed concern about the lack of a cast member of color in the troupe, stressing the importance of black audiences for late-night because, among other reasons, they had "no place to go in the morning—no jobs—so they can stay up as late as they like . . . [also], they can't follow hourlong drama shows—no attention span—so sketches are perfect for them."[67]

The troupe members voted themselves a pay cut and put the savings toward production expenses. Comments in production memos pair the cockiness of their MTV success with the uneasiness of knowing the support they had there no longer existed. In a production memo entitled "Some Things to Ponder Whilst Formulating a Network Special," the troupe formulates a list of questions for Pike, including "What is considered pushing it on CBS? Can we have fun at the network's expense?"[68] The oppositional aesthetic *The State* expressed while at and toward MTV—and MTV's co-option of that oppositionality for sale back to its young audiences—had taken on higher stakes at CBS. But if the first sketch of its Halloween special was any indication, *The State* would critique CBS no matter what the network thought.

MTV's *The State* only occasionally built parodies of the network's shows and branding into its flow of sketches, but the troupe built nearly the entire premise of its Halloween special on the disillusionment it felt at CBS. "*The State*'s 43rd Annual All-Star Halloween Special" (itself a joke about the lack of longevity *The State* assumed it would have) begins with a musical number that expresses this discomfort explicitly. Opening on a close-up of CBS's eye logo prominently displayed on the studio set, effigies of the cast members drop from the rafters in a mock hanging. The cast appears on stage dressed in tuxedos and holding shovels that they then use to begin digging their own graves. The number continues with ominous and discomfiting imagery and lyrics like "CBS is anxious, they're all in a fuss / They scraped the bottom of the barrel, and they found us / They promised us a series if this last one goes well / We've got a better chance of making snowmen in hell." At the number's conclusion, all cast members lay down in the mass grave they have just dug.

Later in the special, cast members Michael Ian Black and David Wain appear on the same set and address the camera to mockingly pay tribute to Desi Arnaz of *I Love Lucy*, one of CBS's early television hits. The gag revolves around their straight-faced reading of misinformation and fuzzy recollections about Arnaz, and it comes across with the same sort of cringe-inducing feeling as the opening musical number. Throughout the special, *The State* relentlessly mocks CBS's sense of television heritage, hoping their edgy aesthetic plays well with the Xer audiences CBS thinks it wants.

Even the presence of musical guest Sonic Youth speaks to *The State*'s Gen X sensibilities and how they seemed simultaneously to bolster and undermine CBS's attempts to reach out to a young adult audience. The network initially suggested pop group Hootie and the Blowfish for the special and eventually booked Blues Traveler, only to have the latter cancel suddenly that week to play the season premiere of—fittingly enough—*Saturday Night Live*. Starr hurriedly nabbed Sonic Youth to fill in, a band that hip Xers (who formed part of the broader slumpy audience courted by broadcast networks) likely embraced, but one that Pike misunderstood as being too obscure. Upon discovering the switch at the show's taping, Pike attempted to call his daughter, according to Lipsky, "Not to see if she *likes* them. To see if she's *heard* of them."[69] The special aired on Friday, October 27, 1995, with virtually no promotion from CBS and earned a paltry six share.[70] In fact, few of CBS's new, slumpy-courting programs succeeded, and Pike ended the network's relationship with *The State*. CBS's audience share plummeted, and in September 1996, it initiated a "Welcome Home" campaign to win back conservative and rural audiences.

After its deal with CBS ended, *The State* found itself without the regular television exposure necessary to support cast members' various side projects. Throughout the winter of 1995–1996, the troupe embarked on a college tour and collected material for a book, *State by State with the State: An Uninformed, Poorly Researched Guide to the United States* (1997). In January, they adjourned to the Bahamas to record a comedy album for Warner Bros., *Comedy for Gracious Living*, which was released over a decade later. Various attempts at extending the life of *The State* brand fizzled or lingered in development throughout the late 1990s, including an internet series not unlike *You Wrote It, You Watch It*, and several film projects (many of which, developed by David Wain, resemble the tone of the troupe's 2001 cult hit, *Wet Hot American Summer*). Most importantly, the CBS debacle exposed weaknesses in the troupe's egalitarian working methods, and various members began pursuing their own projects. Garant, Lennon, Kenney, and Black spun off a *State* sketch into *Viva Variety* on Comedy Central in early 1997, and similar clusters of *State* alumni would continue on the network into the 2000s with *Stella* (2005), *Reno 911!* (2003–2009), and *Michael and Michael Have Issues* (2009) and on film with *Night at the Museum* (2006), *The Ten* (2007), and *Role Models* (2008).

The State's troubled tenure at CBS again points to problematic assumptions about using generation as a basis for cultural identity, as well as how cultural hegemonic forces in the television industry operationalize those assumptions. Caught up in shifting industrial imperatives that prized a particular segment of its idealized audience, CBS may have focused too narrowly on trying to incorporate *The State* into its more broadly appealing fare. Yet the strategy took CBS too far from what had been, up until before that season, working for the network. While in the present day, such a strategy might be considerably less risky given broadcast television's waning audience share, the multichannel context of the 1990s—before cable television and other entertainment outlets had cut as significantly into American viewers' entertainment resources as today—indicated that merging traditional conceptions of television as a mass medium and newer views of it as a niche product would prove difficult.

Even MTV, working exclusively (and with some success) in smaller-scale audience targeting, met with resistance to the notion that it could tell viewers with more and more precision what they wanted. Indeed, the commercial impulses driving both MTV and CBS's respective treatments of *The State* are not as dissimilar as they might seem. MTV and CBS adjusted their production and distribution routines—MTV to look and act more like a broadcast network, and CBS to look and act more like a cable outlet—but both underestimated the volatility of pulling the malleability of sketch comedy on *The State* too far in either direction.

Conclusion

The difficulty of describing the exact relationship among *The State*, MTV in the multi-channel transition, and Generation X viewers further highlights the sketch comedy field as a site of struggles. In this case, perhaps more so than in the previous two chapters, the specific logic through which the show refracted external economic determinants actually defined the positions of its cast members and the cultural meanings they generated. On the one hand, as this chapter has outlined, Generation X was a construction of the very American consumer culture many of its cultural voices critiqued, one built from the top down and whose members rejected any association with it. In this view, Generation X was always already a part of hegemonic cultural forces in the media industries, particularly those aligning the generational identity with the profit-driven practices of niche audience targeting. In this conception, any resistant elements became suppressed or elided in popular figurations of Generation X. The more oppositional discourses of black and feminist Generation X culture, such as those articulated by hip-hop or riot grrrl movements, were marginalized in Xer forums like MTV in favor of those constructing the primary identities of Generation X as those of young, white, men. It is something of a perverse irony that Pike urged *The State* to add a black cast member in some feeble attempt to incorporate that audience into its turn to slumpies. The troupe would also often deflect questions about the extent to which its racial and gender composition (ten white men and one white woman) reflected many of the entrenched social powers it so ruthlessly mocked.[71]

On the other hand, this chapter has also explored the extent to which Gen X sketch comedy provided young people with "a repository of symbols"[72] for the tactics of identity formation that MTV worked so hard to obscure and appropriate. The myriad cultural contexts of young people across two decades is surely too vast and heterogeneous to account for in one signifier, yet such complexity does not align with media industrial interests that need to cut through this complexity in order to program and maintain profitability. Here too, the reflexivity of comedy in *The State* functioned flexibly, inverting the meaning of musical iconography in order to position itself and its viewers as decidedly *not* that which had already been and could be so easily identified. The power of sketch comedy in processes of identity formation is precisely its ability to allow performers and to invite viewers to occupy both positions simultaneously—the Generation X cultural identity and, to invoke Hall again, its constitutive other. At the very least, *The State* offered Generation X a powerful cultural tool for articulating both what young people were at the time and what they were not.

The State further underlines how sketch comedy's reflexive flexibility is both ideal and troubling for many conventional television industry practices. The format's malleable structure, for example, allows comedians to address a wide array of topics and audiences without necessarily having a cohesive, structuring narrative. Producers and performers on sketch programs are freer to experiment with content than those in long-form comedy formats, knowing that if one sketch misses, another might hit just minutes later. At the same time, though, publicity and advertising interests must channel this textual volatility to productive ends, offering viewers a clearly defined reason to watch. In the case of *The State*, it was one built around appeals to youth culture and the contested notion of a Generation X identity that would position the show as fresh and innovative. *The State* certainly endeavored to distinguish itself from the consecrated comedy of sketch predecessors, but its downfall was in not recognizing how these efforts were implicated in broader industrial infrastructures. Resistance defined the show's aesthetic and initially helped brand it as edgy, but *The State* never found a successful way to reconcile its oppositional aesthetic with the commercial impulses driving it toward the mainstream.

For television networks across the multichannel transition and into the post-network era, the long-term viability of a sketch comedy show has depended not just on exposure to broader audiences and the increased profitability that comes with a move from cable to broadcast. It has also meant developing that show (or elements of it) into texts for distribution and consumption across the various outlets housed within the network's parent company. Although this dynamic has been especially true of media texts with expansive, long-form narrative universes, here again, sketch comedy's modularity would seem to be an ideal fit. Comedic internet shorts that have gone viral make for appealing television development projects, while successful television shows can repurpose humorous outtakes for online distribution. Popular recurring sketch characters can serve as the basis for feature-length film comedies or appear as supporting players across a film franchise. Even when sketch comedy is not explicitly testing the boundaries of medium specificity, the cultural meanings generated by agents working in the sketch comedy field can rarely be claimed only by their creators. I explore this dynamic more through the case of Comedy Central and post-network era television in the next chapter.

Notes

1. Stelter, "The Good Ol' Days of 20 Years Ago."
2. Turner, "*Reality Bites*: The Ultimate Sellout?"

3. Lipsitz, *Time Passages*, 42.
4. Wilson, "'My So-Called Adulthood.'"
5. Toffler quoted in Hibberd, "MTV Pushing Out 'Cynical' Generation X."
6. Napoli, *Audience Economics*, 104.
7. Strauss and Howe, *Generations*, 36.
8. Undoubtedly, a driving factor for this was MTV's reluctance to program music videos by black artists in its early years. Though the channel would eventually come to embrace hip-hop music with videos and original programming like *Yo! MTV Raps* (1988–1995), these practices were largely folded into broader audience-targeting strategies that courted viewers who were young, white men.
9. Ritchie, "Get Ready for 'Generation X'; Soon the Primary Market, and Very Unlike Aging Boomers," 21.
10. Epstein, "Introduction: Generation X, Youth Culture, and Identity."
11. Holtz, *Welcome to the Jungle*, 3.
12. Giroux, "Teenage Sexuality, Body Politics, and the Pedagogy of Display," 25.
13. Dunn, "Hanging Out with American Youth," 24. The initiation of the so-called "baby bust"—another pejorative nickname for Generation X often seen in literature of the time—was undoubtedly spurred on by the introduction of commercially produced birth control in the early 1960s and the 1973 U.S. Supreme Court ruling on *Roe v. Wade*.
14. Strauss and Howe, *Generations*, 325.
15. Bernstein with Woodruff, Buell, Peacock, and Thurston, "What Happened to the American Dream?"
16. Leo, "The Unplugged Generation," 22.
17. Strauss and Howe, "The New Generation Gap."
18. Gordinier, *X Saves the World*, xxi.
19. Bob Guccione quoted in Ritchie, *Marketing to Generation X*, ix.
20. Star, "The Twentysomething Myth," 25.
21. Coupland, *Generation X: Tales for an Accelerated Generation*.
22. See, among others: Gaines, *Teenage Wasteland: Suburbia's Dead End Kids*; Kearney, "'Don't Need You:' Rethinking Identity Politics and Separatism from a Grrrl Perspective"; and Shevory, "Bleached Resistance: The Politics of Grunge."
23. Leo, "The Unplugged Generation," 22.
24. Best and Kellner, "Beavis and Butt-Head: No Future for Postmodern Youth, 78.
25. Leland, "Battle for Your Brain," 48.
26. Turow, *Breaking Up America*, 1–17.
27. Mullen, *The Rise of Cable Programming in the United States*, 129.
28. Turow, *Breaking Up America*, 55.
29. Ibid., 76.
30. Curtin, "On Edge," 181–202.
31. See Johnson, *Branding Television*. Johnson's book examines in detail (with MTV as a brief case study) the balancing act for branded television content between emulating what has worked for others, but providing just enough differentiation to matter.
32. Rabinovitz, "Animation, Postmodernism, and MTV," 99–112.
33. Ibid., 101.
34. Ibid., 103.
35. Tetzlaff, "MTV and the Politics of Postmodern Pop," 80.
36. Jameson, *Postmodernism, or the Cultural Logic of Late Capitalism*, 25.

37. See Goodwin, "Fatal Distractions: MTV Meets Postmodern Theory" for a fuller discussion of MTV as postmodern phenomenon.

38. Ibid., 49.

39. Caldwell (in *Televisuality*) notes that postmodern narrative strategies (as seen in programs like *Mystery Science Theater 3000* [1988–1999] and *Beavis and Butt-Head*) of having characters watch and comment on the same thing as the audience are in line with similarly reflexive televisual techniques stretching back to *Texaco Star Theater* in the 1940s.

40. Caldwell, *Televisuality*, 3–31.

41. Ibid., 197.

42. Mullen, *The Rise of Cable Programming in the United States*, 172.

43. Levinson quoted in Donaton and Levin, "The Media Wakes Up to Generation X," 16.

44. Cortez and Cuneo, "Taco Bell Logs Odd Hours to Lure Xers in New Ads," 3.

45. Burns, "Popular Music, Television, and Generational Identity," 130–131.

46. Ibid., 129.

47. Ibid., 131.

48. This logic would include the targeting of children's audiences, as well. The Viacom-owned Nickelodeon also branded itself with "an 'Us versus Them' attitude, where the television programs aired on Nickelodeon are expressly not for adults but *only* for kids" (Banet-Weiser, *Kids Rule! Nickelodeon and Consumer Citizenship*, 59). Viacom's goal, then, was to keep viewers within its family of networks from early childhood to adulthood, moving them along a sequence of seemingly distinct steps of cultural consumption whose profits ultimately flowed back to the same source.

49. Kompare, *Rerun Nation*, 182.

50. Pendleton, "TV Plays It Safe—Just for Laughs."

51. Herzog would go on to serve in a number of capacities for the Viacom empire, including president of Comedy Central.

52. Brodie, "MTV Expands Horizon: In-house Unit to Delve into Films, Network TV," 3.

53. The State, Starr, and Bendis, "Pre-Existing Characters."

54. Gray suggests that DVD commentary tracks most often serve as sites of reclamation on the part of artists looking to rectify studio or network meddling in their work. The troupe's admissions in them go against these preferred uses of commentary tracks, but they highlight the difficulty of characterizing *The State* and Generation X as unequivocally battling against some unified ideology. See Gray, *Show Sold Separately*, 81–116.

55. Gabriel, "Television; Beyond Beavis and Butt-Head, MTV's Sketch Comedy Group."

56. Ibid.

57. Ibid.

58. MTV Networks, "Ratings Report."

59. Herzog, "MTV Networks, Herzog Memo to Starr and Bendis."

60. Beth McCarthy quoted in Marks and Tannenbaum, *I Want My MTV*, 513.

61. Starr, "Starr Pictures Memo RE: THE STATE."

62. Starr, "RE: 'THE STATE'—NETWORK FORMAT."

63. Ibid.

64. Ibid.

65. Ibid.

66. Becker, *Gay TV and Straight America*, 97–107.

67. Pike quoted in Lipsky, "They Died Laughing." The incident ultimately contributed to Pike's resignation.

68. The State, "Some Things to Ponder Whilst Formulating a Network Special."
69. Pike quoted in Lipsky, "They Died Laughing."
70. Lipsky, "They Died Laughing."
71. When asked about the reason behind Kerri Kenney being the only woman member of *The State*, one cast member stated that previous women simply did not work out, and another jokingly remarked, "These are lies. . . . The real reason is, Kerri ate them" (Gabriel, "Television; Beyond Beavis and Butt-Head, MTV's Sketch Comedy Group").
72. Medhurst, *A National Joke*, 39.

4

SKETCH COMEDY'S IDENTITY (POST-)POLITICS

Inside Amy Schumer, Key & Peele, and Comedy Central in the Post-Network Era

"Everyone's talking about feminism. People are getting together, and they're addressing discrimination. Black Lives Matter, transgender activists," laments an angry, middle-aged man played by Carrie Brownstein (in drag) in a 2017 episode of the sketchuational comedy *Portlandia* (2011–2018).[1] "What I hate about it is that none of it's about us, none of these movements are about us. I mean, where's our movement?" replies a friend played by Fred Armisen before the duo launch into a song called "What about Men?" On one level, the sketch lampoons responses by men's rights movements and the alt-right to various identity-based political struggles in the 2010s. The song critiques the notion that although men—particularly straight, white men—have long held cultural, political, and economic power in the United States, they now feel threatened. Of course, the fact that identity-based movements are gaining visibility does little to diminish straight, white men's power—certainly not enough to ask for a falsely equivalent "our movement," as Armisen's character ironically implores.

On another level, the *Portlandia* scene gestures to broader shifts in the relationship among sketch comedy and race- and gender-based identities in television's post-network era. It is no accident that the program's network, IFC, ditched its long-time brand (the Independent Film Channel) in 2010 in order to program hipster comedies like *Portlandia*. In that light, "What about Men?" might also be a jab at competitors like Comedy Central with its core viewership of straight, white men. Indeed, myriad industrial forces have long constructed comedy as a masculine genre, as evidenced by Comedy Central's history of programs like *South Park* (1997–present), *Tosh.o* (2009–present), *Workaholics* (2011–2017), and, of course, *The Man Show* (1999–2004). Despite Comedy Central's strategic forays into developing programs by black comedians, so too have the majority of its hits starred white men.

Although it has long exploited (and contributed to) a presumed link between straight, white men and comedy, Comedy Central has recently taken a different tack. What began as a strategy of narrowcasting for its desired audience during the multichannel transition has now morphed into something seemingly more inclusive. With sketch comedies (and comedies with self-contained scenes amenable to online circulation) like *Inside Amy Schumer* (2013–present), *Broad City* (2014–2019), *Key & Peele, Kroll Show* (2013–2015), and *Nathan for You* (2013–2017), Comedy Central in the post-network era has begun courting more diverse audiences, or at least ones that include viewers who are not straight, white men. What's more, it is doing so without alienating the core viewership of straight, young, white men so important to its brand.

We might call Comedy Central's new strategy, as well as its echoes elsewhere on cable networks in the post-network era, a "post-politics" approach to identity and sketch comedy. Politics in this sense, then, refers not to party affiliations but to broader discourses that construct and circulate identities such as gender, race, class, sexuality, age, and more. By calling these shows post-politics, I do not mean to say that gendered and race-based identities no longer matter in assessing sketch comedy in the post-network era—quite the opposite, in fact. Instead, I hope to highlight how sketch comedy persists in being a particularly salient site of struggle over cultural meaning today, despite superficial markers of representational equality in these programs' humor. In other words, Comedy Central's sketch-heavy comedies *Inside Amy Schumer, Broad City, Key & Peele, Kroll Show*, and *Nathan for You*, among others, reflexively satirize televisual representations of gender and race without positioning any one identity group as dominant over another at the level of the text. The seemingly progressive and feminist meanings of these shows shift, however, when considering their many flexible industrial uses for Comedy Central's distribution and publicity practices, ones that reaffirm the power of its long-time audience of straight, white men.

As I explore below, post-network industrial practices include an emphasis on online distribution, multiscreen and mobile media viewing (behaviors the channel often associates with viewers who are white men), as well as discursive strategies from executives and journalists that reinscribe gendered and raced hierarchies. Today, this din of hegemonic television industry routines is shouting down the distinctive voices of Comedy Central's contemporary woman- and racial/ethnic minority-led sketch shows. Despite the progressive, feminist representational impulses of the programs discussed below, television's post-network industrial discourses have the effect of reaffirming the power of Comedy Central's already powerful core audience: straight, white men.

In the first section of this chapter, I use interviews with founding Comedy Central executives to briefly trace the network's early use of sketch comedy in the creation of an industrial identity, one that has seen increasing challenges from competitors on cable in the post-network era. Given this renewed competition for its format and core audience, the network rebranded in 2011, developing sketch comedies like *Inside Amy Schumer* and *Key & Peele*. The distribution and promotional practices bolstering Comedy Central's newly expanded brand identity, however, encoded preferred meanings in these shows centered on dominant identity groups. In pairing textual and industrial analysis across this chapter's second and third sections, I work within what John Caldwell calls an "integrated cultural-industrial" approach, examining how the "managed self-disclosures" of Comedy Central talent, management, and press about them help shape perceptions about their work.[2] These discourses are particularly important in the post-network era given the intense differentiation tactics necessary at all levels of creative industries to compete with multiplying entertainment options, navigate television's convergence with digital platforms, and attract younger viewers who desire content on their own terms.[3] Generally speaking, this chapter examines how the field of economic power surrounding sketch comedy's identity struggles in the post-network era limit the potentially empowering cultural meanings of the genre today.

Comedy Central's Industrial Identity from the Multichannel Transition to the Post-network Era

Comedy Central has roots in two competing, comedy-centric cable networks that launched in the heart of television's multichannel transition:

The Comedy Channel, which debuted in November 1989, and Ha! in April 1990. Stu Smiley, one of the executives credited with launching The Comedy Channel, indicates that since the networks began so close to one another, "There was a rush to get this product out, and [Ha!] went by the way of licensing and [The Comedy Channel] went by the way of trying to develop something original."[4] As a network owned by HBO, The Comedy Channel sought to take advantage of that premium network's already-robust presence in stand-up comedy and supplement it with edgy, cost-effective original programming. This relationship presented The Comedy Channel with a challenge not only at the level of its industrial identity but also at the level of day-to-day production. According to Art Bell, another HBO executive involved in The Comedy Channel's launch: "I remember when we talked about the fact that we gotta bring some sketch in because it was important, and we started looking around and there wasn't that much. Even though there's a lot of sketch troupes, there were a lot of sketch troupes you're trying to figure out how to shoot them. You couldn't go in and shoot it like standup. You couldn't just set up a couple of cameras and light the place and then you're done. It just was a different undertaking."[5] Among The Comedy Channel's early forays into sketch-like shows were *The Higgins Boys and Gruber* (1989–1991) and *Mystery Science Theater 3000* (1988–1999), both created and cowritten by Joel Hodgson. Though not wholly composed of scripted sketches in the way that many other sketch comedies are, the two programs had a loose, modular aesthetic that regularly incorporated or made fun of short clips from other media. Another show, *Short Attention Span Theater* (1989–1994), hosted by Jon Stewart, was "a precursor to what everybody is watching on YouTube now, in terms of short clips of comedy from movies or television or watching your cat play the piano."[6] With their mix of scripted studio sketches, monologues, semi-improvised remote segments, and borrowed clips, these early Comedy Channel shows would provide a template for many later Comedy Central sketch(-like) comedies of the multichannel transition such as *Exit 57* (1995–1996), *Viva Variety*, and *Upright Citizens Brigade* (1998–2000).

Early on, then, sketch comedy helped distinguish The Comedy Channel from competitor Ha!, which had been relying for the most part on "historical, nostalgic acquired content" like *The Mary Tyler Moore Show, Newhart* (1982–1990), and *Rhoda* (1974–1978).[7] When it quickly became apparent the market would not support two comedy-focused outlets, though, The Comedy Channel and Ha! merged to form Comedy Central in 1991. Like many of its cable contemporaries, the fledgling network continued to rely partially on inexpensive syndicated fare while experimenting with a strange brew of clip shows, stand-up specials, game shows, and formally adventurous sketch comedies.[8] Comedy Central's privileging of original programming like sketch comedy helped the network clearly articulate its demographic focus, too—young men. According to Bell: "When the merger happened, it was really decided that this is going to be a comedy network for young men. That was sort of where we characterized it at the time. Not that we were trying to exclude women, but as an advertising demographic, young men were very hard to get. We found that standup comedy and some other kinds of edgy comedy get young men. So, that was sort of our first target, and that's how we sort of weaned ourselves from the syndicated sitcom stuff."[9] Comedy Central flexibly deployed sketch comedies early on, then, to plug programming gaps, experiment with cheap original content, and target a demographic increasingly prized by television as it moved from the multichannel transition of the 1980s and 1990s to the post-network era. The network's sketch-y shows targeting young men during this time have included, among many others, *The Man Show*, *Crank Yankers* (2002–2005), and *Tosh.o*.

Although Comedy Central has had successful multiseason runs with many of its short-form and sketch comedies, the full range of cultural and industrial ends to which it would program the genre would not come until early in the post-network era. In 2003, Viacom (Ha!'s corporate parent) took full ownership of the network, the same year that the sketch comedy *Chappelle's Show* debuted and quickly became a phenomenon. Around this time, Comedy Central's other nonsketch flagship shows—*The Daily Show with Jon Stewart* (1999–2015) and *South Park*—began to come into their own as powerful voices of political dissent. In the ensuing years, these programs drove increased carriage for Comedy Central and spurred both popular and scholarly debate about everything from culture wars to presidential elections.

Comedy Central's digital strategy began to take shape early in the post-network era too, in ways that would distinguish its brand identity in the increasingly crowded cable marketplace. After Viacom purchased the short-form entertainment website Atom in 2006, Comedy Central used the platform as a farm league of sorts for growing new programming. It developed the Atom web series *Ugly Americans* (2010–2012) into a half-hour television program for the cable network in 2010, and it regularly ran half-hour compilations of Atom short videos (under the title *Atom TV* [2008–2010]) during hours normally reserved for syndicated and paid programming. In keeping with the post-network era's logic of seeing the internet as a complement, rather than a competitor, to conventional television, Viacom and Comedy Central have used their expanding digital presence to allow content to find a following gradually online rather than subject the untested material to the competitive rigors of television scheduling and promotion.[10] By the same token, Comedy Central also utilized Atom as a testing ground for television material in which it was not fully confident. In December 2009, for instance, the network segmented the half-hour pilot for the puppet-cop comedy *The Fuzz* into several minutes-long chunks and released it online. Today, Atom.com has simply been folded into a subsection of Comedy Central's homepage titled, appropriately enough, "Short Form."

The move to produce sketch comedy amenable to both television and the internet echoes Max Dawson's characterization of "unbundling," the process of dismantling television texts and distributing them in self-contained segments for viewing on smart devices.[11] Over the course of the post-network era, the practice has gained traction in high-profile broadcast shows like *Lost* (2004–2010) and *24* (2001–2010, 2014), for example, offering additional content online that extended their respective dieges and kept their loyal viewers engaged beyond the moment of television exhibition. These unbundled television segments circulated across digital platforms in order to serve the repurposing needs of television networks, often at the behest of their conglomerate parent companies.[12] In the case of Comedy Central programming, though, comedy segments have not simply been dependent, extracted parts of a larger textual whole. Instead, sketch comedy and short form comedy for the network—as sketches from the case studies below indicate—have proven useful in their *re*-bundling for television too. By the time Atom's production resources became the in-house digital production hub CC Studios in early 2013, Comedy Central began playing up its programs' roots in—and return to—the internet.

In the post-network era, the most significant industrial function for the many modular moves of Comedy Central shows has been their ability to court and foster intense loyalty in viewers who are young, tech-savvy, men. With *The Daily Show*'s perceived reliability as a nightly news source and *South Park*'s unique ability among animated sitcoms to address current events, Comedy Central has used the two shows' regular viewership as a promotional mechanism in launching and scheduling new programs. After the taxing production schedule of *South Park* drove creators Trey Parker and Matt Stone to half-season orders every fall and spring, for instance, Comedy Central filled its vacated Wednesday timeslot with the second season of *Tosh.o* in 2010. Despite its schedule-hopping, *Tosh.o* has become the network's new flagship for the contemporary digitally driven moment, regularly rating highest for its telecast night among cable viewers eighteen to forty-nine and excelling at attracting men aged eighteen to twenty-four.[13] A 2011 *New York Times* profile of Comedy Central's inaugural Comedy Awards (timed to coincide with the network's twentieth birthday) not only acknowledges the legacy of *South Park* and *The Daily Show* but also quotes a Viacom executive describing *Tosh.o* as "the template for future success stories" due to its multiplatform engagement with young men.[14]

The Comedy Awards, and *Tosh.o*'s emergence as Comedy Central's top program, came on the heels of a 2011 rebrand for the network, one whose publicity reiterated the importance of content moving with modularity, able to be viewed, shared, and commented on by viewers who were either explicitly depicted or implicitly constructed as straight, young men. For instance, promotions showcasing the new logo and design begin with short sequences of men swiping and clicking Comedy Central content on smartphones, computer screens, and tablets.[15] These viewers access clips focused on bawdy bodily humor: *South Park*'s Randy Marsh microwaving his genitals, Jon Stewart mockingly exclaiming "sex with ladies in their vaginas!," and rapidly scrolling text beside the new logo declaring, somewhat perplexingly, "SHIT. BALLS. COMEDY." In addition to these depictions of men and masculine humor, commentary from network and advertising executives about the rebrand reiterated the importance of television content being "screen agnostic," able to be accessed and shared across media platforms.[16] Such rhetoric, particularly in the context of television comedy, constructs a presumed viewership of young men, one whose attention a channel must seek to seize and retain in multiscreen viewing environments through the use of provocative sexual and/or racial humor.[17] Of course, Comedy Central had implemented this strategy long before the post-network era through incendiary characters such as *South Park*'s Eric Cartman. But by early 2011, Comedy Central had (re)declared itself a television and online home for consumers of humor who were young men, one evolving both in programming and distribution to align with the ribald and high-tech habitus of this demographic perceived to hold high value.

Comedy Central trumpeted its status at the end of 2011 as the top non-sports cable network among men eighteen to thirty-four and eighteen to twenty-four, though it faced considerable competition from networks with renewed interest in delivering those same demographics to advertisers.[18] The early 2010s would be a tipping point for cable networks looking to better court young men by rebranding with contentious comedy and by bolstering their digital presences. These strategies were part of a broader move among many networks away from fact-based programming like documentaries toward entertainment programming to compete for viewers who were young men.[19] History, for instance, moved from historical documentaries toward blue-collar reality shows like *Pawn Stars* (2009–present) and *American Pickers* (2010–present). In the comedy realm, TBS increased its original comedic programming by building around *Conan* (2010–present), IFC shifted its focus to alternative comedy programming that same year, and FXX launched in 2013 as a comedy-focused addition to the FOX family of cable outlets. By 2014, even the prestige drama network AMC and the general interest website Yahoo! developed or added comedies, with the latter resurrecting *Community* (2009–2015), the canceled NBC sitcom with an intensely loyal online following. As the cable and digital landscapes became more cluttered in the early 2010s, then, networks increasingly viewed comedy as a way both to stand out from the pack and to attract audiences of young men.

Given the glut of competitors both for its format and its audience by the end of 2012, the nightly average of Comedy Central's total primetime audience had fallen more than 25 percent from 2008, a trend that prompted parent company Viacom to increase the amount of ad time on the network by 9 percent.[20] The network also struggled to develop new programming for its traditional cable channel, despite ongoing efforts to extend its presence into off-screen ventures like merchandising and live tours. Comedic talent began bringing television projects to competitors like Adult Swim, bypassing Comedy Central due to its growing "reputation as perhaps the most professionally thoughtless and creatively obtuse operation in the business."[21] In the midst of this malaise, Comedy Central made two management changes that highlight the relationship between gender identities and multiplatform viewing as ongoing focuses for comedy outlets in the post-network era.

First, the network brought in executive Brooke Posch, who would supervise program development in New York and launch the women-led

Broad City and *Inside Amy Schumer*. Second, Comedy Central consolidated all content development—both television and digital—under programming executive Kent Alterman, a move that later involved dismantling the network's separately run digital department and reforming it as a production studio that would serve as a farm system for television and off-screen opportunities. Although press coverage indicates no direct correlation between Comedy Central's early-2010s stagnation and the management changes, it is rife with what Caldwell, in his study of television production culture, calls "aesthetic status metaphors," or canned responses designed to highlight executives' abilities and trigger "favored cultural and psychological associations" among industry brethren.[22]

Alterman in particular has a habit of performing for press a type of persona one might expect from a comedian, but one that continually effaces his authority in an effort to subvert gender expectations. Of Posch's promotion as his second-in-command in 2014, for instance, Alterman quips that he's "just grateful [Posch]'s letting me be her boss."[23] Of Allison Kingsley's promotion to head of the digital studio, Alterman wryly concedes, "Allison uses techy words I don't understand, so I know she's the right person for the job."[24] Profiles of the executive repeatedly emphasize his sense of humor, implicitly legitimating his decisions both on-screen and off: "Spend time with Kent Alterman, and one can forget that he is not a comedian who appears on Comedy Central shows but rather the executive who programs them."[25]

These managerial moves, and the press discourses about them, also highlight how executive personnel at Comedy Central closely compete with one another for the capital to manage cultural production at the network. They do so by consciously constructing gendered discourses that seek to differentiate themselves from one another and Comedy Central from its competitors. Clearly, Alterman's deflection of authority is meant to assign creative and managerial agency to the women working beneath him. However, it does so in a way that draws attention to his comedic and, in some regard, more important executive voice than the managerial moves on which he is commenting. It is meant to be funny, for instance, that Brooke Posch would be Alterman's boss, and that Allison Kingsley "uses techy words," because both are unexpected inversions of gender norms in the television industry. Despite his progressive intentions, Alterman's lauding of his women colleagues underscores the extent to which men remain the presumed identity group both as executives and as onscreen talent in the world of television comedy.

Aesthetic status metaphors centered on gender pervade press about *Inside Amy Schumer* and *Broad City* as well. As I explore in the next section, incendiary humor from the perspective of women provide the basis for much of the programs' comedy. Although I do not wish to suggest that these shows' stars consciously follow a mandate from executives to engage gender identity in a post-politics way, I do wish to highlight how the programs' reflexive humor serves the network's expanded brand identity without alienating its core audience. The channel touts the many transgressions of its contentious comedies, as well as the diversity of its talent and audience, to contrast itself with the predominantly masculine makeup of competitors. Comedy Central's promotion and distribution strategies, however, ultimately constrain those transgressions, tethering them to the tastes of straight, young men.

"A Sort of Feminist Bent on a Male-skewing Network": Comedy Central's Gender Identities

In order to address the implications of Comedy Central's promotion and distribution of humor first from women comedians, a formal analysis of its programming is best integrated with a deeper understanding of the industrial discourses described above. Such dialogue between television economics and textual representations avoids characterizations of comedic programs as unified, coherent commodities and accounts for their processual, polysemic meanings. In other words, the key to understanding Comedy Central's move to a post-politics treatment of gender identities is to analyze closely both its programs and their industrial contexts. Reading *Broad City* and the sketch comedy *Inside Amy Schumer* solely as products of the network's rebrand neglects their potential for transgressive meanings that might undermine Comedy Central's economic strategy. In the same way, celebrating the programs as transgressive purely based on their comedic critiques ignores the extent to which *Broad City* and *Inside Amy Schumer* circulate as profit-seeking cultural products. The clearest picture of the significance of Comedy Central and its programs emerges only when we see their cultural and industrial contexts as mutually constitutive.

In this way, we can see how Comedy Central shows function as "programme brands" that "invite multiplicity, not just in their formal construction (for example, being made up of multiple segments that can be unbundled and/or transferred onto other products), but also in their address to viewers."[26] Although she uses the term in reference to programs with long-form narratives, Catherine Johnson's concept clearly points to sketch comedy's reflexive flexibility as well. All of the programs discussed below, for instance, use sketch's malleability for different purposes. Though neither is a sketch comedy per se, *Broad City* routinely integrates sketchy, non-sequitiur scenes into its sitcom narratives, and *Nathan for You*'s real-world stunts rely on recurring characters and absurd twists in often unconnected stories. More importantly, each program's modularity supports Comedy Central's mission to unbundle content and quickly push it out across media platforms.

This relationship between form and function puts Comedy Central and its talent in a tricky bind. On the one hand, the network develops shows with segments and sketches that it can easily excerpt from episodes and circulate beyond television. This content is often centered on incendiary humor about race, gender, or other edgy topics that can be empowering to marginalized comedians and viewers. On the other hand, Comedy Central's attempts to court young men via multiscreen viewing, and its jokingly gendered press discourses, ensure that the transgressions of its edgy content remain limited. The hegemonic pull of Comedy Central's promotional and distribution strategies constrain the critique of its programming, despite the shows' investment in satirizing television sketch comedy's politics of representation.

The *Inside Amy Schumer* sketch "Focus Group" (2014) for instance, openly toys with the gender identity politics of sketch comedy and their industrial implications. A nondescript boardroom full of young men gives feedback to a fictional executive about the show while its eponymous star looks on from behind a one-way mirror. The executive asks routine questions ("What do you think about the balance between sketches and stand-up?"), and various participants respond with crass remarks about Schumer's physique or their willingness to sleep with her. After several iterations of the gag, one participant interjects, "I like the routines where she was on the street talking to people, and I appreciated how it had a sort of feminist bent on a male-skewing network. But I must say I would enjoy the routines more if she had a ten percent better 'dumper,'" referring to Schumer's posterior. The focus group ends with the participants receiving payment in beef jerky and energy drinks, but not before we see Schumer behind the mirror with a look of incredulous delight that "a couple of them said they would 'bang' [her]."

Fig. 4.1. Amy Schumer reacts with sarcastic delight at the idea that Comedy Central's audience of young men finds her attractive.

The sketch satirizes a recurrent theme on the show and about Schumer—that her humor works for Comedy Central only insofar as the network's audience of men finds her attractive. Many *Inside* sketches like "Focus Group" similarly invert sexist assumptions about women in comedy—comedians who are men are rarely, if ever, judged first by their appearance the way women comedians are. Men are often the target of satire throughout the show, and gendered jokes function reflexively to critique Comedy Central's audience. The focus group member who briefly breaks from salivating over Schumer to note the "feminist bent" of the interview segments, for instance, highlights the gendered pleasures of television talk.[27]

Similarly, in the case of *Broad City*, idiosyncratic patter between cocreators and series stars Abbi Jacobson and Ilana Glazer underscores the blurry boundary between homosocial friendship and homosexual romance between the two. Jacobson and Glazer often refer to one another with masculine slang like "dude," but just as often decry and deconstruct the sexual or professional shortcomings of men on the show, reasserting their homosocial relationship as the series' driving narrative force. Press celebrate the representational tactics of Schumer, Jacobson, and Glazer as part of a golden age for women's comedy, with profiles highlighting how they foster a dialogic and nurturing creative environment in their respective writers' rooms.[28]

More often, however, publicity and promotion construct the comedians' femininity in a way that positions masculinity as a presumed norm for comedic performers and consumers, implicitly reaffirming patriarchal presumptions about comedy in the process. The home page for *Inside Amy Schumer* on the Comedy Central website, for instance, often features photos of a fully made-up Schumer dressed to accentuate her curvy physique. Thumbnails for episodes available to stream sample salacious sexual material, such as a line-up of bulbous women's buttocks for the sketch "Milk Milk Lemonade" (2015), rather than other sight gags. Elsewhere, one profile of Schumer notes as a matter of course in detailing her ascendance, "Bookers and producers quickly took notice of her long, blonde hair and all-American look."[29] Perhaps attempting to disavow gender as an evaluative criterion, reviewers reiterate that Comedy Central's women stars are "not gendered necessarily in their comedy, they're just funny," an observation that only serves to highlight the already-highly gendered nature of what we presume to be funny.[30] Similarly, a *New Yorker* profile of Jacobson and Glazer suggests that their popularity "seems to arise not only from the calibre of the comedy but also from the apparent authenticity of the women's affection for each other," positioning their gendered affection as extrinsic to high "calibre" comedy.[31] Ultimately, this tension between *Inside* and *Broad's* textual representations and extratextual publicity functions hegemonically, constructing appeals to women viewers in ways that affirm comedy's gendered hierarchies.

The ambivalence of Comedy Central's gender politics in sketch and elsewhere arises, in part, out of the broader context of "post-second-wave" feminism on contemporary cable television. Amanda Lotz's study of "contested" masculinities and gender identities in cable programs like *Breaking Bad* (2008–2013), *Dexter* (2006–2013), and *Men of a Certain Age* (2009–2013) suggests "it is cable's ability to derive commercial success by narrowcasting to smaller and specific audience niches that allowed these unconventional characters."[32] The contested femininities *of Inside Amy Schumer* and *Broad City*, however, indicate that narrowcasting to small audience niches may not be enough as competition for that same niche—young men—intensifies.

Comedy Central's post-politics turn represents an unconventional tweak to the type of narrowcasting Lotz describes, one that many cable competitors increasingly programming sketch comedy embrace in the post-network era. In some ways, it is taking the opposite tack of narrowcasting in its attempt to supplement a viewership of young men with women. In the hypercompetitive cable environment, Comedy Central is attempting to expand the boundaries of its audience of young men without alienating it, a dynamic borne out by ratings data and comments from executives. Alterman notes of Jacobson and Glazer, for instance, that he "saw with them an opportunity to expand our audience . . . but never at the expense of our core audience."[33] Posch, the woman executive responsible for shepherding the shows, similarly highlights the balancing act, noting that "Our ad buys are for men, so we can't lose them," but also touts Schumer's femininity: "Amy celebrates being a girl and being girly. Amy gets 50–50 male-female demos."[34] Similarly, *Inside Amy Schumer* writer Kurt Metzger notes that "It's a pretty even split of male and female viewers. I wanted to make it not, like, a 'chick show.'"[35] Stories elsewhere play up the woman stars' internet bona fides, stressing the authenticity of *Broad City*'s origins as a web series and touting the streaming numbers of advanced episodes of *Inside Amy Schumer* via the network's app.[36] In keeping with Comedy Central's rebrand, the programs' digital mobility implicitly constructs an audience of tech-savvy men whose attention incendiary sexual humor seeks to seize and refocus on television as the most important screen in the room.

Importantly, Lotz notes, the same hypercompetitive cable environment that fostered contested, post-politics gender identities also enables the production of programs "targeting audiences desiring unreconstructed, patriarchal masculinities."[37] Indeed, Comedy Central's primetime schedule has long showcased heteronormative masculinities; but in attempting to broaden its appeal to women, Comedy Central is essentially trying to have it both ways—that is, showing both men and women in a position of comedic, cultural power. This tension is why it remains crucial to consider the industrial context of comedic programming, particularly sketch, as the format most amenable to post-network practices of mobility across media. From this broader perspective, *Inside Amy Schumer* and *Broad City* lampoon the network's tradition of targeting men, but through their industrial circulation, the shows revalue that very demographic. Comedy Central's post-politics identity work is not limited to gender, however, as I explore in the next section.

"Remember, You're a Gangster!": Racial and Ethnic Identities on Comedy Central

In much the same way that *Schumer* contests comedic representations of gender, so too have *Key & Peele*, *Kroll Show*, and *Nathan for You* served as sites of struggle over cultural constructions of race and ethnicity. As biracial actors, eponymous stars Keegan-Michael Key and Jordan Peele have used sketch comedy's reflexive flexibility to explore a broader range of racial identities than perhaps any other comedians of the post-network era. In *Key & Peele*'s sketch "Thug English Actor" (2013), for instance, the duo portrays gangsters with guns pointed at each other in a gritty urban setting. They use African American slang to trade violent threats as the scene builds to a climax before an off-screen voice yells "Cut!" The scene's director, played by Colin Hanks (an actor known for roles as a vanilla everyman), compliments the performance of Key's character Nigel, who acknowledges with an English accent the joy of playing "an American tough." The director then notes to Peele's character Antoine that he does not "buy" his performance as a black Brooklyn native, an insult to which Antoine replies with a list of his criminal credentials. The scene escalates through several iterations of the gag, with the director exaggeratedly complimenting Nigel's affected urban patois. "Antoine, remember, you're a gangster!" Hanks's director shouts in urging an increasingly incredulous Antoine to "transform" into something he already is. Even after Antoine physically assaults him with genuine rage, the director still tells the actor, "I just . . . I don't believe you."

"Thug English Actor" debates the existence of authentic blackness, but the sketch—like many on *Key & Peele*—satirizes more directly the television industry's pursuit of black as a coherent, fully formed identity and demographic category. In a broad sense, Hanks's clueless director is a stand-in for above-the-line media personnel urging African American performers to "black it up."[38] The sketch reflexively satirizes this industrial discourse, suggesting that it is a commercially motivated construction that privileges performances confoming to prevailing, hegemonic ideas about race. One of *Key & Peele*'s preferred tactics is to explore the tension of racial signifiers in genre parodies where they might not be expected—black characters in predominantly white genres like science fiction and fantasy, for instance. Another common theme of their sketches is the use of racial signifiers like cuisine, athletic prowess, or names (as in the "East/West College Bowl" sketches, [2012, 2013]) to invert assumptions about race-based identities.

In the sketch "Substitute Teacher" (2013), for instance, the eponymous teacher—played by an exasperated and stern-looking Key—enters a high school classroom, declares that he has "taught school for 20 years in the inner city," and begins to take roll. "Jay-KWEL-un. Where's Jay-KWEL-un at? No Jay-KWEL-un here?" he asks. A white teenaged girl tentatively raises her hand: "Uh, do you mean 'Jacqueline?'" The sketch proceeds through another iteration of the joke before escalating to the following exchange between Key's Mr. Garvey and another white girl student:

Mr. Garvey: "Dee-Nice." Is there a "Dee-Nice?" If one of y'all says some silly ass name, this whole class is gonna feel my wrath. Now, "Dee-Nice!"

[Denise, a white, girl student, hesitantly raises her hand.]

Denise: Do you mean "Denise?"

[Mr. Garvey furiously breaks the clipboard over his knee.]

Mr. Garvey: Son of a bitch! You say the name right, right now.

Denise: "Denise?"

Mr. Garvey: Say it right.

Denise: "Denise."

Mr. Garvey: Correctly.

Denise: "Denise."

Mr. Garvey: Right.

Denise: "Denise."

Mr. Garvey: Right.

Denise: "Dee-Nice."

[Mr. Garvey gives a sarcastic, exaggerated bow.]

Mr. Garvey: That's better. Thank you.

The sketch's flexible identity play offers at least two plausible readings. One highlights an otherness of black culture, as the exaggeratedly silly mispronunciations from Mr. Garvey differentiate him from the normative expectations of his white students (and viewers), making him the butt of the joke. An alternative reading, conversely, interrogates the inequality of power between the black and white creators and consumers of sketch comedy. In this reading, the sketch mines name mispronunciation for laughs as a way to understand the constructed, artificial nature of racial hierarchy. The black Mr. Garvey is supposed to know and utilize the "correct" pronunciation of names assumed by his white students. After all, these are "normal" names in American culture, to be contrasted with more ethnically or racially marked names whose mispronunciation by a white teacher would be excusable. By not abiding by these assumed rules, the sketch, in

Fig. 4.2. Keegan-Michael Key toys with racist assumptions about names in the *Key & Peele* sketch "Substitute Teacher."

this latter reading, confronts viewers with the arbitrary way something as innocuous as a name can create and reinforce race-based power differentials. It shows us that the naming and pronunciation norms of the dominant, largely white American culture are not natural or eternal. The sketch's humor in this reading, then, comes from making this assumed, implicitly white norm explicit and, in doing so, it asks Comedy Central's desired white audience to grapple with this possibility.

Undoubtedly, *Key & Peele* is critical of dominant racial power in their sketches again and again, just as *Schumer* continuously calls attention to gendered power differentials. And it's entirely possible—perhaps even likely—that audiences might understand simultaneous, conflicting meanings of a sketch, or that they might even process it with a range of readings other than the ones discussed above. When considering *Key & Peele*'s critiques of race-based power differentials in the context of Comedy Central's broader industrial imperatives, though, these critiques become less salient. As Herman Gray describes in his study of *In Living Color*, racial jokes in the sketch comedy negotiate two competing tensions, both perpetuating and critiquing race-based social hierarchies, resulting in a politics of representation that is fundamentally ambivalent. For some, Gray says, the ambivalence of race-based humor "contests hegemonic assumptions and representations of race in general and blacks in particular in the American social order; for others, it simply perpetuates troubling images of blacks."[39] Sketch comedy's reflexive flexibility similarly cuts both ways—empowering both comedians from marginal identity groups to voice cultural critiques and television networks to channel those critiques toward profitable ends.

Despite its clearly critical edge, the ultimate ambivalence of *Key & Peele*'s humor is due in no small part to Comedy Central's efforts to make race, gender, sketch comedy, and politics accessible in the same field of cultural mash-ups made possible by multiplatform viewing environments. The network's distribution and promotional strategies undermine *Key & Peele*'s critique of racial representation, making it merely a signifier of humor like so many other readily available jokes and products from the network. Interstitial advertisements on the show, in press, and on the Comedy Central website direct viewers to purchase football jerseys based on the recurring "East/West College Bowl" sketches, tout the program's multiplatform mobility, and urge viewers to seek out the duo's spin-off web series, *Vandaveon and Mike* (2012).

Network and creative personnel on the show tout *Key & Peele*'s internet presence (not unlike the dynamic described above with *Broad City*), going so far as to place the sketch comedy's television home on equal footing with its circulation online. As former Comedy Central president Michele Ganeless recalls: "I remember the show really blowing up online. The ad campaign we did for season three was literally Keegan and Jordan doing a video for YouTube, saying, "Hey, this is a TV show!" People discovered that show in its pieces, and then came back to watch it on linear TV."[40] Similarly, cocreator and star Jordan Peele says: "It's the full realization of the fact that in some ways we are more of an internet show than we are a television show. We were sort of the first of our kind and straddled both, and now that every single sketch is online, we've done this interesting culmination that I think is really cool."[41] In other promotional discourses, Alterman (as is his wont in commenting on gender and women performers) jokingly foregrounds the duo's race in interviews, encoding it as a light object of humor and neutralizing it as a possible point of contention. Of *Key & Peele*'s second season renewal, he quips, "I was worried if we didn't give the show a quick pick up, people might accuse me of being racist."[42] By rearticulating racial referents in the service of publicity and distribution practices, these industrial discourses constrain the critical potential of *Key & Peele*'s humor.

Kroll Show and *Nathan for You* similarly also use racial/ethnic and gendered humor to critique white, heteronormative masculinity. Like *Key &*

Peele, *Kroll*, and *Nathan* revel in parodies of genres—the woman-targeted lifestyle reality shows of Bravo, the working-class reality dating competitions of VH1, and the makeover programming of myriad home- and cooking-focused outlets—that are normally beyond the habitus of Comedy Central's core audience. *Kroll*, for instance, manically maneuvers among semiconnected sketches that see the eponymous star portraying, among others, a boisterous Latino disc jockey, a vapid animal plastic surgeon, an officiously entitled scenester, and an uncouth teenager of undetermined ethnicity. The recurring characters most engaged in deconstructing representational norms, though, are the ditzy publicist Liz and gigolo Bobby Bottleservice, around whom Nick Kroll constructs a deep storyworld that satirizes Hollywood fame-mongering.

Nathan for You similarly contests white heternormativity through having star Nathan Fielder—a stiff, staid business expert—awkwardly enact real business makeover scenarios with working-class people who are often nonwhite. In the sketch "Focus Group" (2014), Fielder seeks feedback about why his personality as host rubs would-be guests the wrong way. He assembles a group composed of many of the demographics Comedy Central strives to court—women, black, Asian, Hispanic, and "old." The panelists speak into Fielder's earpiece while he's shooting, urging him to smile or acknowledge the camera more. The bit builds to Fielder getting a makeover to resemble reality hosts like *Diners, Drive-ins and Dives*' (2007–present) Guy Fieri or the *Property Brothers*' (2011–present) Scott twins, complete with hair gel, trendy clothing, and exaggerated displays of masculinity. In the sketch's resolution, however, Fielder tests his new look with a former client who chastises his facile attempt at manliness, further highlighting the contested nature of race and gender identity within sketch comedy.

Although *Kroll Show* and *Nathan for You* rarely address ethnicity explicitly, their representational strategies are grounded in the Jewish heritages of their stars. As Vincent Brook notes, Jewish television comedians have a long history of effacing explicit ethnic markers in order to align with mainstream conceptions of hegemonic whiteness.[43] This flexibility provides Fielder and Kroll room to perform myriad identities, often explicitly critiquing their industrial circulation in sketches like "Focus Group," "PubLIZity," and "Gigolo House." Yet, the economic imperatives of contemporary cable television and digital convergence consistently circumscribe the potential of the programs' cultural critiques. Comedy Central reduces Kroll's characters in promotions online and via the network's app to seconds-long catchphrases—Liz's nasally "Ameeezing!"; Bobby's idiosyncratic repetition of "Very much . . ."—and removes their critiques from much-needed context. As promotional mechanisms, the catchphrases circulate as incendiary, gendered caricatures designed for fleeting consumption by a presumed audience of men in a distracted, multiscreen viewing environment. Promotion for Fielder has similarly eschewed the show's ambivalent address to men and played up its sexualized or hashtag-worthy stunts. The season one finale saw Fielder threatening to expose himself to children, while publicity for the "Dumb Starbucks" (2014) stunt strove to rise above the social media din and drive a viewership of men to the Comedy Central app. Both *Nathan for You* and *Kroll Show*, despite the contested nature of their racial/ethnic and gendered representations, ultimately circulate as comedic signifiers aiming to seize and retain the attention of Comedy Central's core audience of straight, young, white men.

Conclusion

It is no accident that cable networks like Comedy Central, IFC, and TBS seeking to distinguish themselves from competition are increasingly turning to sketch comedy. The format is often cheap to develop, ideal for post-network practices of differentiation and branding, attractive to performers prone to experimentation, and amenable to the drawing of clearly identifiable boundaries around a desired audience. Both culturally and industrially, sketch comedy in the post-network era can serve as a powerful marker of difference, to paraphrase Medhurst, "a prime testing ground for ideas about belonging and exclusion."[44] *Inside Amy Schumer, Broad City, Kroll Show, Nathan for You*, and *Key & Peele* all serve as testing grounds for how many different performers and viewers place themselves among hierarchies of cultural power. Humor has traditionally aimed to laugh up at those in positions of power, a crucial, ongoing function of comedy in American culture. However, as comedic referents multiply and compete for our attention, the temptation exists to overlook how they are anchored in specific technological and industrial contexts, to see only fleetingly that much comedic content appears to make fun of everything equally.

Of course, characterizing the identity work of the shows discussed in this chapter as "post-politics" risks reproducing the same false progress narrative as accounts of comedy that "makes fun of everything equally" or engages in any pluralist conception of "post-"ness, for that matter. Instead, as I have argued, comedic television's recent proliferation and expansion across digital platforms further stratifies the power relations among its new and diverse audiences. In the case of Comedy Central's sketch shows, this dynamic can and often does give voice to identity groups peripheral to its core economic imperatives. Just as often, however, those voices serve as "nonhegemonic poses" for the network to test the boundaries of its core.[45]

By no means must sketch comedy in the post-network era always serve the hegemonic purposes I have described in this chapter. Comedy Central's use of it is likely a hedge by the old media cable channel as it grapples with the emergent industrial practices of digital convergence. As the distribution and promotional practices of television and/as digital media continue to evolve, sketch comedy will undoubtedly continue to play a role in shaping them. In doing so, the format's flexible identity politics can incorporate more and different representations of who belongs and who does not.

Notes

1. Ess, "Nick Kroll Talks 'Kroll Show' Season 2 with Seth Meyers."
2. Caldwell, "Cultures of Production," 200.
3. Lotz, *The Television Will Be Revolutionized*, 16–19.
4. Stu Smiley, author interview, September 22, 2011.
5. Art Bell, author interview, September 26, 2011.
6. Bell quoted in Seabaugh, "*Night after Night* to *@midnight*: An Oral History of Comedy Central (Part 1)."
7. Ganeless quoted in Seabaugh, "*Night after Night* to *@midnight*: An Oral History of Comedy Central (Part 1)."
8. Boone, "The Origin and Early Programs of Comedy Central."
9. Bell, author interview, September 26, 2011.
10. Weprin, "Comedy Central Bets Big on Web Development."
11. Dawson, "Little Players, Big Shows," 231–250.
12. Caldwell, "Convergence Television," 41–74.
13. Gelt, "Comedy Central Renews 'Tosh.o' for Three Seasons."
14. Stelter, "Comedy Central Still Strong at 20."
15. See Kiffer Keegan; Jaeger, "In-depth: Comedy Central Re-brand."
16. See Jaeger, 2011.
17. Sienkiewicz and Marx, "Click Culture."
18. Gorman, "Comedy Central Ends 2011 as the #1 Entertainment Network in Cable among Men 18–34 and 18–24."
19. Hamilton, "U.S. Cable Networks: What Do Males Want? Content? Or Entertainment? Who's Delivering Which?"
20. Chozik, "A Comedy Show That Comes via a Hashtag"; Vranica and Jannarone, "Viacom Loads More Ads on Channels."

21. Morgan, "What's Wrong with Comedy Central?"
22. Caldwell, *Production Culture*, 205.
23. Alterman quoted in Andreeva, "Brooke Posch Upped to SVP Original Programming at Comedy Central."
24. Alterman quoted in O'Connell, "Comedy Central Launches Digital Production Studio, Taps Allison Kingsley as VP."
25. Quoted in Rose, "Comedy Central's Kent Alterman on Leno, Rape Jokes and a Jon Stewart-Free 'Daily Show.'"
26. Johnson, *Branding Television*, 165.
27. Fiske, *Television Culture*, 183; Shattuc, *The Talking Cure*, 1–12.
28. Stewart, "Amy Schumer and the Women of *Broad City*: Paving the Way for a Female 'Golden Age'"; and Zinoman, "Amy Schumer, Funny Girl."
29. Quoted in Seabaugh, "*Variety*'s 2014 Breakthrough in Comedy Winner: Amy Schumer."
30. Quoted in Greenwald, "The Andy Greenwald Podcast: Comedy Central Programming Head Kent Alterman."
31. Quoted in Paumgarten, "Id Girls."
32. Lotz, *Cable Guys*, 32.
33. Alterman quoted in Greenwald, "The Andy Greenwald Podcast: Comedy Central Programming Head Kent Alterman."
34. Posch quoted in Zinoman, "Amy Schumer, Funny Girl."
35. Metzger quoted in Seabaugh, "*Night after Night* to *@midnight*: An Oral History of Comedy Central (Part 3)."
36. Berkowitz, "How the Creators of *Broad City* Turned Their Web Series into a TV Show"; Petski, "*Inside Amy Schumer* Renewed for Fifth Season on Comedy Central—TCA."
37. Lotz, *Cable Guys*, 32.
38. Racquel Gates uses this term in reference to both the explicit mandates and implicit pressures from *Saturday Night Live* executives on Eddie Murphy to conform to a prevailing notion of blackness for the show. See Gates, "Bringing the Black: Eddie Murphy and African American Humor on *Saturday Night Live*."
39. Gray, *Watching Race*, 130.
40. Ganeless quoted in Seabaugh, "*Night after Night* to *@midnight*: An Oral History of Comedy Central (Part 1)."
41. Peele quoted in Seabaugh, "*Night after Night* to *@midnight*: An Oral History of Comedy Central (Part 2)."
42. Weisman, "Comedy Central Renews 'Key.'"
43. Brook, *Something Ain't Kosher Here*, 1–22.
44. Medhurst, *A National Joke*, 39.
45. Elkins, "Cultural Identity and Subcultural Forums," 607.

CONCLUSION
Sketch Comedy and Cultural Cohesion

I BEGAN THIS BOOK BY DISCUSSING EXAMPLES FROM *Saturday Night Live* that highlighted sketch comedy's reflexive flexibility as it relates to identities centered in and around political discourse. The popularity of that show, perhaps more so than any other scripted entertainment program on television, tends to rise and fall according to the electoral cycles of American politics. Undoubtedly, the identities created and exploited by *SNL*'s anti-Trump turn were at least partially a product of their coming on the heels of his contentious campaign and election. In any other era, interest in and ratings for the show precipitously fall off soon after an election. In the case of *SNL*'s 2016–2017 season, however, the show sustained its highest levels of viewership in 23 years.[1] *SNL* responded to the mounting success of its postelection season with a revolutionary (for the show) idea in support of national unity: starting in April 2017, *SNL* broadcast live coast to coast, without the customary delays for NBC's affiliates in the mountain and Pacific time zones. *SNL*'s success aligned with surprising viewership upticks elsewhere on television, particularly cable news, regardless of the network's political ideology. "Despite a dizzying array of new media choices," the *New York Times* observed, "viewers are opting for television's mass gathering spots, seeking the kind of shared experience that can validate and reassure."[2]

On their surface, these trends would seem to undermine the arguments and historical trajectories I have been developing over the course of this book—that sketch comedy's reflexive flexibility has arisen out of, mirrored, and even facilitated the gradual fragmentation of American television and culture over the last several decades. Considered in a different light, however, I would offer them as evidence of what happens once the edges of those fragments have dulled. Indeed, looming in the background of this book's focus on flexible identity work is its constitutive other, a sort of cultural coagulation. If networks, comedians, and viewers turn to sketch comedy to differentiate from one another, so too do they use it to cohere once again and express something—anything—collectively. This is not to say, of course, that the recent political past has reversed decades of balkanizing efforts on the part of American commercial media industries. It is only to suggest that one result of sketch comedy's many struggles over cultural identities and social power might be unification in places we least expect it.

And yet, this book's broad understanding of sketch comedy as a site of struggle over the resources for identity formation might be missing more elemental—and possibly more important—functions of the format. Elsewhere, Matt Sienkiewicz and I have traced the recent history of comedy scholarship as a reflection both of the proliferation of political humor across media and of the maturation of comedy studies as a subfield within the academic discipline of media studies.[3] For better or for worse, this book is certainly a product of both trends. At the same time, we suggest, a focus on comedy's identity politics might be overlooking questions "about the aesthetics of comedy, comedy's relationship to the lived experiences of modern society, and even comedy's ability to address the joys and terrors of being a solitary human being in a vast, complex, and often deeply confusing universe."[4] In other words, might sketch comedy's power to unify us lie in something much simpler, a universalizing quality that speaks to all human beings, regardless of one's identity or political affiliation?

To answer this question, we might turn one final time to an example of sketch comedy's reflexive flexibility, its self-obsession and/about its malleability and modularity. In an *SNL* sketch called "Darrell's House" (2013), host Zach Galifianakis plays Darrell, an awkward, easily flustered cable access talk show personality. Darrell stands in his living room and directly addresses the camera with top-of-show small-talk—"Hi! Hello! I'm Darrell, this is the first time I'm having house over to my people." With every mistake, though, Darrell glances off-camera and asks an unseen producer to make specific edits—"Cut that . . . I want a shot of snacks there, okay?" The sketch proceeds through several iterations of the gag, including having black cast member Keenan Thompson stand in for white actor Jon Hamm, who Darrell intends to insert later on. The sketch quickens the pace of Darrell's flubs and the absurdity of his requests to the producer to fix them before it ends on the same cheap cable access–style title sequence with which it began.

"Darrell's House" is an amusing spin on Galifiankis's host character from the Funny or Die mock talk show and internet series *Between Two Ferns* (2008–present), one that parodies analogue aesthetics and

Fig. 5.1. The *SNL* sketches "Darrell's House" toy with televisual conventions and point to the constructed nature of cultural meanings.

sycophantic talk show banter through absurd non sequiturs and sight gags. The sketch's full significance wouldn't come until later in the very same episode, when *SNL* ran "Darrell's House" again, this time with all of his requested edits—snacks inserted on an empty platter, Hamm awkwardly replacing Thompson, and so forth—from the earlier live sketch. In doing so, the two "Darrell's House" sketches laid bare just about every one of *SNL*'s longstanding aesthetic and industrial conventions, reinserting a "sense of live-television danger" into the show.[5]

Though certainly not centered on cultural identity in the same way I have discussed in this book, "Darrell's House" displays reflexive flexibility in several ways. Most obviously, the sketches poke fun at how fungible televisual meanings can be with even modest manipulation of their conditions of production. That this central comedic premise is grounded in the guise of a cable access show is perhaps meant to funnel *SNL* viewers' admiration toward the behind-the-scenes crew members savvy enough to pull that premise off, ones such as editor/director Oz Rodriguez, who made the "Darrell's House" edits in less than half an hour in the middle of a live broadcast. The sketches certainly demonstrate sketch comedy's formal malleability too, one combining both the semi-improvisational performance of Galifianakis with the formal experimentation that has long been a hallmark of post–"Weekend Update" sketches. Finally, the sketches highlight both the intratextual and cross-media modularity of sketch comedy, as the "Darrell's House" bits recurred both within that evening's episode and across digital platforms in the following days.

It seems silly to call any of these meanings "dangerous," but I would suggest that their superficial silliness belies a much more potentially galvanizing idea: that there is an inherent artifice to all cultural activities and the everyday lived experiences of which they are a part. In other words, sketches like "Darrell's House" offer—in a very small way—a reminder to us that there is nothing natural or eternal in television and culture, especially not in a constantly shape-shifting format like sketch comedy. In doing so, sketch comedy offers us a sort of postmodern media literacy, an instruction manual for how to assemble meanings, representations, and identities out of the myriad cultural fragments increasingly cluttering our collective consciousness. That we tend to quickly disassemble these pieces for a variety of personal and political purposes makes their fleeting concatenation no less salient.

Speaking personally, my attraction to sketch comedy both as a fan and scholar is rooted in its ability to declare differences based in identity. However, I would be lying if I did not admit that the genre has given me just as many experiences of joyful unity with others wholly unlike me. Sketch comedy's flexible identity work often gives me pleasure that I keep private, but its ability to bring me close to others engages me on a much bigger emotional and intellectual scale. The more I meet and discuss sketch comedy television with students, friends, colleagues, family, and even strangers, the more I suspect that the genre taps into a similar push and pull of atomization and collectivization for them too.

My analyses throughout this book bear this suspicion out, even if only implicitly, again and again. More than any other genre or performative mode, sketch comedy seems to take on extra special importance to those involved at the specific terminals of creation and consumption. It can articulate a specific kind of worldview or assert a sense of self where other cultural discourses fall short. Indeed, part of what attracts many producers and performers to sketch comedy is the sense that other cultural expressions are inadequate to capture their voices. As those voices multiply, and as they do so through sketch comedy, continued consideration of the myriad forces bearing on their creation will hopefully bring us together just as often as they keep us apart.

Notes

1. Rose, "*SNL*'s Yuuuge Year."
2. Grynbaum and Koblin, "For Solace and Solidarity in the Trump Age, Liberals Turn the TV Back On."
3. Marx and Sienkiewicz, "Volume Introduction: Comedy as Theory, Industry, and Academic Discipline," 11–15.
4. Ibid., 14.
5. Voss, "Is 'Saturday Night Live' Becoming 'Saturday Night Pretaped'?"

BIBLIOGRAPHY

Acham, Christine. *Revolution Televised: Prime Time and the Struggle for Black Power.* Minneapolis: University of Minnesota Press, 2004.
Adorno, Theodor W. "Culture Industry Reconsidered." In *The Culture Industry: Selected Essays on Mass Culture*, edited by J. M. Bernstein, 98–106. London: Routledge, 1991.
Agee, James. "Comedy's Greatest Era." *Life*, September 1949.
Allen, Robert C. *Horrible Prettiness: Burlesque and American Culture.* Chapel Hill: University of North Carolina Press, 1991.
Althusser, Louis. *Lenin and Philosophy and Other Essays.* New York: Monthly Review, 1971.
Anderson, Christopher. *Hollywood TV: The Studio System in the Fifties.* Austin: University of Texas Press, 1994.
Anderson, Christopher, and Michael Curtin. "Writing Cultural History: The Challenge of Radio and Television." In *Media History: Theories, Methods and Analysis*, edited by Niels Brügger and Søren Kolstrup, 15–32. Aarhus, Denmark: Aarhus University Press, 2001.
Andreeva, Nellie. "Brooke Posch Upped to SVP Original Programming at Comedy Central." *Deadline Hollywood*, February 27, 2014. http://www.deadline.com/2014/02/brooke-posch-upped-to-svp-original-programming-at-comedy-central/.
Balio, Tino. "'A Major Presence in All of the World's Important Markets': The Globalization of Hollywood in the 1990s." In *Contemporary Hollywood Cinema*, edited by Steve Neale and Murray Smith, 58–73. London: Routledge, 1998.
Banet-Weiser, Sarah. *Kids Rule! Nickelodeon and Consumer Citizenship.* Durham, NC, and London: Duke University Press, 2007.
Barnum, Pete. "Interdepartment Correspondence to Sam Fuller: *Colgate Comedy Hour*, February 2, 1954." Unpublished archival document, Sam Fuller Files, Box 380, Folder 31, NBC Archives, Wisconsin Center for Film and Theater Research, Wisconsin Historical Society.
Bauder, David. "Lack of Black Women on 'Saturday Night Live' Becomes Major Issue." *Huffington Post*, November 3, 2013. https://www.huffingtonpost.com/2013/11/03/snl-black-women_n_4208192.html.
Baumgartner, Jody, and Jonathan S. Morris. "*The Daily Show* Effect: Candidate Evaluations Efficacy, and American Youth." *American Politics Research* 34, no. 3 (2006): 341–367.
Baym, Geoffrey. "*The Daily Show*: Discursive Integration and the Reinvention of Political Journalism." *Political Communication* 22, no. 3 (2005): 259–276.
Becker, Ron. *Gay TV and Straight America.* New Brunswick, NJ: Rutgers University Press, 2006.
Berardinelli, James. "Step Brothers." *ReelViews*, July 2008. http://www.reelviews.net/php_review_template.php?identifier=1258.
Berkowitz, Joe. "How the Creators of *Broad City* Turned Their Web Series into a TV Show." *Fast Company*, February 5, 2014. https://www.fastcompany.com/3025672/how-the-creators-of-broad-city-turned-their-web-series-into-a-tv-show.

Bernstein, Aaron, with David Woodruff, Barbara Buell, Nancy Peacock, and Karen Thurston. "What Happened to the American Dream?" *Business Week*, August 19, 1991. http://www.businessweek.com/archives/1991/b322758.arc.htm.

Berry, Richard. "Will the iPod Kill the Radio Star? Profiling Podcasting as Radio." *Convergence* 12, no. 2 (2006): 143–162.

Best, Steven, and Douglas Kellner. "Beavis and Butt-Head: No Future for Postmodern Youth." In *Youth Culture: Identity in a Postmodern World*, edited by Jonathan S. Epstein, 74–99. Malden, MA: Blackwell, 1998.

Bodroghkozy, Aniko. *Groove Tube: Sixties Television and the Youth Rebellion*. Durham, NC, and London: Duke University Press, 2001.

———. "*The Smothers Brothers Comedy Hour* and the Youth Rebellion." In *The Revolution Wasn't Televised: Sixties Television and Social Conflict*, edited by Lynn Spigel and Michael Curtin, 201–220. New York: Routledge, 1997.

Bogle, Charles. "*Date Night* and *City Island*: One Comedy That Knows Where It's Going, Another That Can't Seem to Decide." *World Socialist Web Site*, June 10, 2010. http://www.wsws.org/articles/2010/jun2010/date-j10.shtml.

Bogle, Donald. *Toms, Coons, Mulattoes, Mammies, and Bucks: An Interpretive History of Blacks in American Films*. New York and London: Continuum, 1973.

Bond, Julian. "Civil Rights Leader Julian Bond's *SNL* Hosting Regret (Guest Column)." *Hollywood Reporter*, January 15, 2014. https://www.hollywoodreporter.com/news/snl-civil-rights-leader-julian-671054.

Boone, Brian. "The Origin and Early Programs of Comedy Central." *Splitsider*, January 11, 2012. http://splitsider.com/2012/01/the-origin-and-early-programs-of-comedy-central/.

Bordwell, David, Janet Staiger, and Kristin Thompson. *The Classical Hollywood Cinema: Film Style and Mode of Production to 1960*. New York: Columbia University Press, 1985.

Bourdieu, Pierre. *Distinction: A Social Critique of the Judgment of Taste*. Translated by Richard Nice. Cambridge, MA: Harvard University Press, 1987.

———. *The Field of Cultural Production*. Columbia, NY: Columbia University Press, 1993.

———. *The Rules of Art: Genesis and Structure of the Literary Field*. Translated by Susan Emanuel. Stanford, CA: Stanford University Press, 1996.

Brodie, John. "MTV Expands Horizon: In-house Unit to Delve into Films, Network TV." *Daily Variety*, May 4, 1993.

Brook, Vincent. *Something Ain't Kosher Here: The Rise of the "Jewish" Sitcom*. New Brunswick, NJ: Rutgers University Press, 2003.

Burgess, Jean, and Joshua Green. *YouTube: Online Video and Participatory Culture*. Cambridge, UK: Polity, 2010.

Burns, John. "Popular Music, Television, and Generational Identity." *Journal of Popular Culture* 30, no. 3 (1996): 129–141.

Burr, Ty. "Will Ferrell Is the Ultimate Blow-dried Blowhard in the Silly, Spotty 'Anchorman.'" *Boston Globe*, July 9, 2004. http://www.boston.com/movies/display?display=movie&id=4492.

Busis, Hillary. "'Saturday Night Live': Each Season's Best Sketch." *Entertainment Weekly*, August 4, 2017. http://ew.com/article/2014/09/24/saturday-night-live-best-sketches/.

Caldwell, John Thornton. "Convergence Television: Aggregating Form and Repurposing Content in the Culture of Conglomeration." In *Television after TV: Essays on a Medium in Transition*, edited by Lynn Spigel and Jan Olsson, 41–74. Durham, NC: Duke University Press, 2004.

———. "Cultures of Production: Studying Industry's Deep Texts, Reflexive Rituals, and Managed Self-disclosures." In *Media Industries: History, Theory, and Method*, edited by Jennifer Holt and Alisa Perren, 199–212. Malden, MA: Wiley Blackwell, 2009.
———. *Production Culture: Industrial Reflexivity and Critical Practice in Film and Television*. Durham, NC: Duke University Press, 2007.
———. *Televisuality: Style, Crisis, and Authority in American Television*. New Brunswick, NJ: Rutgers University Press, 1995.
Carter, Bill. "In the Tastes of Young Men, Humor Is Most Prized, a Survey Finds." *New York Times*, February 19, 2012. http://www.nytimes.com/2012/02/20/business/media/comedy-central-survey-says-young-men-see-humor-as-essential.html.
Chorba, Frank J. "Ernie Kovacs." In *The Encyclopedia of Television*, edited by Horace Newcomb, 1285–1287. New York: Routledge, 2013.
Chozik, Amy. "A Comedy Show That Comes via a Hashtag." *New York Times*, April 21, 2013. http://www.nytimes.com/2013/04/22/business/comedy-central-to-host-comedy-festival-on-twitter.html?pagewanted=all.
Claessens, Nathalie, and Alexander Dhoest. "Comedy Taste: Highbrow/Lowbrow Comedy and Cultural Capital." *Participations* 7, no. 1 (2010): 49–72.
Clifford, Stephanie. "The Funny Side of What Can Go Wrong at the Big Meeting." *New York Times*, March 17, 2010. http://www.nytimes.com/2010/03/18/business/media/18adco.html?adxnnl=1&adxnnlx=1269190937-q+cxnqo//I4YuO570OucVw.
Cogan, Brian. *Deconstructing South Park: Critical Examinations of Animated Transgression*. Lanham, MD: Lexington Books, 2011.
Connelly, Sherryl. "'Comedy at the Edge' Looks at '70s Standup Explosion." *New York Daily News*, January 13, 2008. http://www.nydailynews.com/entertainment/music-arts/comedy-edge-70s-standup-explosion-article-1.345455.
Cortez, John P., and Alice Z. Cuneo. "Taco Bell Logs Odd Hours to Lure Xers in New Ads." *Advertising Age*, May 10, 1993.
Cotton, Jen, Andrei Kallaur, Margaret Lyons, and Josh Wolk. "See Vulture's Map of the Comedy Zeitgeist." *Vulture*, April 30, 2012. http://www.vulture.com/2012/04/comedy-zeitgeist-map-apatow-stiller.html.
Coupland, Douglas. *Generation X: Tales for an Accelerated Generation*. New York: St. Martin's Press, 1991.
Crafton, Donald. "Pie and Chase: Gag, Spectacle and Narrative in Slapstick Comedy." *Classical Hollywood Comedy*, edited by Kristine Brunovska Karnick and Henry Jenkins, 106–199. New York: Routledge, 1995.
Curtin, Michael. "Matrix Media." In *Television after "TV": Understanding Television in the Post-Broadcast Era*, edited by Graeme Turner, 9–19. London: Routledge, 2009.
———. "On Edge: Culture Industries in the Neo-Network Era." In *Making and Selling Culture*, edited by Richard Ohmann, Gage Averill, Michael Curtin, David Shumway, and Elizabeth Traube, 181–202. Hanover, CT: Wesleyan University Press, 1996.
Curtin, Michael, and Thomas Streeter. "Media." In *Culture Works: Essays on the Political Economy of Culture*, edited by Rick Maxwell, 225–250. Minneapolis: University of Minnesota Press, 2001.
D'Acci, Julie. "Cultural Studies, Television Studies, and the Crisis in the Humanities." In *Television after TV: Essays on a Medium in Transition*, edited by Michael Curtin, Lynn Spigel, and Jan Olsson, 418–445. Durham, NC, and London: Duke University Press, 2004.

"DATELINE 4.07." *Mediaweek*, April 7, 2008, 3.

Dawson, Max. "Little Players, Big Shows: Format, Narration, and Style on Television's New Smaller Screens." *Convergence* 13, no. 3 (2007): 231–250.

Deveau, Danielle Jeanine. *English Canadian Stand-Up Comedy as a Field of Cultural Production*, PhD dissertation, Simon Fraser University, 2012.

Dominus, Susan. "Can Kristen Wiig Turn On the Charm?" *New York Times*, April 28, 2011. https://www.nytimes.com/2011/05/01/magazine/mag-01wiig-t.html.

Donaton, Scott, and Glenn Levin. "The Media Wakes Up to Generation X." *Advertising Age*, February 1, 1993.

Douglass, James C. "Letter to Sam Fuller, March 2, 1955." Unpublished archival document, Sam Fuller Files, Box 380, Folder 28, NBC Archives, Wisconsin Center for Film and Theater Research, Wisconsin Historical Society.

Drake, Philip. "Low Blows?: Theorizing Performance in Post-Classical Comedian Comedy." In *Hollywood Comedians: The Film Reader*, edited by Frank Krutnik, 187–198. London and New York: Routledge, 2003.

Dunn, William. "Hanging Out with American Youth." *American Demographics* 12, no. 2 (1992): 24.

Elkins, Evan. "Cultural Identity and Subcultural Forums: The Post-network Politics of Adult Swim." *Television & New Media* 15, no. 7 (2014): 595–610.

Epstein, Jonathon S. "Introduction: Generation X, Youth Culture, and Identity." In *Youth Culture: Identity in a Postmodern World*, edited by Jonathan S. Epstein, 1–23. Malden, MA: Blackwell, 1998.

Ess, Ramsey. "Nick Kroll Talks 'Kroll Show' Season 2 with Seth Myers." *Vulture*, November 15, 2013. http://www.vulture.com/2013/11/nick-kroll-talks-kroll-show-season-2-with-seth-meyers.html.

Everett, Anna. "Golden Age of Television Drama." In *The Encyclopedia of Television*, edited by Horace Newcomb, 1001–1004. New York: Routledge, 2013.

Fiske, John. *Television Culture*. London: Routledge, 1987.

Foucault, Michel. *The Archaeology of Knowledge*. New York: Pantheon Books, 1972.

———. *The History of Sexuality Volume 1: An Introduction*. New York: Vintage Books, 1990.

Friedman, Sam. "The Cultural Currency of a 'Good' Sense of Humour: British Comedy and New Forms of Distinction." *British Journal of Sociology* 62, no. 2 (2011): 347–370.

Gabriel, Trip. "Television; Beyond Beavis and Butt-Head, MTV's Sketch Comedy Group." *New York Times*, January 8, 1995. http://www.nytimes.com/1995/01/08/arts/television-beyond-beavis-and-butt-head-mtv-s-sketch-comedy-group.html?pagewanted=all&src=pm.

Gaines, Donna. *Teenage Wasteland: Suburbia's Dead End Kids*. Chicago: University of Chicago Press, 1998.

Gates, Racquel. "Bringing the Black: Eddie Murphy and African American Humor on *Saturday Night Live*." In *Saturday Night Live and American TV*, edited by Nick Marx, Matt Sienkiewicz, and Ron Becker, 151–172. Bloomington: Indiana University Press, 2013.

Gelt, Jessica. "Comedy Central Renews 'Tosh.0' for Three Seasons." *Los Angeles Times*, December 13, 2013. http://articles.latimes.com/2013/dec/10/entertainment/la-et-st-comedy-central-renews-tosho-for-three-seasons-20131210.

Giddens, Anthony. *Beyond Left and Right: The Future of Radical Politics*. Palo Alto, CA: Stanford University Press, 1994.

Giroux, Henry A. "Teenage Sexuality, Body Politics, and the Pedagogy of Display." In *Youth Culture: Identity in a Postmodern World*, edited by Jonathan S. Epstein, 24–55. Malden, MA: Blackwell, 1998.

Gomery, Douglas. "Hollywood Corporate Business Practice and Periodizing Contemporary Film History." In *Contemporary Hollywood Cinema*, edited by Steve Neale and Murray Smith, 47–57. London: Routledge, 1998.

Goodwin, Andrew. "Fatal Distractions: MTV Meets Postmodern Theory." In *Sound & Vision: The Music Video Reader*, edited by Simon Firth, Andrew Goodwin, and Lawrence Grossberg, 37–56. New York: Routledge, 1993.

Gordinier, Jeff. *X Saves the World: How Generation X Got the Shaft But Can Still Keep Everything from Sucking*. New York: Viking Penguin, 2008.

Gorman, Bill. "Comedy Central Ends 2011 as the #1 Entertainment Network in Cable among Men 18–34 and 18–24." *TV by the Numbers*, December 21, 2011. http://tvbythenumbers.zap2it.com/2011/12/21/comedy-central-ends-2011-as-the-1-entertainment-network-in-cable-among-men-18-34-and-men-18-24/114431/.

Gournelos, Ted. *Popular Culture and the Future of Politics: Cultural Studies and the Tao of South Park*. Lanham, MD: Lexington Books, 2009.

Gramsci, Antonio. *Selections from the Prison Notebooks*, edited by Quintin Hoare and Geoffrey Nowell Smith. New York: International Publishers, 1971.

Gray, Herman. *Watching Race: Television and the Struggle for "Blackness."* Minneapolis: University of Minnesota Press, 1995.

Gray, Jonathan. *Show Sold Separately: Promos, Spoilers, and Other Media Paratexts*. New York and London: New York University Press, 2010.

———. *Watching with The Simpsons*. New York: Routledge, 2005.

Gray, Jonathan, Jeffrey P. Jones, and Ethan Thompson, eds. *Satire TV: Politics and Comedy in the Post-Network Era*. New York: New York University Press, 2009.

Greenwald, Andy. "The Andy Greenwald Podcast: Comedy Central Programming Head Kent Alterman." *Grantland*, April 23, 2014. http://grantland.com/hollywood-prospectus/the-andy-greenwald-podcast-comedy-central-president-kent-alterman/.

Greshler, Abby. "Memo to Fred Wile Jr., January 19, 1954." Unpublished archival document, Sam Fuller Files, Box 380, Folder 28, NBC Archives, Wisconsin Center for Film and Theater Research, Wisconsin Historical Society.

Grossberg, Lawrence. "On Postmodernism and Articulation: An Interview with Stuart Hall." *Journal of Communication Inquiry* 10, no. 47 (1986): 45–60.

Grynbaum, Michael M., and John Koblin. "For Solace and Solidarity in the Trump Age, Liberals Turn the TV Back On." *New York Times*, March 12, 2017. https://www.nytimes.com/2017/03/12/business/trump-television-ratings-liberals.html.

Gunning, Tom. "Response to Pie and Chase." In *Classical Hollywood Comedy*, edited by Kristine Brunovska Karnick and Henry Jenkins, 120–122. New York: Routledge, 1995.

Haggins, Bambi. *Laughing Mad: The Black Comic Persona in Post-Soul America*. New Brunswick, NJ: Rutgers University Press, 2007.

Hale, Mike. "Showtime's 'Short Stories' Tries to Reach the Web Generation." *New York Times*, February 18, 2011. http://www.nytimes.com/2011/02/20/arts/television/20watchlist.html?src=twrhp.

Hall, Stuart. "Encoding, Decoding." In *The Cultural Studies Reader*, edited by Simon During, 90–103. London and New York: Routledge, 1993.

———. "Who Needs Identity?" In *Questions of Cultural Identity*, edited by Stuart Hall and Paul du Gay. London: Sage, 1996.

Hamilton, Peter. "U.S. Cable Networks: What Do Males Want? Content? Or Entertainment? Who's Delivering Which?" *Documentary Television*, October 26, 2011. http://www.documentarytelevision.com/commissioning-process/u-s-cable-networks-what-do-males-want-content-or-entertainment-whos-giving-what/.

Harris, Will. "Garrett Morris on *SNL, 2 Broke Girls*, and Singing Arias for Walter Matthau." *AV/TV Club*, May 4, 2014. https://tv.avclub.com/garrett-morris-on-snl-2-broke-girls-and-singing-arias-1798268909.

Havig, Alan. *Fred Allen's Radio Comedy*. Philadelphia: Temple University Press, 1990.

Haygood, Daniel M. "A Status Report on Podcast Advertising." *Journal of Advertising Research* 47, no. 4 (2007): 518–523.

Heisler, Steve. "Are We Nearing Comedy Podcast Overload?" *The Onion A.V. Club*, March 2, 2012. http://www.avclub.com/articles/are-we-nearing-comedy-podcast-overload,70194/.

Herzog, Doug. "MTV Networks, Herzog Memo to Starr and Bendis." Unpublished archival document, Starr Collection, M98-128, Box 3, Folder 35, Wisconsin Center for Film and Theater Research, Wisconsin Historical Society.

Hesmondhalgh, David. "Bourdieu, The Media and Cultural Production." *Media, Culture & Society* 28, no. 2 (2006): 211–231.

Hibberd, James. "MTV Pushing Out 'Cynical' Generation X." *Hollywood Reporter*, February 23, 2010. http://www.thrfeed.com/2010/02/mtv-pushing-out-cynical-generation-x-.html.

Hill, Doug, and Jeff Weingrad. *Saturday Night: A Backstage History of Saturday Night Live*. New York: Beech Tree Books, 1986.

Hilmes, Michele. "Fanny Brice and the Schnooks Strategy." *Spectator* 25, no. 2 (Fall 2005): 11–25.

———. *Only Connect: A Cultural History of Broadcasting in the United States*. Belmont, CA: Wadsworth, 2002.

———. "Pay Television: Breaking the Broadcast Bottleneck." In *Hollywood in the Age of Television*, edited by Tino Balio, 297–310. Boston: Unwin Hyman, 1990.

———. *Radio Voices: American Broadcasting, 1922–1952*. Minneapolis: University of Minneapolis Press, 1997.

Holtz, Geoffrey T. *Welcome to the Jungle: The Why Behind "Generation X."* New York: St. Martin's Press, 1995.

Itzkoff, Dave. "The All Too Ready for Prime Time Players." *New York Times*, January 2, 2005. http://www.nytimes.com/2005/01/02/arts/television/the-all-too-ready-for-prime-time-players.html.

Jaeger, Doug. "In-depth: Comedy Central Re-brand." *Motionographer*, January 5, 2011. http://motionographer.com/2011/01/05/in-depth-comedy-central-re-brand/.

Jameson, Frederic. *Postmodernism, or the Cultural Logic of Late Capitalism*. Durham, NC: Duke University Press, 1990.

Jenkins, Henry. "Rowan and Martin's Laugh-in." Museum of Broadcast Communications *Encyclopedia of Television*, accessed June 30, 2012, http://www.museum.tv/archives/etv/R/htmlR/rowanandmar/rowanandmar.htm.

———. *What Made Pistachio Nuts? Early Sound Comedy and the Vaudeville Aesthetic*. New York: Columbia University Press, 1992.

Johnson, Catherine. *Branding Television*. New York and London: Routledge, 2011.

Kane, Margaret. "HBO Invests in Will Ferrell's FunnyorDie.com." *CNET News*, June 11, 2008. http://news.cnet.com/8301-10784_3-9965649-7.html.

Kearney, Mary Celeste. "'Don't Need You': Rethinking Identity Politics and Separatism from a Grrrl Perspective." In *Youth Culture: Identity in a Postmodern World*, edited by Jonathan S. Epstein, 148–188. Malden, MA: Blackwell, 1998.

Kiffer Keegan, "Comedy Central Rebrand," accessed April 18, 2019, http://www.kifferkeegan.com/Comedy-Central-Rebrand.

Kompare, Derek. *Rerun Nation: How Repeats Invented American Television*. New York: Routledge, 2005.

Krutnik, Frank. "General Introduction." In *Hollywood Comedians: The Film Reader*, edited by Frank Krutnik, 1–18. London and New York: Routledge, 2003.

———. "Introduction Part Five: Post-classical Comedian Comedy." In *Hollywood Comedians: The Film Reader*, edited by Frank Krutnik, 167–170. London and New York: Routledge, 2003.

Kuipers, Giselinde. "Television and Taste Hierarchy: The Case of Dutch Television Comedy." *Media, Culture and Society* 28, no. 3 (2006): 359–378.

LaSalle, Mick. "Flip the Channel on 'Anchorman,' a Comedy Sketch Stretched Too Far." *San Francisco Chronicle*, July 9, 2004. https://www.sfgate.com/movies/article/Flip-the-channel-on-Anchorman-a-comedy-sketch-2743131.php.

Leland, John. "Battle for Your Brain." *Newsweek*, October 11, 1993.

Leo, John. "The Unplugged Generation." *U.S. News and World Report*, July 20, 1992.

Lipsitz, George. *Time Passages: Collective Memory and American Popular Culture*. Minneapolis: University of Minnesota Press, 1990.

Lipsky, David. "They Died Laughing." *Details*, January-February 1996. http://davidwain.com/details-article/.

Lotz, Amanda. *Cable Guys: Television and Masculinities in the 21st Century*. New York: New York University Press, 2014.

———. *The Television Will Be Revolutionized*. New York and London: New York University Press, 2007.

Loviglio, Jason. "Sound Effects: Gender, Voice and the Cultural Work of NPR." *Radio Journal: International Studies in Broadcast & Audio Media* 5, no. 2/3 (2007): 67–81.

Marc, David. *Comic Visions: Television Comedy and American Culture*. London: Unwin Hyman, 1989.

———. "Lending Character to American Comedy." *Television Quarterly* 25 (1992).

Marks, Craig, and Rob Tannenbaum. *I Want My MTV: The Uncensored Story of the Music Video Revolution*. New York: Dutton, 2011.

Marx, Karl. "The German Ideology." In *Karl Marx: Selected Writings*, edited by David McLellan. New York and London: Oxford University Press, 2000.

Marx, Nick. "Expanding the Brand: Race, Gender, and the Post-Politics of Representation on Comedy Central." *Television & New Media* 17, no. 3 (2016): 272–287.

———. "'The Missing Link Moment': Web Comedy in New Media Industries." *Velvet Light Trap* 68 (2011): 14–23.

Marx, Nick, and Matt Sienkiewicz. "Volume Introduction: Comedy as Theory, Industry, and Academic Discipline." In *The Comedy Studies Reader*, edited by Nick Marx and Matt Sienkiewicz, 1–16. Austin: University of Texas Press, 2018.

McAvity, Thomas. "Memo to *Colgate Comedy Hour* Staff, January 25, 1954." Unpublished archival document, Sam Fuller Files, Box 380, Folder 29, NBC Archives, Wisconsin Center for Film and Theater Research, Wisconsin Historical Society.

McFadden, Margaret T. "America's Boy Friend Who Can't Get a Date: Gender, Race, and the Cultural Work of the Jack Benny Program, 1932–1946." *Journal of American History* 8, no. 1 (1993): 9–35.

Medhurst, Andy. *A National Joke: Popular Comedy and English Cultural Identities*. New York: Routledge, 2007.
Miege, Bernard. "The Logics at Work in the New Cultural Industries." *Media, Culture & Society* 9, no. 3 (1987): 273–289.
Miller, Jeffrey S. "What Closes on Saturday Night: NBC and Satire." In *NBC: America's Network*, edited by Michele Hilmes, 192–208. Berkeley and Los Angeles: University of California Press, 2007.
Minow, Newton. "Television and the Public Interest." Speech delivered to the National Association of Broadcasters, May 9, 1961. https://americanrhetoric.com/speeches/newtonminow.htm.
Mittell, Jason. *Genre and Television: From Cop Shows to Cartoons in American Culture*. New York: Routledge, 2004.
Morgan, Richard. "What's Wrong with Comedy Central?" *Splitsider*, March 19, 2012. http://splitsider.com/2012/03/whats-wrong-with-comedy-central/.
"Movie Review: 'Step Brothers' Is Men Behaving Badly." *Mac News*, accessed April 18, 2019, http://preserve.mactech.com/content/movie-review-step-brothers-men-behaving-badly.
MTV Networks. "Ratings Report." Unpublished archival document, Starr Collection, M95-204, Box 2, Folder 4, Wisconsin Center for Film and Theater Research, Wisconsin Historical Society.
Mullen, Megan. *The Rise of Cable Programming in the United States*. Austin: University of Texas Press, 2003.
———. *Television in the Multichannel Age: A Brief History of Cable Television*. Malden, MA: Blackwell, 2008.
Murphy, Caryn. "'Is this the Era of the Woman?': *SNL*'s Gender Politics in the New Millennium." In *Saturday Night Live and American Television Culture*, edited by Nick Marx, Matt Sienkiewicz, and Ron Becker, 173–190. Bloomington: Indiana University Press, 2013.
Murray, Susan. *Hitch Your Antenna to the Stars: Early Television and Broadcast Stardom*. New York: Routledge, 2005.
Napoli, Philip. *Audience Economics: Media Institutions and the Audience Marketplace*. New York: Columbia University Press, 2003.
Neale, Steve. *Monty Python's Flying Circus* sidebar in "Sketch Comedy." In *The Television Genre Book*, edited by Glen Creeber, 64. London: British Film Institute, 2001.
———. "Sketch Comedy." In *The Television Genre Book*, edited by Glen Creeber, 61–65. London: British Film Institute, 2001.
Neale, Steve, and Frank Krutnik. *Popular Film and Television Comedy*. London: Routledge, 1990.
Newcomb, Horace M., ed. *Encyclopedia of Television*. 2nd ed. 4 vols. New York and London: Fitzroy Dearborn, 2004.
Newcomb, Horace M., and Paul M. Hirsch. "Television as a Cultural Forum: Implications for Research." *Quarterly Review of Film Studies* 8, no. 3 (1983): 45–55.
Newman, Andrew Adam. "National Lampoon Stakes Revival on Making Own Films." *New York Times*, June 25, 2007. https://www.nytimes.com/2007/06/25/business/media/25lampoon.html.
O'Connell, Michael. "Comedy Central Launches Digital Production Studio, Taps Allison Kingsley as VP." *Hollywood Reporter*, January 31, 2013. http://www.hollywoodreporter.com/news/comedy-central-launches-digital-production-417123.

O'Rourke, Daniel J., III, and Pravin A. Rodrigues. "The Onion's Call for Healing." *Society* 42, no. 1 (2004): 19–27.
Park, Ed. "Ferrell and Unbalanced: Non Sequiturs Nearly Anchor Spoof." *Village Voice*, June 29, 2004. https://www.villagevoice.com/2004/06/29/ferrell-and-unbalanced-non-sequiturs-nearly-anchor-spoof/.
Paul, William. *Laughing Screaming: Modern Hollywood Horror and Comedy*. New York: Columbia University Press, 1994.
Paumgarten, Nick. "Id Girls." *New Yorker*, June 23, 2014. http://www.newyorker.com/magazine/2014/06/23/id-girls.
Pendleton, Jennifer. "TV Plays It Safe—Just for Laughs." *Daily Variety*, February 16, 1993.
Petski, Denise. "*Inside Amy Schumer* Renewed for Fifth Season on Comedy Central—TCA." *Deadline Hollywood*, January 6, 2016. http://deadline.com/2016/01/inside-amy-schumer-renewed-fifth-season-comedy-central-amy-schumer-1201676749/.
Phillips, Michael. "Steve Carell, Tina Fey Deserve a Better 'Date Night.'" *Chicago Tribune*, April 8, 2010. http://articles.chicagotribune.com/2010-04-08/entertainment/chi-100406-date-night-review_1_carell-and-fey-date-night-tina-fey.
Poniewozik, James. "All-Time 100 TV Shows." *Time*, September 6, 2007. http://entertainment.time.com/2007/09/06/the-100-best-tv-shows-of-all-time/slide/saturday-night-live/#saturday-night-live.
Promotional Materials, Unpublished archival document, Broadcast Publicity Files, Box 133, Folder 61, NBC Archives, Wisconsin Center for Film and Theater Research, Wisconsin Historical Society.
Rabinovitz, Lauren. "Animation, Postmodernism, and MTV." *Velvet Light Trap* 24 (1989): 99–112.
Richmond Times-Dispatch Staff. "'Baby Mama' Seems Like a Long, Bad 'SNL' Sketch." *Richmond Times Dispatch*, April 26, 2008. http://www.richmond.com/entertainment/baby-mama-seems-like-a-long-bad-snl-sketch/article_618a4ff9-e076-5633-a6db-9136bea03020.html.
Ritchie, Karen. "Get Ready for 'Generation X'; Soon the Primary Market, and Very Unlike Aging Boomers." *Advertising Age*, November 9, 1992.
———. *Marketing to Generation X*. New York: Lexington Books, 1995.
Rolling Stone. "My Favorite 'Saturday Night Live' Sketch." *Rolling Stone*, March 16, 2017. https://www.rollingstone.com/tv/lists/saturday-night-live-cast-members-on-most-memorable-sketches-w468140.
Rose, Frank. "The Lost Boys." *Wired*, August 1, 2004. http://www.wired.com/wired/archive/12.08/lostboys.html.
Rose, Lacey. "Comedy Central's Kent Alterman on Leno, Rape Jokes and a Jon Stewart–Free 'Daily Show.'" *Hollywood Reporter*, May 1, 2013. http://www.hollywoodreporter.com/news/comedy-centrals-kent-alterman-leno-448317.
———. "'*SNL*'s' Yuuuge Year: 20 Insiders Reveal Alec Baldwin's Future as Trump, 'Spicey' Secrets and Lorne Michaels' Election Pep Talk." *Hollywood Reporter*, May 15, 2017. https://www.hollywoodreporter.com/features/snl-trump-ratings-bump-you-almost-feel-like-a-war-profiteer-1003540.
Rottinghaus, Brandon, Kenton Bird, Travis Ridout, and Rebecca Self. "'It's Better Than Being Informed': College-Aged Viewers of *The Daily Show*." In *Laughing Matters: Humor and American Politics in the Media Age*, edited by Jody C. Baumgartner and Jonathan S. Morris, 279–294. New York: Routledge, 2008.
Saul, Scott. *Becoming Richard Pryor*. New York: HarperCollins, 2014.

Seabaugh, Julie. "*Night after Night* to *@midnight*: An Oral History of Comedy Central (Part 1)." *AV/TV Club*, April 4, 2016. https://tv.avclub.com/night-after-night-to-midnight-an-oral-history-of-come-1798252706.

———. "*Night after Night* to *@midnight*: An Oral History of Comedy Central (Part 2)." *AV/TV Club*, June 20, 2016. https://tv.avclub.com/night-after-night-to-midnight-an-oral-history-of-come-1798248939.

———. "*Night after Night* to *@midnight*: An Oral History of Comedy Central (Part 3)." *AV/TV Club*, August 22, 2016. http://www.avclub.com/article/night-after-night-midnight-oral-history-comedy-cen-240741.

———. "Variety's 2014 Breakthrough in Comedy Winner: Amy Schumer." *Variety*, January 6, 2014. http://variety.com/2014/tv/news/amy-schumer-a-year-for-living-dangerously-1201029531/.

Seidman, Steve. *Comedian Comedy: A Tradition in Hollywood Film*. Ann Arbor, MI: UMI Research Press, 1981.

Setoodeh, Ramin. "Movie Review: Adam Sandler's 'Jack and Jill' Is the Worst Movie Ever Made." *Daily Beast*, November 11, 2011. https://www.thedailybeast.com/movie-review-adam-sandlers-jack-and-jill-is-the-worst-movie-ever-made.

Shales, Tom, and James Andrew Miller. *Live from New York: An Uncensored History of Saturday Night Live*. Boston: Little, Brown, 2002.

Shattuc, Jane M. *The Talking Cure: TV Talk Shows and Women*. New York: Routledge, 1997.

Shedd, Matt. "Diversity in the Spotlight on *SNL*: From Pryor to Zamata." *Peabody*, February, 15, 2015. http://www.peabodyawards.com/stories/story/diversity-in-the-spotlight-on-snl-from-richard-pryor-to-sasheer-zamata.

Shevory, T. C. "Bleached Resistance: The Politics of Grunge." *Popular Music and Society* 19 no. 2 (1995): 23–48.

Sienkiewicz, Matt. "Speaking Too Soon: *SNL*, 9/11 and the Remaking of American Irony." In *Saturday Night Live and American TV*, edited by Nick Marx, Matt Sienkiewicz, and Ron Becker, 93–111. Bloomington: Indiana University Press, 2013.

Sienkiewicz, Matt, and Nick Marx. "Click Culture: The Perils and Possibilities of *Family Guy* and Convergence-Era Television." *Communication and Critical/Cultural Studies* 11, no. 2 (2014): 103–119.

Silver, Dan. "YouTube HOF: Great Moments in Selling Out." *Grantland*, February 1, 2012. http://grantland.com/hollywood-prospectus/youtube-hof-great-moments-in-selling-out/.

Simons, Seth. "The Strange Persistence of Sketch Comedy." *Paste Magazine*, April 12, 2016. http://www.pastemagazine.com/articles/2016/04/the-strange-persistence-of-sketch-comedy.html.

Smith, Chris. "Comedy Isn't Funny: *Saturday Night Live* at Twenty—How the Show That Transformed TV Became a Grim Joke." *New York Magazine*, March 13, 1995. http://nymag.com/arts/tv/features/47548/.

Smith, Eve. "Selling Terry Pratchett's Discworld: Merchandising and the Cultural Economy of Fandom." *Participations: Journal of Audience and Reception Studies* 8, no. 2 (2011): 239–256.

Smith, Greg M. "'To Waste More Time, Please Click Here Again': Monty Python and the Quest for Film/CD-ROM Adaptation." In *On a Silver Platter: CD-ROMs and the Promises of a New Technology*, edited by Greg M. Smith, 58–86. New York: New York University Press, 1999.

Snickars, Pelle, and Patrick Vonderau, eds. *The YouTube Reader*. Stockholm: National Library of Sweden, 2009.
Spigel, Lynn. *Make Room for TV: Television and the Family Ideal in Postwar America*. Chicago: University of Chicago Press, 1992.
Spigel, Lynn, and Michael Curtin, eds. *The Revolution Wasn't Televised: Sixties Television and Social Conflict*. New York: Routledge, 1997.
Stam, Robert. *Subversive Pleasures: Bakhtin, Cultural Criticism, and Film*. Baltimore, MD: Johns Hopkins University Press, 1989.
Star, Alexander. "The Twentysomething Myth." *New Republic*, January 4, 1993.
Starr, Steven. "RE: 'THE STATE'—NETWORK FORMAT." Unpublished archival document, Starr Collection, M95-204, Box 3, Folder 37, Wisconsin Center for Film and Theater Research, Wisconsin Historical Society.
———. "Starr Pictures Memo RE: THE STATE." Unpublished archival document, Starr Collection, M98-128, Box 3, Folder 35, Wisconsin Center for Film and Theater Research, Wisconsin Historical Society.
State, The. "Some Things to Ponder Whilst Formulating a Network Special." Unpublished archival document, Starr Collection, Box 2, Folder 4, Wisconsin Center for Film and Theater Research, Wisconsin Historical Society.
State, The, Steven Starr, and Jon Bendis. "Pre-Existing Characters." Unpublished archival document, Starr Collection, M98-128, Box 3, Folder 35, Wisconsin Center for Film and Theater Research, Wisconsin Historical Society.
Stelter, Brian. "Comedy Central Still Strong at 20." *New York Times*, April 11, 2011. http://www.nytimes.com/2011/04/11/business/media/11comedy.html.
———. "The Good Ol' Days of 20 Years Ago." *New York Times*, July 18, 2011. https://www.nytimes.com/2011/07/19/arts/television/teennicks-90s-nostalgia-fest.html.
———. "The Rise of Web Video, Beyond 2-Minute Clips." *New York Times*, July 5, 2009. http://www.nytimes.com/2009/07/06/business/media/06video.html.
———. "YouTube Videos Pull in Real Money." *New York Times*, December 10, 2008. http://www.nytimes.com/2008/12/11/business/media/11youtube.html.
Sternberg, Joel. "The *Colgate Comedy Hour*." Museum of Broadcast Communications. http://www.museum.tv/archives/etv/C/htmlC/colgatecomed/colgatecomed.htm.
Stewart, Sara. "Amy Schumer and the Women of *Broad City*: Paving the Way for a Female 'Golden Age.'" *Indiewire*, May 7, 2014. https://www.indiewire.com/2014/05/amy-schumer-and-the-women-of-broad-city-paving-the-way-for-a-female-golden-age-206768/.
Strauss, William, and Neil Howe. *Generations: The History of America's Future, 1584 to 2069*. New York: William Morrow, 1991.
———. "The New Generation Gap." *Atlantic Monthly*, December 1992. http://www.theatlantic.com/past/docs/issues/92dec/9212genx.htm.
Streeter, Thomas. "Blue Skies and Strange Bedfellows: The Discourse of Cable Television." In *The Revolution Wasn't Televised: Sixties Television and Social Conflict*, edited by Lynn Spigel and Michael Curtin, 221–242. New York and London: Routledge, 1997.
Tatge, Mark. "A Funny Thing." *Forbes*, January 31, 2005. https://www.forbes.com/forbes/2005/0131/071.html#51fcadcb166f.
Tetzlaff, David. "MTV and the Politics of Postmodern Pop." *Journal of Communication Inquiry* 10, no. 1 (1986), 80–91.

Thompson, Ethan. *Parody and Taste in Postwar American Televeision Culture*. New York and London: Routledge, 2011.
Thompson, Ethan, and Ethan Tussey. "Andy Samberg's Digital Success Story and Other Myths of the Internet Comedy Club." In *Saturday Night Live and American TV*, edited by Nick Marx, Matt Sienkiewicz, and Ron Becker, 233–253. Bloomington: Indiana University Press, 2013.
Travers, Peter. "Anchorman: The Legend of Ron Burgundy." *Rolling Stone*, July 14, 2004. http://www.rollingstone.com/movies/reviews/anchorman-the-legend-of-ron-burgundy-20040709.
———. "Date Night." *Rolling Stone*, April 8, 2010. http://www.rollingstone.com/movies/reviews/date-night-20100408.
Turner, Gustavo. "*Reality Bites*: The Ultimate Sellout?" *LA Weekly*, January 5, 2012. http://www.laweekly.com/film/reality-bites-the-ultimate-sellout-2173518.
Turow, Joseph. *Breaking Up America: Advertisers and the New Media World*. Chicago: University of Chicago Press, 1997.
Voss, Erik. "Is 'Saturday Night Live' Becoming 'Saturday Night Pretaped'?" *Vulture*, May 9, 2014. http://www.vulture.com/2014/05/is-saturday-night-live-becoming-saturday-night-pretape.html.
Vranica, Suzanne, and John Jannarone. "Viacom Loads More Ads on Channels." *Wall Street Journal*, August 12, 2012. http://online.wsj.com/news/articles/SB10000872396390444082904577609893517491070.
Weaver, Simon. *The Rhetoric of Racist Humour: US, UK and Global Race Joking*. Farnham, UK: Ashgate, 2011.
Weinstein, David. *The Forgotten Network: Dumont and the Birth of American Television*. Philadelphia: Temple University Press, 2004.
Weisman, Jon. "Comedy Central Renews 'Key.'" *Variety*, February 14, 2012. http://variety.com/2012/tv/news/comedy-central-renews-key-1118050241/.
Wenner, Kathryn S. "Peeling the Onion." *American Journalism Review* 24, no. 7, (2002): 48–53.
Weprin, Alex. "Comedy Central Bets Big on Web Development." *Broadcasting & Cable*, December 7, 2009. https://www.broadcastingcable.com/news/comedy-central-bets-big-web-development-35842.
Wertheim, Arthur Frank. *Radio Comedy*. New York: Oxford University Press, 1979.
Whalley, Jim. *Saturday Night Live, Hollywood Comedy, and American Culture*. London: Palgrave Macmillan, 2010.
Wile, Fred, Jr. "Memo: *Colgate Comedy Hour*, February 2, 1954." Unpublished archival document, Sam Fuller Files, Box 380, Folder 28, NBC Archives, Wisconsin Center for Film and Theater Research, Wisconsin Historical Society.
———. "Memo: *Colgate Comedy Hour* Proposal, February 11, 1954." Unpublished archival document, Sam Fuller Files, Box 380, Folder 31, NBC Archives, Wisconsin Center for Film and Theater Research, Wisconsin Historical Society.
Williams, Raymond. "Base and Superstructure in Marxist Cultural Theory." In *Media and Cultural Studies Keyworks*, edited by Meenakshi Gigi Durham and Douglas M. Kellner, 152–165. Malden, MA: Blackwell, 2001.
———. *Resources of Hope: Culture, Democracy, Socialism*. London: Verso, 1989.
Wilson, Carl. "'My So-Called Adulthood.'" *New York Times*, August 4, 2011. https://www.nytimes.com/2011/08/07/magazine/the-gen-x-nostalgia-boom.html.

Wyatt, Justin. *High Concept: Movies and Marketing in Hollywood.* Austin: University of Texas Press, 1994.

Young, Susan. "TV's Golden Age of Sketch Draws Comic Minds out of the Woodwork." *Variety*, June 17, 2015. http://variety.com/2015/tv/awards/tvs-golden-age-of-sketch-comedy-1201521301/.

Zinoman, Jason. "Amy Schumer, Funny Girl." *New York Times*, April 18, 2013. https://www.nytimes.com/2013/04/21/arts/television/amy-schumers-comedy-central-show-from-the-inside.html.

INDEX

Page numbers in italics refer to figures

Abbott, Bud, 27, 46, 52
ABC, 28–29, 92n4, 102–3
absurdisms, 1, 7, 11, 109, 135
Acham, Christine, 72
Adult Swim, 91–92, 132
advertisers: baby boomers, 33, 102; *The Colgate Comedy Hour* (1950–1955), 40, 48, 50; Comedy Central, 129, 131–32, 138; cultural identities, 98–99; Ferrell, Will, 87; gender, 129, 131–32, 138; generations, 97–98; Generation X, 33, 98–99, 101, 102–3, 107–8; identities, 23, 98; *Key & Peele* (2012–2015), 142; MTV, 104–9; multichannel transition:1980s–1990s, 102–3, 129; networks, 28–29, 102–3, 132; post-network: 2000s–Present, 35, 129; recurring characters, 43; recursive practices, 24–25; reflexive flexibility, 5; sketch comedy, 24, 121; Turow, Joseph, 33; vaudeo, 46, 53; vaudeville, 43; young adult audiences, 33, 102–3, 131–32
Allen, Robert, 41
All in the Family (1971–1979), 29–30, 76
Allison, Kevin, 110
Alterman, Kent, 132–33, 138, 142
AMC, 132
American television industry, 2, 5–6, 7, 24, 25, 37, 147. *See also* industrial identities; *individual eras*
Amon, Ruth, 115
anarchistic comedies, 27, 42
Anchorman (2004), 80–81, 84, 88–89, *89*
animal comedy, 65–66
Animal House (1978), 65, 82
"Argument to Beethoven's Fifth" (sketch), 10
Armisen, Fred, 125
Arnaz, Desi, 118
art v commerce, 4–5, 14. *See also* advertisers; consumerism; economics

Atom (website)/*Atom TV* (2008–2010), 129–30
Aukerman, Scott, 36
Austin Powers franchise (1997, 1999, 2002), 80
Aykroyd, Dan, 66, 77, 78

baby boomers: advertisers, 33, 102; *All in the Family* (1971–1979), 76; *The Ben Stiller Show* (MTV 1989–1990, FOX 1992), 103–4; definitions, 98; Generation X, 97, 98–100, 102, 108, 112; media, 100, 112; *Monty Python's Flying Circus* (1969–1974), 63; MTV, 108; network era:1950s–1970s, 54, 57–59; Nick at Nite/TV Land, 109; 1990s nostalgia, 96–97; *SNL* (1975–), 30, 58–59, 61–62, 64, 67–68; VH1, 108–9
Baby Mama (2008), 80
Baldwin, Alec, 1, 3–4
Ball, Lucille, 26, 44, 52
Barnum, Peter, 50–51
Beavis and Butt-Head (1993–1997, 2011), 97, 101–2, 107, 108, 109–10, 114, 123n39
Becker, Ron, 116
Bell, Art, 128, 129
Belushi, John, 8–9, 31, 62, 64, 65, 66, 77, 78, 82, 88
Bendis, Jonathan, 110, 114–15, 116
Ben Stiller Show, The (MTV 1989–1990, FOX 1992), 33, 103–4, 109
Berle, Milton, 47–48
Between Two Ferns (2008–present), 148–49
Billy Madison (1995), 82
Black, Michael Ian, 110, 118, 119
blackness, 139–41; Chappelle, Dave, 22–23; Comedy Central, 138–44; economics, 22; "Election Night" (sketch), 1–2, 3; FOX, 22; Generation X, 120; Gray, Herman, 141–42; identities, 22–23, 68–69, 72–77, 138–44;

167

blackness (*Cont.*)
  Key & Peele (2012–2015), 139–41; *In Living Color* (1990–1994), 22–23, 33, 103, 141–42; MTV, 105, 122n8; network era:1950s–1970s, 68–69; oppositionality, 33; Pryor, Richard/"Racist Word Association Interview" (sketch), 73–76; satire, 139; *SNL* (1975–), 18–20, 68–77, 146n38; The State (comedy troupe), 117, 120. *See also* race
blackouts, 7, 11–12, 55
"Black Perspective" (sketches), 69–72, 73, 76
Blues Brothers, The (1980), 78
Blues Brothers 2000 (1998), 80
Bob Newhart Show, The (1961–1962), 54–55
Bond, Julian, 70–71, 76
Bourdieu, Pierre, 3, 14–21, 24, 42
Bravo, 142–43
Breaking Bad (2008–2013), 137
breaking character, 7, 10
Brice, Fanny, 43
Broad City (2014–2019), 126, 132–33, 134–38, 144
Broadway Video, 78
Brook, Vincent, 143
Brooks, Albert, 73
Brownstein, Carrie, 125
burlesque, 11, 41–42. *See also* vaudeville
Burnett, Carol, 10, 28
Bush, George W., 83

cable. *See* post-network: 2000s–Present
Cable Music Channel, 105
Caesar, Sid, 10, 47–48
Caesar's Hour (1954–1957), 10
Caldwell, John, 106–7, 123n39, 127, 133
Canadian comedy, 7, 16, 77–78, 115
Cantor, Eddie, 27, 40, 42–44, 46, 49, 57
Carell, Steve, 85–86, 89
Carol Burnett Show, The (1967–1978), 10, 28
Carson, Johnny, 30, 63
Cartoon Network, 91–92
Carvey, Dana, 78, 79
cast members. *See* performers
CBS, 4, 28–29, 30, 47–48, 55, 96, 102–3, 115–19. *See also State, The* (1995, CBS)
CC Studios, 130
Chaplin, Charlie, 26, 81

Chappelle, Dave, 1–3, 8, 22–23
Chappelle's Show (2003–2006), 1–2, 3, 11, 22–23, 129
Chase, Chevy, 31, 62, 64–69, 72–76, 78, 80, 82, 88
"Chippendales" (sketch), 10
class, 14, 22, 29, 40, 42, 98, 126
Clayton Bigsby sketch, 11, 22
Cleese, John, 8
Clinton, Hillary, 2
Coca, Imogene, 47–48
Coe, Fred, 25–26
Colgate Comedy Hour, The (1950–1955), 27–28, 40–41, 42, 44, 46–53
Colgate Variety Hour, The, 47, 52
comedian comedy films, 81–82
comedians. *See* performers
comedy, 148. *See also* sketch comedy
Comedy Bang! Bang! (2012–2016), 36
Comedy Central, 125–51; advertisers, 129, 131–32, 138; Alterman, Kent, 132–33; Atom (website), 129–30; blackness/race, 22–23, 36, 125–27, 131, 135, 138–44; CC Studios, 130; cultural identities, 36, 126; economics, 134, 145; ethnicities, 127, 138–44; Ganeless, Michael, 142; gender, 22, 36, 125–27, 129–38, 142–44; Ha! (network), 127–28; identities, 22–23, 127, 132, 134–45; IFC, 125–26; industrial identities, 36, 127–34; internet, 129–33, 142, 143–44; media, 131–32, 135, 138, 144–45; MTV, 107; multichannel transition:1980s–1990s, 126, 127–34; politics, 129, 142; Posch, Brooke, 132–33; post-network: 2000s–Present, 36–37, 121, 125–34; post-politics, 36–37, 126, 134, 137–38; presidential elections, 129; reflexive flexibility, 126; sitcoms, 128–29; sketch comedy, 32, 36–37, 126–30, 142, 144–45; unbundled content, 134–35; Viacom, 129–30, 132; young adult audiences, 36, 129, 130, 131–32, 134, 144. *See also individual shows*
Comedy Channel, The, 127–28
Comedy for Gracious Living (album), 118
"Comedy Isn't Funny: *Saturday Night Live* at Twenty—How the Show That

Transformed TV Became a Grim Joke"
  (article), 79
Community (2009–2015), 132
Coneheads (1993), 78
conflict, 8, 9–11, 12
consumerism: early television: 1940s–1950s,
  43–44, 45; ethnicities/gender, 43–44;
  generations, 97–98; Generation X, 33–34,
  95, 99, 100–101, 112, 120; *The State* (1993–
  1995, MTV), 33–34, 94–95; vaudeo, 46. *See
  also* advertisers; economics
Costello, Lou, 27, 46, 52
Coupland, Douglas, 100, 109
Crank Yankers (2002–2005), 129
Cross, David, 12–13
Crystal, Billy, 77
cultural identities, 96–102; advertisers,
  98–99; Brice, Fanny, 43; *The Colgate
  Comedy Hour* (1950–1955), 28, 41; Comedy
  Central, 36, 126; generations, 96–102, 109,
  119; Generation X, 94–95, 96–102, *104*,
  111, 119–21; network era:1950s–1970s, 29;
  performers, 4, 24; sketch comedy, 2–4, 6,
  14–24, 34, 41, 126, 146n38, 148, 150; *SNL*
  (1975–), 1, 58, 61, 92, 149; *The State* (1993–
  1995, MTV), 120. *See also* identities
cultural politics, 63–68, 75–76
cultural production, 13–24, 41, 62
Curtin, Michael, 32–33, 34, 35, 60n30, 103

Daily Show with Jon Stewart, The (1999–
  2015), 129, 130, 131
"Darrell's House" (sketch), 148–50
Date Night (2010), 84, 85–87
Dawson, Max, 130
"Dead Parrot" (sketch), 8–9
Details (magazine), 100, 117
Deveau, Danielle Jeanine, 16
Dexter (2006–2013), 137
Dick Van Dyke Show, The (1961–1966), 29
digital platforms. *See* internet; media
*Distinction: A Social Critique of the
  Judgment of Taste* (Bourdieu), 14–15
Dixon, James, 116
Doumanian, Jean, 77
Downey, Robert, Jr., 78
Drake, Philip, 81, 85–86

Dratch, Rachel, 84
"Dumb Starbucks" (sketch), 144
Durante, Jimmy, 46, 52, 57
Dylan, Bob, 112, 114

early television: 1940s–1950s, 40–60;
  consumerism, 43–44, 45; economics, 46;
  industrial identities, 25–28; live audiences,
  26, 39n30, 52–53; networks, 25; performers,
  25–27, 44, 46; sketch comedy, 25–28,
  44–53; vaudeo, 27; vaudeville, 40–44. *See
  also individual shows*
"East/West College Bowl" (2012, 2013)
  (sketches), 139, 142
Ebersol, Dick, 63, 77, 78
economics: art v commerce, 4–5, 14;
  blackness, 22; Bourdieu, Pierre, 16; *The
  Colgate Comedy Hour* (1950–1955), 48, 50;
  Comedy Central, 134, 145; early television:
  1940s–1950s, 46; gender, 125; Generation
  X, 98–99; identities, 21, 23–24; industrial
  identities, 24–25; internet, 143–44; large
  and small-scale production, 17; MTV,
  105, 107; multichannel transition:1980s–
  1990s, 32; networks, 23–24, 28–29, 58;
  performers, 4; sitcoms, 53; sketch comedy,
  5, 15, 16, 24–25, 37–38, 50–51, 52, 95–96, 127;
  SNL (1975–), 19, 64; *The State* (1993–1995,
  MTV), 95–96, 119–21; vaudeo, 46. *See also*
  consumerism
Ed Sullivan Show, The (1948–1971), 29
"Election Night" (sketch), 1–3
Entertainment Weekly, 73
Ernie Kovacs Show, The (1952–1962), 54
ethnicities, 40, 42–44, 98, 127, 138–44
Exit 57 (1995–1996), 128

Fabray, Nanette, 10
Fallon, Jimmy, 10, 15–16, 84
Farley, Chris, 10, 78, 79, 80, 81
females. *See* gender
Ferrell, Will, 34–35, 80–81, 82–91
Fey, Tina, 15, 80, 81, 82–87, 91
Fielder, Nathan, 143–44
films: *The Colgate Comedy Hour* (1950–1955),
  48, 50, 51–52; comedian comedy films,
  81–82; recurring characters, 15, 121; sketch

films (Cont.)
    comedy, 26, 40–44, 58, 62–63, 77–82; *SNL* (1975), 15, 31, 61–63, 65, 77–91; *The State* (1993-1995, MTV), 94–95, 111; *The State* (1995, CBS), 118–19. See also individuals; individual films
Fletch (1985), 80
flexibility, 3, 18, 84, 87–88, 143. See also reflexive flexibility
Flip Wilson Show, The (1970-1974), 28, 72
"Focus Group" (sketch) (*Inside Amy Schumer*), 135–36
"Focus Group" (sketch) (*Nathan for You*), 143
Foley, Dave, 7–8, 9, 11–12
Ford, Gerald, 64–65
Ford Theater (1952-1956), 25–26
Four Star Playhouse (1952-1956), 25–26
FOX, 22, 33, 94, 103, 132
Franken, Al, 79
Fuller, Sam, 51
Funny or Die (website), 34–35, 36, 87, 90, 148–49
Fuzz, The (online), 130
FXX, 132

Galifianakis, Zach, 148–49
Game of Thrones (2011-2019), 17
Ganeless, Michael, 142
Garant, Robert Ben, 110, 119
Garofalo, Janeane, 79
Gates, Racquel, 146n38
gender: advertisers, 129, 131–32, 138; Alterman, Kent, 133, 142; Bravo, 142–43; Brice, Fanny, 43; *Broad City* (2014-2019), 134–38; *Chappelle's Show* (2003-2006), 3; Comedy Central, 22, 36, 125–27, 129–38, 142–44; consumerism, 43–44; economics, 125; generations, 98; Generation X, 120; Hall, Stuart, 20; identities, 20–22, 91, 125–26, 132, 133, 134–38, 143; *Inside Amy Schumer* (2013-present), 4, 134–38; MTV, 105, 107, 120, 122n8; multichannel transition:1980s-1990s, 33; *Nathan for You* (2013-2017), 143; networks, 132; "Oval Office" (sketch), 19–20; performers, 136–37; politics, 125; *Portlandia* (2011-2018), 125–26; Posch, Brooke, 132–33; post-network: 2000s–Present, 125–27, 132, 137; satire, 135–36; sketch comedy, 18, 40, 43–44, 91, 125–26, 135, 137, 143; *SNL* (1975–), 18, 31, 62, 63–68, 69, 70–71, 76–77, 79, 82, 91; *The State* (1993-1995, MTV), 96; The State (comedy troupe), 120, 124n71; *Tosh.o* (2009–present), 131
generations: advertisers/consumerism, 97–98; as concept, 95; cultural/identities, 96–102, 109, 114, 119, 120; gender/media, 98; multichannel transition:1980s-1990s, 109; network era:1950s-1970s, 29, 101; race, 98; sketch comedy, 24, 114; *SNL* (1975–), 92; *The State* (1993-1995, MTV), 33–34, 111–13, 114. See also baby boomers; millennials
Generation X, 96–102; advertisers, 33, 98–99, 101, 102–3, 107–8; baby boomers, 97, 98–100, 102, 108, 112; *The Ben Stiller Show* (MTV 1989-1990, FOX 1992), 33; blackness, 120; CBS, 118; consumerism, 33–34, 95, 99, 100–101, 112, 120; cultural identities, 94–95, 96–102, 104, 111, 119–21; definitions, 98, 99–100; economics, 98–99; gender, 120; grunge, 103–4; Howe/Strauss, 100; identities, 33–34, 98–99, 101, 105, 107, 120–21; media, 99, 101, 103, 120; MTV, 97, 103–5, 107–8, 113, 120; multichannel transition:1980s-1990s, 96–102, 119–21; oppositionality, 94–95, 99, 100–101, 109, 111–13, 120; pejorative nickname, 122n13; presidential elections, 101; race, 98; Ritchie, Karen on, 98–99; sketch comedy, 94–95, 119, 120; *SNL* (1975–), 30; *The State* (1993-1995, MTV), 95, 102, 105, 111–13, 119–21; *The State* (1995, CBS), 118; young adult audiences, 102
Generation X: Tales for an Accelerated Generation (Coupland), 100
"Get Off the Shed" (sketch), 87–88
"Gigolo House" (sketch), 143–44
Glazer, Ilana, 136–38
Gleason, Jackie, 45, 48, 52
Goodwin, Andrew, 106
Gordinier, Jeff, 100
Gottfried, Gilbert, 77
Gray, Herman, 22, 141–42. See also Nickelodeon
Gray, Jonathan, 86–87, 123n54

Grier, David Allen, 22
Groundlings, The (improvisational troupe), 82
grunge, 95, 98, 103–5, 115–16
Guest, Christopher, 77

Ha! (network), 127–28
Haggins, Bambi, 22–23
Hall, Anthony Michael, 78
Hall, Stuart, 3, 20–21, 120
Hamm, Jon, 148
Hanks, Colin, 139
Hartman, Phil, 78
Hawn, Goldie, 56, 65
HBO, 32, 35, 36, 94, 128
Headbangers Ball (1987–1995; MTV2, 2003–2012), 97
Herzog, Doug, 109, 114–15
Hesmondhalgh, David, 17
Higgins Boys and Gruber, The (1989–1991), 128
Hills, The (2006–2010), 97
Hilmes, Michele, 25, 43, 59n29
hip-hop, 95, 98, 105, 120, 122n8
History (network), 132
Hodgson, Joel, 128
Holoubek, Todd, 110
"Homeboy Shopping Network" (sketch), 22–23
homosexuality, 22, 79, 136
Honeymooners, The (1955–1956), 45, 52
Howe, Neil, 100

identities, 125–51; advertisers, 23, 98; blackness/race, 20, 22–23, 68–69, 72–77, 125–26, 138–44; Cantor, Eddie, 42–43; Chappelle, Dave, 22–23; Comedy Central, 22–23, 127, 132, 134–45; economics, 21, 23–24; ethnicities, 138–44; Fielder, Nathan, 143; gender, 20–22, 91, 125–26, 132, 133, 134–38, 143; generations, 98, 99, 109, 114, 119, 120; Generation X, 33–34, 98–99, 101, 105, 107, 120–21; Gray, Herman, 22; Hall, Stuart, 3, 20–21; Kroll, Nick, 143; Medhurst, Andy, 21; multichannel transition:1980s–1990s, 94–95, 102–9; networks, 107; performers, 83; politics, 125–26, 148; post-network: 2000s–Present, 125–26; reflexive flexibility, 15, 20, 142; sketch comedy, 3, 15, 17, 20–24, 40, 120, 125, 127, 135, 142, 143, 145, 148, 150; *SNL* (1975–), 30, 58, 62–63, 64, 68, 72–73, 76–77, 79, 91, 147; *The State* (1993–1995, MTV), 33–34, 120; *30 Rock* (2006–2013), 85. *See also* cultural identities; industrial identities
Idiot Box, The (1990–1991), 106, 109
IFC, 125–26, 132, 144
I Love Lucy (1951–1957), 44, 52, 118
improvisational comedy, 13, 82–83, 85–87, 89–90. *See also individual improvisational troupes*
industrial identities, 24–37; Comedy Central, 36, 127–34; early television: 1940s–1950s, 25–28; economics, 24–25; MTV, 95, 102–9, 120; multichannel transition:1980s–1990s, 32–34, 94–95, 102–9, 127–34; network era:1950s–1970s, 28–32; networks, 107; post-network: 2000s–Present, 34–37, 127–34
In Living Color (1990–1994), 10, 22–23, 33, 94, 103, 141–42
Inside Amy Schumer (2013–present), 36–37, 126–27, 132–33, 134–38, 144
internet: *Broad City* (2014–2019), 138; Comedy Central, 129–33, 142, 143–44; *Inside Amy Schumer* (2013–present), 138; *Key & Peele* (2012–2015), 142; NBC, 35; networks, 3, 35, 132; performers, 36; post-network: 2000s–Present, 34–35, 127, 130, 143; sketch comedy, 34–36, 41, 121, 130, 144–45; *SNL* (1975–), 90; *The State* (1995, CBS), 118–19; unbundled content, 130. *See also* media; *individual websites*
interstitial bits, 7, 8, 37, 67–68, 104–6, 142

Jacobson, Abbi, 136–38
Jann, Michael, 110
Jenkins, Henry, 27, 42, 55, 57, 82
Jewishness, 29, 42–43, 143. *See also* ethnicities; *individuals*
Joe's Apartment (1992), 109–10
Johnson, Arte, 57
Johnson, Catherine, 122n13, 135
Jones, Leslie, 18, 76
Jon Stewart Show, The (1993–1995), 113

Katz, Eileen, 114, 115
Kenney, Kerri, 110, 119, 124n71
Key, Keegan-Michael, 8, 139, *141*
Key & Peele (2012–2015), 8, 36–37, 126–27, 138–44
Kids in the Hall, The (1989–1994), 7–8, 9, 11–12, 115
Killam, Taran, 18–19
Kingsley, Allison, 133
Klausner, Josh, 86
Koechner, David, 89
Korman, Harvey, 10
Kovacs, Ernie, 10, 12, 53–54
Kraft Television Theater (1953–1955), 25–26
Kroll, Nick, 143–44
Kroll Show (2013–2015), 126, 138–39, 142–44

Landis, John, 65
Late Night with David Letterman (1982–1993), 54
Lear, Norman, 76
Lennon, Thomas, 110, 111, 113–14, 119
Levinson, Sara, 107
Lewis, Jerry, 27, 40, 46, 48–49, 52, 81
Lipsitz, George, 96
Lipsky, David, 117, 118
Liquid Television (1991–1994), 108, 109
live audiences, 6, 11, 12, 26, 28, 30, 39n30, 40, 52–53. See also vaudeville; *individual shows*
Live From New York (Shales and Miller) (oral history), 62, 77
Lonely Island, The (comedy team), 35
Lotz, Amanda, 39n30, 137–38
Love Guru, The (2008), 80
low v high comedy, 40–42
Lux Video Theater (1954–1957), 25–26

Mad TV (1995–2009, 2016), 6–7
Magicoms, 29
males. *See* gender
Man Show, The (1999–2004), 126, 129
Marc, David, 29
Marino, Ken, 110, 111
Martin, Dean, 27, 46, 48–49, 52
Martin, Dick, 55–56. *See also* Rowan and Martin's Laugh-In (1968–1973)
Marx Brothers, 26–27

Mary Tyler Moore Show, The (1970–1977), 29–30, 128
Maude (1972–1978), 29–30
Maya & Marty (2016), 12
"Mayhem Inc. Annual Awards Dinner" (sketch), 48–49
McAvity, Thomas, 50
McKay, Adam, 84, 87, 90
Medhurst, Andy, 21, 144
media: advertisers, 102; baby boomers, 100, 112; comedy, 148; Comedy Central, 131–32, 135, 138, 144–45; The Comedy Channel, 128; Ferrell, Will, 87; generations, 98; Generation X, 99, 101, 103, 120; grunge, 104; MTV Prods., 109–10; multichannel transition:1980s–1990s, 37; *New York Times* on, 147; performers, 31–32, 61, 82–83, 85; politics, 147–48; post-network: 2000s–Present, 36–37, 127, 138; sketch comedy, 31, 34–35, 37–38, 50–51, 82, 83, 91, 138, 149–50; *SNL* (1975–), 77, 78, 82–83, 85, 87, 90–91; *The State* (1993–1995, MTV), 94–95, 111; young adult audiences, 120. *See also* internet; *individual media*
Mencia, Carlos, 6–7
Men of a Certain Age (2009–2013), 137
"Men On . . ." (sketch), 22
Metzger, Kurt, 138
Michaels, Lorne, 1, 15, 18, 61–63, 66, 73–74, 77–79, 82
"Milk Lemonade" (sketch), 136–37
millennials, 97–98
Miller, James Andrew, 62
Miller, Jeffrey S., 54, 59n29, 77, 79
Mind of Mencia (2003–2008), 6–7
Minow, Newton, 29, 54, 59n29
misunderstandings, 7, 8–9
Monkees, The (1966–1968), 103–4
Monty Python's Flying Circus (1969–1974), 8–9, 63, 77–78, 108
Mooney, Paul, 73–74
Morris, Garrett, 31, 68–72, 73, 76
Mr. Show (1995–1998), 12–13, 36, 54, 94, 102
MTV, 94–124; advertisers, 104–9; baby boomers, 108; blackness/race, 105, 107, 120, 122n8; CBS, 115–16, 119; economics, 105, 107; gender, 105, 107, 120, 122n8; Generation X, 97, 103–5, 107–8, 113, 120;

Herzog, Doug, 109, 114–15; industrial identities, 95, 102–9, 120; interstitial bits, 104–6; Katz, Eileen, 114, 115; Levinson, Sara, 107; multichannel transition:1980s–1990s, 102–9, 119; music, 115–16; music videos, 97, 104–7, 108, 109, 122n8; NBC, 114–15; 1990s nostalgia, 97; politics, 106; postmodernism, 105–7, 108; recurring characters, 110–11; Remote Productions, Inc., 110; sketch comedy, 32; televisuality, 106–7; Viacom, 105, 108–9; young adult audiences, 97, 103–9, 119, 122n8. *See also individual shows*

MTV Prods., 109–10

Mullen, Megan, 107

multichannel transition:1980s–1990s, 94–124; absurdisms, 11; advertisers, 102–3, 129; CBS, 119; Comedy Central, 126, 127–34; economics, 32; gender/race, 33; generations, 109; Generation X, 96–102, 119–21; industrial/identities, 32–34, 94–95, 102–9, 127–34; Lotz, Amanda, 39n30; media, 37; MTV, 102–9, 119; networks, 32–33, 121; oppositionality, 95; sketch comedy, 32–34, 94, 121; *SNL* (1975–), 90–92, 94; *The State* (1993–1995, MTV), 92, 94, 109–15, 119; *The State* (1995, CBS), 115–19; televisuality, 106–7; young adult audiences, 101–3, 132. *See also individual cable channels*

Murdoch, Rupert, 33

Murphy, Caryn, 66

Murphy, Eddie, 68, 76–77, 146n38

Murray, Bill, 66, 88

Murray, Susan, 45–46, 48, 52

music, 101, 105, 115–16, 118, 120

music videos, 97, 104–7, 108, 109, 122n8

Myers, Mike, 78, 79, 80

Mystery Science Theater 3000 (1988–1999), 128

"Nairobi Trio" sketches (1957), 10

Nathan for You (2013–2017), 126, 135, 138–39, 142–44

NBC: advertisers, 102–3; *The Bob Newhart Show* (1961–1962), 54; Bourdieu, Pierre, 15; CBS, 116; Coe, Fred, 25–26; *The Colgate Comedy Hour* (1950–1955), 27, 42, 46–53;

Community (2009–2015), 132; internet, 35; MTV, 114–15; network era:1950s–1970s, 28–29; "Racist Word Association Interview" (sketch), 73–74; *Rowan and Martin's Laugh-In* (1968–1973), 55, 63; satire, 59n29; Schlosser, Herb, 63; *30 Rock* (2006–2013), 84–85; *The Tonight Show* (1962-1992), 63; young adult audiences, 3, 116. *See also SNL* (1975–)

Neale, Steve, 6–7, 38n5, 63

network era:1950s–1970s, 53–58; baby boomers, 54, 57–59; blackouts, 12; generations, 29, 101; industrial identities, 28–32; Lotz, Amanda, 39n30; race, 29–30, 68–69, 72, 75–76; sitcoms, 58; sketch comedy, 53–58; *SNL* (1975–), 30–31, 91; young adult audiences, 30, 55. *See also SNL* (1975–); *individual networks*

networks: advertisers, 28–29, 102–3, 132; early television: 1940s–1950s, 25; economics, 23–24, 28–29, 58; gender, 132; industrial identities, 107; internet, 3, 35, 132; multichannel transition:1980s–1990s, 32–33, 121; 1960s, 29, 60n30; sitcoms, 53; sketch comedy, 3, 4, 26, 31–32, 35–36, 41, 121; young adult audiences, 30, 132. *See also post-network: 2000s–Present; individual networks*

Newhart (1982–1990), 128

Newhart, Bob, 54–55, 128

Newman, Laraine, 31, 66–67, 68

New Show, The (1984), 78

New Yorker, The, 137

New York Magazine, 65, 79

New York Times, 114, 131, 147

"Next-Door Neighbors" (sketch), 49

Nick at Nite, 109

Nickelodeon, 96, 97, 123n48

"Niggar Family, The" (sketch), 22. *See also* blackness; race

1990s nostalgia, 96–97

Obama, Michelle and Barack, 18–20

O'Connor, Donald, 46, 50

O'Donoghue, Michael, 64

online. *See* internet; media

oppositionality: blackness, 22, 33, 75; Generation X, 94–95, 99, 100–101, 109,

oppositionality (*Cont.*)
111–13, 120; multichannel transition:1980s–1990s, 95; performers, 103; *The State* (1993–1995, MTV), 33–34, 94–95, 103, 109–15, 117, 121; *The State* (1995, CBS)/young adult audiences, 117
"Oval Office" (sketch), 18–20

Palin, Michael, 8
Palin, Sarah, 83, 84
paratextual materials, 86–87, 113, 123n54
Parker, Trey, 130–31
parodies: *Beavis and Butt-Head* (1993–1997, 2011), 101; *The Ben Stiller Show* (MTV 1989–1990, FOX 1992), 104; *Chappelle's Show* (2003–2006), 11; Clayton Bigsby sketch, 11, 22; *Key & Peele* (2012–2015), 139; Kovacs, Ernie, 54; *Kroll Show* (2013–2015), 142–43; *In Living Color* (1990–1994), 10; *Nathan for You* (2013–2017), 142–43; politics, 1; recurring characters, 9; sketch comedy, 7–8, 10; *The Smothers Brothers Comedy Hour* (1967–1969), 55; *The State* (1993–1995, MTV), 114, 117; *You Wrote It, You Watch It* (1992–1993), 109
Paul, William, 65–66
Peele, Jordan, 8, 139, 142. See also *Key & Peele* (2012–2015)
performers: Bourdieu, Pierre, 14–15; breaking character, 10; *The Colgate Comedy Hour* (1950–1955), 27, 28, 40–41, 46–52; conflict, 9; cultural identities, 4, 24; cultural production, 13–18; Deveau, Danielle Jeanine, 16; early television: 1940s–1950s, 25–27, 44, 46; economics, 4; gender, 136–37; identities, 83; internet, 36; media, 31–32, 61, 82–83, 85; oppositionality, 103; post-network: 2000s–Present, 36; reflexive flexibility, 5, 7–8, 83–84; reflexivity, 8, 46; sitcoms, 45–46; sketch comedy, 7, 9, 37, 44, 46, 121; *SNL* (1975–), 15–16, 30–32, 57–58, 61–63, 65, 76–77, 78; *The State* (1993–1995, MTV), 95, 103, 114; *The State* (1995, CBS), 117–19; vaudeo, 27, 45–46. See also *individuals*; recurring characters
Pharaoh, Jay, 18–19
physical virtuosities, 7, 10–11

Pike, John, 115–18, 123n67
Piscopo, Joe, 77
Plympton, Bill, 107–8
Poehler, Amy, 15, 80, 84
politics: absurdisms/parodies, 1; Bourdieu, Pierre, 16; Comedy Central, 129, 142; gender, 125; identities, 125–26, 148; media, 147–48; MTV, 106; post-network: 2000s–Present, 19; *Rowan and Martin's Laugh-In* (1968–1973), 56; sketch comedy, 16, 135, 145, 147–48, 150; *The Smothers Brothers Comedy Hour* (1967–1969), 57; *SNL* (1975–), 1–4, 16, 19, 147. See also cultural politics; post-politics; presidential elections
Portlandia (2011–2018), 125–26
Posch, Brooke, 132–33, 138
postmodernism, 105–7, 108, 113, 123n39
post-network: 2000s–Present, 127–51; absurdisms, 11; advertisers, 35, 129; Comedy Central, 36–37, 121, 125–34; gender, 125–27, 132, 137; identities, 125–26; industrial identities, 34–37, 127–34; internet, 34–35, 127, 130, 143; Lotz, Amanda, 39n30; media, 36–37, 127, 138; networks, 121; performers, 36; politics, 19; race, 125–27; reflexive flexibility, 34, 37; sketch comedy, 34–37, 41, 121, 127, 137, 144–45; unbundled content, 130; young adult audiences, 127, 132
post-politics, 36–37, 126, 134, 137–38, 144–45
premise, 8–9, 12
presidential elections, 1–4, 101, 129, 147
"Pre-taped Call-in Show" (sketch), 12–13
Pryor, Richard, 4, 31, 72–76
"PubLIZity" (sketch), 143–44
punchlines, 11–14

Quaid, Randy, 78

Rabinovitz, Lauren, 105–6
race: Alterman, Kent, 142; "Black Perspective" (sketches), 69–72, 73, 76; *Chappelle's Show* (2003–2006), 3, 11, 22–23; Clayton Bigsby sketch, 11, 22; Comedy Central, 22–23, 36, 125–27, 131, 135, 138–44; "Election Night" (sketch), 1–3; *The Flip Wilson Show* (1970–1974), 72; Generation X/generations, 98; Gray, Herman,

141–42; Hall, Stuart, 20; identities, 20, 22–23, 68–69, 72–77, 125–26, 138–44; *Key & Peele* (2012–2015), 139–42; *In Living Color* (1990–1994), 22–23, 33, 103, 141–42; Magicoms, 29; Michaels, Lorne, 18, 73–74; MTV, 105, 107, 120, 122n8; multichannel transition:1980s–1990s, 33; network era:1950s–1970s, 29–30, 68–69, 72, 75–76; "The Niggar Family" (sketch), 22; "Oval Office" (sketch), 18–20; post-network: 2000s–Present, 125–27; Pryor, Richard, 4, 72–76; reflexive flexibility, 142; sitcoms, 29; sketch comedy, 18, 40, 72, 125, 142, 143; *SNL* (1975–), 18–20, 31, 62, 68–77, 146n38; *The State* (1993–1995, MTV), 96; The State (comedy troupe), 117, 120; "Substitute Teacher" (sketch), 139–41. *See also* blackness

"Racial Draft" (sketch), 22

"Racist Word Association Interview" (sketch), 72–76

radio, 25–26, 40, 41–44, 58

Radner, Gilda, 31, 67–68, 78, 91

Reality Bites (1994), 96

recurring characters: advertisers/Brice, Fanny, 43; *The Colgate Comedy Hour* (1950–1955), 48; films, 15, 121; Kovacs, Ernie, 54; *Kroll Show* (2013–2015), 143; MTV, 110–11; *Nathan for You* (2013–2017), 135; Newman, Laraine on, 66; parodies, 9; performers, 15, 110–11, 116; Radner, Gilda, 67–68; Samurai Futaba sketches, 8–9; sketch comedy, 7, 9; *The Smothers Brothers Comedy Hour* (1967–1969), 30, 55; *SNL* (1975–), 66–67, 78–79, 80; *The State* (1993–1995, MTV), 34, 110–11, 116; vaudeo, 27

recurring scenarios, 27, 40–41, 48

reflexive flexibility, 1–39; advertisers, 5; Comedy Central, 126; cultural identities, 2–4; cultural production, 17; "Darrell's House" (sketch), 149–50; identities, 142; performers, 5, 7–8, 83–84; post-network: 2000s–Present, 34, 37; race, 142; *SNL* (1975–), 2–4, 8, 58, 61–62, 67–68, 77, 80–81, 82, 147; *The State* (1993–1995, MTV), 114, 120–21. *See also* sketch comedy and reflexive flexibility

reflexivity, 2–3, 8, *13*, 20, 46, 59, 64, 67–77

Reilly, John C., 89–90

Reiner, Carl, 29

Remote Control (1987–1990), 106–7, 109

Remote Productions, Inc., 110

Ren & Stimpy (1991–1995), 97

resolution, 8, 11–14

Revolution Wasn't Televised: Sixties Television and Social Conflict, The (Spigel and Curtin), 60n30

Rhoda (1974–1978), 128

Richard Pryor Show, The (1977), 72

Ritchie, Karen, 98–99

Rock, Chris, 1–3

Rodriguez, Oz, 149

Rosie Live (2008), 25

Rowan, Dan, 55–57

Rowan and Martin's Laugh-In (1968–1973), 28, 55–57, 63

Rudd, Paul, *89*

Rudolph, Maya, 84

Samurai Futaba sketches, 8–9

Sandler, Adam, 79, 80, 82

satire, 54–55, 57, 59n29, 102, 126, 135–36, 139

Saturday Night Live. *See SNL* (1975–)

Saul, Scott, 73–74, 76

Schlosser, Herb, 63

Schumer, Amy, 4, 8, 135–38. *See also Inside Amy Schumer* (2013–present)

Second City (improvisational troupe), 82

Second City Television (1976–1981), 77–78, 85–86

Seidman, Steve, 81–82

sexuality, 29, 126, 131. *See also* gender; homosexuality

Shales, Tom, 62, 77, 79

Short, Martin, 77

Short Attention Span Theater (1989–1994), 128

Showalter, Michael, 110, 111, *113*, 114

Sienkiewicz, Matt, 148

sitcoms, 29, 43–46, 52–53, 58, 79, 128–29. *See also individual shows*

sketch comedy, 125–51; absurdisms, 1, 7, 11, 109, 135; advertisers, 24, 121; art v commerce, 4–5, 14; blackouts, 7, 11–12, 55; Bourdieu, Pierre, 19; Comedy Central, 32, 36–37, 126–30, 142, 144–45; The Comedy

sketch comedy (*Cont.*)
  Channel, 128; conflict, 8, 9–11, 12; cultural identities, 2–4, 6, 14–24, 34, 41, 126, 146n38, 148, 150; cultural production, 13–24, 41, 62; *Date Night* (2010), 86; definitions, 2–4, 6, 7–14; *Distinction: A Social Critique of the Judgment of Taste* (Bourdieu), 15; early television: 1940s-1950s, 25–28, 44–53; economics, 5, 15, 16, 24–25, 37–38, 50–51, 52, 95–96, 127; films, 26, 40–44, 58, 62–63, 77–82; Funny or Die (website), 34–35, 36, 87; gender, 18, 40, 43–44, 91, 125–26, 135, 137, 143; generations, 24, 114; Generation X, 94–95, 119, 120; HBO, 32, 35; identities, 3, 17, 20–24, 40, 120, 125, 127, 135, 142, 143, 145, 148, 150; internet, 34–36, 41, 121, 130, 144–45; interstitial bits, 7; Kovacs, Ernie, 53–54; live audiences, 11, 12; low v high comedy, 40–42; media, 31, 34–35, 37–38, 50–51, 82, 83, 91, 138, 149–50; Michaels, Lorne, 61, 62; misunderstandings, 7; MTV, 32; multichannel transition:1980s–1990s, 32–34, 94, 121; Neale, Steve, 7; network era:1950s–1970s, 53–58; networks, 3, 4, 26, 31–32, 35–36, 41, 121; parodies, 7–8, 10; performers, 7, 9, 37, 44, 46, 121; physical virtuosities, 7, 10–11; politics, 16, 135, 145, 147–48, 150; post-network: 2000s–Present, 34–37, 41, 121, 127, 137, 144–45; post-politics, 144–45; premise, 8–9, 12; punchlines, 11–14; race, 18, 40, 72, 125, 142, 143; radio, 25–26, 40, 41–44, 58; recurring characters, 7, 9; reflexivity, 20; resolution, 8, 11–14; *Second City Television* (1976–1981), 77–78; shelf life, 4–5; transgression, 22–24; variety shows, 45–48, 58; vaudeo, 27–28, 40–41, 45–47, 58; vaudeville, 10–12, 26–28, 40–44. *See also* industrial identities; *individual shows*; *individual sketches*
"Sketch Comedy" (sketch), 7–8, 11
sketch comedy and reflexive flexibility, 1–39; American television industry, 7, 25, 147; art v commerce, 5; Comedy Central, 37; cultural identities, 2–4; "Darrell's House" (sketch), 148–50; definitions, 2–4; early television: 1940s-1950s, 58; economics, 96; films, 81; generations, 114; identities, 15, 20, 114, 142; Johnson, Catherine, 135; *Key & Peele* (2012–2015), 139; post-network: 2000s–Present, 34, 37; race, 142; radio, 58; "Sketch Comedy" (sketch), 7–8; *SNL* (1975–), 2–4, 77, 81, 147; *The State* (1993–1995, MTV), 96, 114, 120–21; variety shows, 58; vaudeo, 41, 58
Smiley, Stu, 128
Smothers Brothers Comedy Hour, The (1967–1969), 30, 55–57, 58, 63
SNL (1975–), 61–93, 147–50; ABC, 92n4; baby boomers, 30, 58–59, 61–62, 64, 67–68; blackness/race, 18–20, 31, 62, 68–77, 146n38; Broadway Video, 78; CBS, 118; "Comedy Isn't Funny: *Saturday Night Live* at Twenty—How the Show That Transformed TV Became a Grim Joke" (article), 79; cultural identities, 1, 58, 61, 92, 149; cultural politics, 63–68, 75–76; economics, 19, 64; films, 15, 31, 61–63, 65, 77–91; gender, 18, 31, 62, 63–68, 69, 70–71, 76–77, 79, 82, 91; generations, 92; Generation X, 30; identities, 30, 58, 62–63, 64, 68, 72–73, 76–77, 79, 91, 147; interstitial bits, 8, 67–68; live audiences, 6, 28, 30; The Lonely Island (comedy team), 35; media, 77, 78, 82–83, 85, 87, 90–91; *Monty Python's Flying Circus* (1969–1974), 63; multichannel transition:1980s-1990s, 90–92, 94; NBC, 61, 63, 64, 73, 77, 78, 79, 92n4; network era:1950s-1970s, 30–31, 91; performers, 15–16, 30–32, 57–58, 61–63, 65, 76–77, 78; politics, 1–4, 16, 19, 147; presidential elections, 1–4, 147; recurring characters, 66–67, 78–79, 80; reflexive flexibility, 2–4, 8, 58, 61–62, 67–68, 77, 80–81, 82, 147; reflexivity, 2–3, 59, 64, 67–77; sitcoms, 79; sketch comedy, 2–4, 28, 30–32, 57–59, 63, 77–82, 90–91, 94, 147; *The State* (1993–1995, MTV), 92, 114–15; vaudeo, 58, 94; young adult audiences, 4, 30, 64. *See also individuals; individual sketches*
"Soda Jerk" (sketch), 49
So I Married an Axe Murderer (1993), 80
South Park (1997– present), 126, 129, 130–31
Spade, David, 79
Spigel, Lynn, 43, 60n30
sponsors, 24–25. *See also* advertisers

Starr, Steven, 96, 110, 114–16
State, The (1993–1995, MTV), 109–15, 119–21; absurdisms, 109; Bendis, Jonathan, 110, 114–15; consumerism, 33–34, 94–95; cultural identities, 120; economics, 95–96, 119–21; films, 94–95, 111; gender, 96; generations, 33–34, 111–13, 114; Generation X, 95, 102, 105, 111–13, 119–21; identities, 33–34, 120; media, 94–95, 111; MTV, 33–34, 94–96, 103, 105, 109–15; multichannel transition:1980s–1990s, 92, 94, 109–15, 119; oppositionality, 33–34, 94–95, 103, 109–15, 117, 121; paratextual materials, 113, 123n54; parodies, 114, 117; performers, 95, 103, 114; postmodernism, 113; race, 96; recurring characters, 34, 110–11, 116; reflexive flexibility, 114, 120–21; sketch comedy, 95–96, 119–21; SNL (1975–), 92, 114–15; Starr, Steven, 96, 110, 114–15; young adult audiences, 103, 115–16, 121
State, The (1995, CBS), 4, 34, 95–96, 102, 115–19
State, The (comedy troupe), 109–10, 114–19, 120, 124n71
State by State with the State: An Uninformed, Poorly Researched Guide to the United States (The State comedy troupe), 118
Step Brothers (2008), 84, 89–91
Stewart, Jon, 109, 113, 115, 128, 129, 130, 131
Stiller, Ben, 33, 103–4, 109, 115
Stone, Matt, 130–31
Strauss, William, 100
"Substitute Teacher" (sketch), 139–41
Sullivan, Ed, 47–48, 50, 52. *See also Ed Sullivan Show, The* (1948–1971)
"Supermarket Checker" (sketch), 10
Sweeney, Julia, 79

Taco Bell, 107–8
Tarkenton, Fran, 69–70
Tashlin, Frank, 51
TBS, 132, 144
Teen Mom (2009–2012, 2015–), 97
TeenNick, 96–97
television. *See* American television industry; individual eras
Television Will Be Revolutionized, The (Lotz), 39n30

televisuality, 106–7
Texaco Star Theatre (1948–1956), 47–48, 123n39
30 Rock (2006–2013), 84–85
Thompson, Keenan, 148
"Thug English Actor" (sketch), 139
Toffler, Van, 97
Tommy Boy (1994), 81
Tonight Show, The (1962-1992), 30, 63, 64
Tonight Show with Jimmy Fallon, The (2014–present), 15–16
Tookes, LaKendra, 18, 76
Tosh.0 (2009–present), 126, 129, 130–31
transgression, 22–24
Truglio, Joe Lo, 110
Trump, Donald, 1–2, 3–4, 147
Turner, Ted, 105
Turow, Joseph, 33
TV Land, 109
Tyson, Cicely, 70–71, 72

Ugly Americans (2010–2012), 129–30
unbundled content, 130, 134–35
Upright Citizens Brigade (1998–2000), 128
Upright Citizens Brigade (improvisational troupe), 82

Vandaveon and Mike (2012), 142
Van Dyke, Dick, 29
variety shows, 26, 28, 45–48, 50, 54, 55, 58. *See also individual shows*
vaudeo (video vaudeville), 27–28, 40–41, 45–48, 53–54, 58, 94. *See also Colgate Comedy Hour, The* (1950–1955)
vaudeville, 10–12, 26–28, 40–44, 82. *See also individuals*
VH1, 108–9, 142–43
Viacom: Atom (website), 129; *The Ben Stiller Show* (MTV 1989–1990, FOX 1992), 33; Comedy Central, 129–30, 132; Ha! (network), 129; Herzog, Doug, 109; internet, 35; MTV, 105, 108–9; Nickelodeon, 97, 123n48; *The State* (1993–1995, MTV), 34, 103; *Tosh.0* (2009–present), 131; VH1, 108–9; young adult audiences, 103, 108–9, 123n48
Viva Variety (1997-1999), 119, 128

Wain, David, 110, 118–19
Washington, Kerry, 18–20
Wayans brothers, 22–23
"Wayne's World" (sketches), 79
Weaver, Sylvester "Pat," 47–48, 49
Wiig, Kristen, 80, 84
Wile, Fred, Jr., 49–50, 51
Wilson, Flip, 28, 72, 74
Winfrey, Oprah, 18–20
"Wolverines" (sketch), 64
Workaholics (2011–2017), 126

Yahoo! 132
young adult audiences: advertisers, 33, 102–3, 131–32; *Beavis and Butt-Head* (1993–1997, 2011), 101–2; CBS, 96, 115–18; Comedy Central, 36, 129, 130, 131–32, 134, 144; media, 120; millennials, 97–98; MTV, 97, 103–9, 119, 122n8; multichannel transition:1980s–1990s, 101–3, 132; NBC, 3, 116; network era:1950s–1970s, 30, 55; networks, 30, 132; oppositionality, 117; post-network: 2000s–Present, 127, 132; *Rowan and Martin's Laugh-In* (1968–1973), 56; *The Smothers Brothers Comedy Hour* (1967–1969), 58; *SNL* (1975–), 4, 30, 64; *The State* (1993–1995, MTV), 103, 115–16, 121; *Tosh.o* (2009–present), 131; VH1, 108–9; Viacom, 103, 108–9, 123n48. *See also* baby boomers; Generation X
Your Show of Shows (1950–1954), 12, 47–48
YouTube, 36, 90, 128, 142
You Wrote It, You Watch It (1992–1993), 109, 110, 118–19

Zamata, Sasheer, 18, 76

NICK MARX is Assistant Professor of Media and Visual Culture in the Department of Communication Studies at Colorado State University. He is coeditor (with Matt Sienkiewicz and Ron Becker) of *Saturday Night Live and American TV* and (with Matt Sienkiewicz) *The Comedy Studies Reader*.

www.ingramcontent.com/pod-product-compliance
Lightning Source LLC
Chambersburg PA
CBHW020849160426
43192CB00007B/849